THE THEORY AND TECHNIQUE
OF FAMILY THERAPY

THE THEORY AND TECHNIQUE OF FAMILY THERAPY

By

CHARLES P. BARNARD, Ed.D.

Graduate Program Director
Marriage and Family Counseling
University of Wisconsin—Stout
Menomonie, Wisconsin

and

RAMON GARRIDO CORRALES, Ph.D.

Director of Family Therapy Training and Research
Counseling Center for Human Development
Kansas City, Missouri

CHARLES C THOMAS · PUBLISHER
Springfield · Illinois · U.S.A.

Published and Distributed Throughout the World by
CHARLES C THOMAS • PUBLISHER
Bannerstone House
301-327 East Lawrence Avenue, Springfield, Illinois, U.S.A.

© 1979, by CHARLES C THOMAS • PUBLISHER
ISBN 0-398-03859-7
Library of Congress Catalog Card Number: 78-10587

With THOMAS BOOKS *careful attention is given to all details of
manufacturing and design. It is the Publisher's desire to present books
that are satisfactory as to their physical qualities and artistic possibilities
and appropriate for their particular use.* THOMAS BOOKS *will be true
to those laws of quality that assure a good name and good will.*

Printed in the United States of America
W-2

Library of Congress Cataloging in Publication Data
Barnard, Charles P

   The theory and technique of family therapy.

   Bibliography: p.
   Includes index.
   1. Family psychotherapy.   2.   Social systems.
I.   Corrales, Ramon Garrido, joint author.   II.   Title.
[DNLM: 1. Family therapy. 2. Family. WM430.5.F2
B259t]
RC488.5.B35   616.8'915   78-10587
ISBN 0-398-03859-7

PREFACE

THE OBJECTIVE OF this book is to present our form of family therapy. As the book is read, names such as Bowen, Whitaker, Satir, Watzlawick, Haley, and Minuchin, among others, appear frequently, as a reflection of the influence these individuals have had upon the practice of family therapy. The reader familiar with these writers recognizes that they all have as their primary target for intervention the family system. This book is an elucidation of the theory and technique of intervention at the level of the family system.

In educating people in regard to the family therapy process, we frequently referred them to a plethora of books. Each time participants mentioned the difficulty of acquiring several books, we became more motivated to write our own idiosyncratic synthesis. The field of family therapy is dynamic, exciting, and expanding, both personally and professionally.

The ideas incorporated within this book have been used in university classes, workshops, and seminars. Among the populations that have attended these workshops and seminars, the following professions have been represented: social workers, clergymen, psychiatrists, psychologists, nurses, school counselors, teachers, and others. This kind of "field testing," in conjunction with clinical practice, has led to the thought that the contents of this book are appropriate for the student as well as experienced clinician. The student will find a comprehensive perspective of the field of family therapy that will enlighten and, hopefully, excite. The experienced clinician may find some of the material a review, but may also find portions as new and hopefully exciting as the novice. The ideas have not come as a result of superior knowledge or experience, but as a result of our differences as individuals from each other and the readers, which results in varying perceptions and insights. Hopefully, these differences can be used to enhance others' perceptions and in the process draw us closer together in our endeavor to help others and ourselves.

The book begins with a theoretical base we believe is sound for practicing family therapy. The reader is encouraged to integrate this base as thoroughly as possible prior to moving into the chapters that deal more specifically with the process and technique of family therapy. Doing so is important to facilitate the actual practice in order to be more like the skilled organist at the keyboard making beautiful music, as opposed to the well-intentioned individual without the theoretical background seated at the keyboard and making random noises.

Our hope is that the reading of this book will be as energizing and exciting to the reader as the writing of it was to us. While there were the apparently inevitable periods of being "bogged" down, we were able to recalibrate and move on, just as the family that is "stuck" must do if they want to grow and change. While there were times when one or the other of us assumed more initiative for stimulating movement and direction, overall, we agreed that the book was truly co-authored. Perhaps the strength of our feelings regarding the joint effort involved is best illustrated by the means in which we determined whose name would appear first for authorship of our work. After discussing various alternatives, we arrived at the "scientific" procedure of flipping a coin.

R.C.
C.P.B.

INTRODUCTION

This book is designed primarily for the beginner in family therapy and especially as a basic text in a masters' level course in marriage and family therapy. A variety of disciplines are currently offering such a course, most of them at the graduate level. We think that the best use of this book in a course involves treating it as the core set of readings around which a more specialized variety of readings can be built. In a field growing as fast as family therapy, it is very difficult to produce a book which, at publication time, is still up-to-date. The reader and the teacher are therefore encouraged to supplement the text with the more current material being published in various journals.

We found that writing a basic text was no simple matter, particularly in a field which reflected so many theoretical models of family functioning and such a variety of principles of change. The end result is that the reader will get an adequate sense of the mainstream approaches to family therapy but certainly not a mastery of any one system. We recommend going to the original sources when a particular way of working with families appeals to you.

The first four chapters in this book we characterize as the theory sections. Chapter 1 views the family as a two-generational interactional unit; it begins the process of helping the reader think interactionally so that he can begin to see the "dance patterns," not just the dancers. Chapter II builds upon these principles but extends their application to include more dancers: Key members of the extended family, with special emphasis upon the families of origin of each parent. Chapter III is an attempt to pull together many theoretical strands of individual and family functioning. Chapter IV is a theoretical treatise on the role of the therapist in the therapeutic system.

With Chapters V and VI, we begin dealing with the therapy

process as such. Chapter V covers aspects of the process at the initial, middle, and termination phases. Chapter VI offers a variety of techniques that the beginning therapist might examine, evaluate, experiment with, and eventually adapt, adopt, or eliminate from his repertoire of intervention strategies.

The remaining chapters go into more specialized areas of family work; communication training for couples and families has become an important aspect of family life education. We have drawn from those endeavors and applied them to a therapy context. Couples groups and multiple family groups have become alternative ways of doing systems therapy; Chapter VIII provides the basic principles and techniques for these contexts of therapy. Chapter IX provides an interesting juxtaposition of two critical phases of family process: premarital and divorce processes. This is followed by a chapter which focuses on the parent-child relationship. Chapter XI discusses family therapy concerning three very sensitive issues: sex, alcohol, and death in the family. The final chapter addresses the training of the family therapist.

In the majority of the chapters, you will find *inserts*; these are related ideas and suggested activities designed to complement and supplement the main ideas in the text. Take these *inserts* as launching pads for alternative activities that could enhance the learning process for you. Adapt them to the specific context in which you are.

CONTENTS

THE THEORY AND TECHNIQUE
OF FAMILY THERAPY

CHAPTER 1

THE FAMILY AS AN
INTERACTIONAL SYSTEM

In TALKING ABOUT the nuclear family, the extended family, or one of the emerging variants in marriage and family life-styles, the common denominator is a group of closely interrelated individuals. This group has a history of past interactions that carry an impact upon its present relationship patterns; it also has a set of expectations regarding future interactions. It seems extremely important for the family therapist to have a solid conceptual grasp of the way a family behaves as a *system* of highly related individuals. This chapter presents such a view.

THE INDIVIDUAL IN THE SYSTEM

Traditionally, therapists have focused on the individual person as the primary locus or site of health or disturbance. The person was regarded as crazy, neurotic, or delinquent. It was as if certain "nuts and bolts" were out of place *inside the head*. With the impact that psychiatry and psychology have had on the professional and lay public, it became difficult to think about relationships as other than mere reflections of intrapersonal concerns. The flow was from intrapersonal to relationship patterns and not from relationship to intrapersonal or a back-and-forth (cybernetic) causal interchange between the two. A family therapist working only with individual-oriented concepts is partially handicapped because he most likely misses many interactional patterns that are vital to the understanding of the family and its members and vital to diagnostic and treatment issues. This is not to say that intrapersonal theories are unimportant; they are important because ultimately the individual is paramount. The person is the subjective base of conscious and unconscious experience, and he or she, after all, forms a crucial part of the family system. Many intrapersonal experiences are unintelligible when they are isolated from the interpersonal context in which they are inseparably embedded. There are vital causal connections between intra- and interpersonal realities that need to be understood.

In order to grasp the connections, a new set of conceptual lenses is needed, in addition to those that individual-oriented theories have generated. Concepts are needed that enable therapists to capture interactional characteristics and events that belong to relationship systems and not merely to the personal system. It is one thing to recognize depression in a person; it is quite another to recognize a sequence of events in which this person is typically pulled in as referee to the habitual conflicts between two family members who rarely resolve their conflicts but who never call upon this person for any other reason. The following is an illustration to capture the interconnections between interpersonal and personal levels.

Imagine a Saturday morning in the Arbor family. Mr. Arbor is reading the paper in the family room. Mrs. Arbor goes into her daughter's room and discovers that the room is a mess. Susie, the daughter, is fifteen years old. Mother gets very angry and proceeds to scold Susie, who fights back. As father hears the fight, his "guts" begin to churn; he then pops two tablets into his "Rolaid stomach." Before the quarrel gets too far underway, Mr. Arbor decides to leave for a round of golf—escape of some kind is his usual reaction to any overt conflict in the family. He leaves with a vague realization that, somehow, his wife's outburst may be partially related to the marital conflicts and tensions that have been smoldering for years. Mother, too, feels guilty because the vehemence of her anger does not match the event (the messy room); she may subconsciously sense her overreaction as an overflow of the unresolved tension in the marital relationship.

Furthermore, Mrs. Arbor becomes angry when she realizes that once again father has escaped the emotional field. She resents having to shoulder the full brunt of the disciplinarian role, silently saying to herself, "Why do I have to be the bad person all the time? Why can't he shoulder the family leadership sometimes? Every time it gets hot around here, he abandons me." Susie, on the other hand, although primarily aware of the present intrusion into her personal boundaries, has sensed the underlying but unresolved tension between her parents. So she, too, feels somewhat victimized by being made the dumping ground of the marital relationship. However, more significant than the resentment, she feels the insecurity of living in a situation in which her intimate world (her family) is sitting on so shaky a foundation as her parents' brittle marriage. She also resents father's rarely coming to her aid, as well as his being so emotionally unavailable.

What started as a simple quarrel over a messy room is based on a complex and powerful set of emotional links that affected every member in that family. An understanding of the linkages in the family system and the causal interconnections with individual members is vital to proper diagnosis and to setting up of an appropriate treatment design. For example, in order to understand the mother-daughter interaction more completely, it is important to understand it in the context of the husband-wife relationship. This framework of understanding is also required to comprehend father's ulcerated stomach and his pattern of interpersonal withdrawal.

A Slice of Family Interaction

As illustrated, Mother, Father, and Susie comprise the Arbor family. Have three people in the class assume the roles of these family members. Role players are encouraged to do the following: (1) assign yourselves an appropriate age and first name; (2) review the interpersonal dynamics within which each person is involved; (3) spend about five minutes in thoughtful meditation as a way to develop the role; and (4) create an historical background for each of the family members.

Have two class members volunteer as therapists. Imagine an ongoing therapy relationship with these clients. Therapists and clients in this session are in the process of discussing the messy room and the quarrel it triggered between mother and daughter. Whether you are an observer or a role player, try to experience, at least vicariously, the systemic interconnections of this interpersonal drama. Let the role playing go for about fifteen to twenty minutes. Discuss family dynamics that emerge, as well as the behavior of the therapists.

Keep this slice of family interaction in mind as the more abstract concepts involved in understanding the family as a system are discussed. It is also important to make a clear distinction between theory and therapy as a prelude to grasping the flow between the two. The purpose of *theory* is to understand and conceptualize; the purpose of *therapy* is to change. One does not necessarily lead to the other. However, theory should ideally guide and permeate therapeutic strategy and therapy sometimes enables testing of theoretical premises.

This chapter stresses theory, with a sensitive eye to therapeutic implications. Therapy is the major concern in this book. Therefore, the theoretical sections always anticipate therapeutic applications.

THE CONCEPT OF SYSTEM

What makes the family a system? In order to answer this, a fundamental question must be asked: *What is a system? At its most basic, the concept of system denotes a number of parts that are relatively organized so that a change in one or more parts is usually accompanied by a change in the other parts of a system* (Bertalanffy, 1966). This definition encompasses any kind of system, mechanical, biological, or social. The central concept is that of organization of components into systemic relationships.

An analogy is presented by Virginia Satir (Big Sur Tape No. 1.) She perceives process, the basic building block of systems, as being similar to the wind. One cannot see or touch the wind, and yet its impact is evident. The same can be said of process in human systems; it cannot be seen or touched but is continually operational in human systems. Satir elaborates by saying relationships are like icebergs in that one-eighth is evident and overt while the other seven-eighths are submerged. She contends that the way we develop an understanding of that submerged seven-eighths of individuals with whom we are involved is through our perceptions of the process in their relationships. Although it is possible to physically see and touch the individual family member, it makes no sense to think of the person as "more real" than the systemic family relationships that cannot be seen or touched directly. Otherwise, it can be argued that the human body is not "as real as" the nuclear particles of which it is composed. To follow Buckley's (1967) thinking on this matter:

> Thus, if social groups are not "real entities" then neither are individual organisms, organs, cells, molecules or atoms, since they are all "nothing but" the constituents of which they are made. But this "nothing but" hides the central key to modern thinking— the fact of *organization* of components into systemic relationships. When we say that "the whole is more than the sum of its parts," the meaning becomes unambiguous and loses its mystery: the "more than" points to the fact of *organization,* which imparts to the aggregate characteristics that are not only *different* from, but often not found in the components alone: and the "sum of the parts" must be taken to mean, not their numerical addition, but their organized aggregation. [P. 42]

The type of system being dealt with, when thinking of the family, is the sociocultural, which, in Buckley's typology, falls under the complex, adaptive system. Buckley describes this system as "a complex of elements or components directly or indirectly related in a causal network, such that each component is related to at least some others in a more or less stable way within any particular period of time" (Buckley, 1967, P. 41). As in the earlier illustration, a ripple in the mother-daughter relationship led to a network of causally related impacts upon the individual members and their interrelationships, including father, who, overtly, was only indirectly related to the event.

There are additional qualities of a social system that are important to keep in mind. Social systems are organizationally complex, purposive, adaptive, and information processing. Some of these elements and how each applies to the family are discussed.

Components of the Family as a Social System

The "components" or "parts" of the family social system are the persons who occupy the highly interrelated positions. A *position* is defined as a location within a social structure. A *social structure* is the recurring interactions between two or more people. Each position in a social structure (whether a family or business firm) contains a number of roles, each of which is reciprocally related to at least one other role attached to another position. This is one base for saying that the family is a social system.

ROLE: First, it is important to understand the concept of *role* as the term is used here. A *role* is a more or less related set of expectations attached to a position in a social structure. For example, in most North American families, the husband-father position, has the breadwinner role. The other family members, as well as society, *expect* from the occupant of that position certain types of characteristics and behaviors that result in the bringing in of a salary adequate to meet the family's physical and social-emotional needs. Even in today's fluid modern society, the husband-father who is substantially derelict in the performance of his role is generally confronted with serious sanctions ranging from informal sanctions, e.g. anger from family members, to formal, legal ones, e.g. as grounds for divorce. The wife-mother is also able to take on this role, but the sanction on her underperformance is currently not as strong as those usually handed to the husband-father.

For every role, there is a reciprocal role in at least one other position. The husband's role as sex partner for example, is inconceivable without the spouse's reciprocal role as his sex partner, and vice versa. The companionship role is again unintelligible apart from a companionship role in another family member, spouse, or child. The disciplinarian role presupposes the existence of one who is the object of the discipline. When one of those roles is not performed as expected by one or more of the family members, at least one other member is affected. When it is realized that a family is generally composed of several members, each of whom performs a good many roles that are intricately interwoven in a network of reciprocally related roles, the systemness of the family can begin to be grasped.

Describing and Assessing Roles

Take at least two positions that you are currently occupying, e.g. son, daughter, husband, wife fiancé(e), employer, employee, organization president or member, teacher, and so forth. Write down at least five roles associated with each position. Remember that roles are a group of related expectations attached to a position. Some of your roles may be unique; use your own terms to describe these roles. After describing these roles, review each one and make a judgment whether a particular role is mostly of your own making, imposed upon you, or a combination. A row of your written material may look like this:

Position	Role	Degree of Role Making or Role Taking
Husband	Launderer	Combination. Initially, my spouse nudged me to take this role; as I began to enact it, she continued to worry and take responsibility for how this was to be done. I fought my way into making the role my major responsibility and carrying it out in the way I saw fit, but keeping myself open to feedback from my wife.

In Class

In groups of about five or less, share your role assessment with class members.

FAMILY AND IDENTITY: The concept of role, although useful, does not always give existential or gut-level sense of the power and meaning of relationships in the family, For this, it is useful to look upon the family as the *matrix of identity* (Minuchin, 1974)—the primary source of the self. We adopt the social-psychological view that *the self is primarily the result of the countless interactions between an individual and his significant others.* The latter are people who are so vitally related to a person that they hold survival value to him socially, emotionally and, ultimately, through psychosomatic mechanisms, physically as well.

The members of one's family are one's significant others par excellence. Particularly in the formative years, the development of a person's self-concept is highly connected to the manner in which family members related to him or her. How do I know that I am a lovable person unless someone important to me dared to love me along the way. As Chapter 2 demonstrates in explaining Laing's (1969) concept of mystification, this process works negatively as well. The quality of the personal affirmation (or lack of it) in the formative years has impact upon the adult person's behavior patterns regarding friends, occupation, mate selection, and the formation of his own marriage and family system.

In the development of a person's identity, psychologists have long pointed to two basic, crucial human experiences: belongingness and separateness. Belongingness is the basic human need for affirmation and acceptance by a group of important people. As the child grows, he knows that he belongs to, for example, the Bender family and that in this group he occupies a certain position in the system with a number of roles. He begins to sense a "we" and a "they." He learns a range of meanings, values, and behaviors that are acceptable to his family and a range of those that are not.

Inseparable from his experience of belongingness is the person's basic need to be recognized as unique or different and relatively autonomous. He is not just a Bender, but he is Bob Bender. A family's style of responding to individual differences in thoughts, feelings, intentions, and actions have important consequences in Bob's personality development. When this existential dimension is added to the concept of role reciprocity or interrelatedness, one is better able to appreciate the tremendous importance of family interaction patterns.

Energy Links to Information Links

In mechanical and biological systems, the relations among the components are primarily a function of the transmission of energy from one component to another. However, in a social system, relations among components (persons) depend more and more on the transmission of information. Although the transmission of information depends on some physical base or energy flow (such as sounds or gestures), the energy base is subordinate to the form or structure that communicates the information in human systems (Buckley, 1967).

The implications of this are central in systems theory. Once energy-based relationships are transcended, the potential fluidity of a system—its capacity to change and elaborate—is increased. Furthermore, a minute amount of structured energy (a gentle touch or the spoken words "I hate you!") is able to selectively trigger a large amount of activity in the receiver of the message, overcoming limitations of spatial and temporal dimensions. Another implication is that a social system is able to develop self-consciousness and, with it, the capacity for self-regulations and self-direction.* Much as a person's self-awareness gives him the capacity for self-direction.

Dependence on information exchange similarly makes a system much more open to environmental influences. In fact, that "a system is open means, not simply that it engages in interchanges with the environment, but that this interchange is an essential factor underlying the system's viability, its reproductive ability or continuity, and its ability to change" (Buckley, 1967, P. 50). The family, like the individual, cannot exist in isolation from other physical and social systems. It has vital ties with the neighborhood, educational, religious, political, and economic systems. The family, therefore, must find ways to maintain its unique boundaries and yet open itself up to meaningful interchange with its environment. The environment in this sense constitutes the larger social system, such as the community, the city, the state, the nation, or the world. It may now become obvious to the reader that he may choose the level of system appropriate for study and for therapy. Throughout this book, the case is made for the family system (nuclear and extended) as the most effective level for the focus of therapeutic intervention.

Feedback: Mechanisms for Maintenance and Elaboration

Because people are different, they are not always matched in terms of goals, ways to achieve those goals, and rhythms and moods, and interpersonal tension is ever-present in some form and intensity in all social systems. How, then, does the family, as a system, deal with these varied actual and potential tensions and still manage to act as a *purposive system;* a system that is goal directed and strives to be responsive to the needs of the group and of its individual members? The concept of feedback has been useful.

Feedback is "a process by which a system informs its component parts how to relate to one another and to the external

---

* The word *self* refers to social systems; in this case, the family.

environment in order to facilitate the correct or beneficial execution of certain system functions" (Kantor and Lehr, 1975, P. 12). To illustrate, the family has expectations about how a ten-year-old daughter ought to behave, for example, in terms of how much autonomy and independence she shows in her behavior. Normally, a ten-year-old girl who decides she should wear nylons and mascara and go out on a date unchaperoned until the early morning hours is viewed as deviating from the family norms. If the family receives such mismatched information (mismatch between desired goal state and actual behavior), it typically goes into the process of bringing the "deviant" back in line. For example, the disciplinarian's role may be activated and the daughter is grounded or given a long lecture, or perhaps the family members as a group reexamine the family's goals and ways of achieving them. In short, the stimulus (daughter's behavior) was sensed by the system and compared to its reference map (values, norms, and habits, etc.). Since there was an error signal, i.e. deviation from the norm, the system acted to bring one of its members back in line with its norms or to look at the possibility of changing its expectations and its typical behavior. This is the process referred to as the *feedback loop*.

Homeostasis and Morphogenesis

Because social scientists once used the model of mechanical or biological systems for studying social systems, they assumed that the typical response of a system to any deviation was to counteract it in order to reestablish the previous "equilibrium." The system was conceived as striving toward a fixed or steady goal state and that all efforts would be directed at maintaining or reestablishing it. Significant deviations from the family's norms were, at least implicitly, seen as necessarily dysfunctional for the family. Although change was ubiquitous, the theory could not account for it except as a source of stress and dysfunction. The tendency of a system to maintain constancy is often referred to as *homeostasis* or as *negative feedback*.*

---

* The term *negative* has no necessary connection to something undesirable but simply to a deviation-counteracting tendency.

Despite its limitations, the concept of homeostasis has proved invaluable to family theory and therapy. There is no question, for example, that families devote considerable energy to maintaining a certain amount of order and stability. Security seems to be tied with a certain amount of stability and predictability. When I go home at the end of a working day, I fully expect to still be married to my present wife and that she remains my companion, sex partner, and coresponsible with me for parental roles. If the realities change daily, it is possible that I will at best be dissatisfied and at worst become psychotic. It is assumed that there is a basic need in the human organism, as well as in the social system, for some range of stability and predictability. As seen later, this range varies from individual to individual and from family to family.

The concept of homeostasis, furthermore, provides a firm grasp of the concept of the family as a highly interrelated network of relationships. Don Jackson (1957) of the Palo Alto group developed this concept extensively. Satir (1967), one of Jackson's most renowned students, summarizes Jackson's thought as follows:

a. According to the concept of family homeostasis, the family acts to achieve a balance in relationships.
b. Members help to maintain this balance overtly and covertly.
c. The family's repetitious, circular, predictable communication patterns reveal this balance.
d. When the family homeostasis is precarious, members exert much effort to maintain it. [P. 1]

These tendencies to maintain balance at whatever cost become especially apparent when working with families who have one or more symptomatic individuals. The more severe the disturbance, the more rigid and unvarying the family patterns appear to be. In fact, the birth of family therapy is partially the result of early work with schizophrenics. When the schizophrenic child who was hospitalized recovered enough to warrant going home, several interesting phenomena were observed: (1) the child became schizophrenic again; (2) someone else in the family showed the symptoms; or (3) the parents separated or obtained a divorce. It seemed that the system could not long stand the change. Either some members maintained the pattern (having a "sick" member), or the system fell apart.* This enabled therapists to talk about a sick or disturbed system rather than a sick individual.

Although the concept of homeostasis enabled theorists and therapists to understand a great deal of family phenomena, it fell short of reality as a model by itself. The family, after all, undergoes many changes and transition points throughout its life cycle. When a husband and wife have their first baby, they literally enter a new ballgame. The system is complicated tremendously. The addition of a new member increases the number of relationships from one to three (husband and wife, father and child, and mother and child). Note that, for the first time, a set of parental roles are added to the husband position (now husband-father) and to the wife position (wife-mother). The store of time, space, and energy previously available to the marital relationship has to be shared with the parent-child relationships. Economic pressures increase with potentially significant impacts on the self-image of the breadwinner(s). These added economic pressures cut into resources that could otherwise have been used for recreation and accumulation of other service and material goods.

As the child moves from infancy to toddlerhood, to the preschool and school-age years, and all the way through adolescence and adulthood, families undergo significant changes. The manner in which families cope with these changes has important consequences for all its members. This is where the mechanical and organismic systems models fall apart. Machines or biological systems cannot typically survive radical restructuring, whereas social systems are able to elaborate and restructure themselves.

The tendency in a social system to elaborate and to change has been referred to as *positive** feedback or morphogenesis*. A positive feedback loop, therefore, is that tendency in a system to be sensitive to a deviation from the usual relationship of

---

* There is of course, the alternative that the family system accommodates to the change; this is discussed as the second type of feedback.

** The term *positive* does not necessarily connote desirability but simply the tendency to amplify a deviation.

component parts and to amplify that deviation. If processed for a long enough period of time and amplified intensively enough, that new attitude or behavior may be incorporated as an acceptable pattern in the family system. Families differ in ways of coping with change. Systems theorists generally agree that for a system to be viable, it must have both homeostatic and morphogenic feedback mechanisms available to it. The basic need of security and stability and hence the importance of homeostasis has been discussed previously. However, without deviation-amplifying forces (change mechanisms), a family becomes vulnerable precisely because change is inevitable for it to survive without the presence of pathology. If the family rules that applied to Johnny when he was five still apply when he is twenty-five, Johnny is probably showing some maladaptive symptoms. If Mrs. Jones decides that she would like to become gainfully employed, and should her relationship with Mr. Jones not have the behavioral flexibility to handle such a change, it could mean serious trouble for the two of them and eventually for the entire family.

Recognizing Feedback Mechanisms

Taking your present family as your focus (your own or your parents'), think about two events that illustrate homeostatic feedback and two that manifest morphogenic feedback. Be clear about what the present homeostatic balance is and what form the deviation from that balance is beginning to take. Try to describe the stances and the strategies being taken by all the members of your present family, including yourself. In other words, describe the *who* and the *how* in the processes of moving, opposing, and amplifying.

Stability combined with flexibility appears to constitute the healthy range of family behavior. Conversely, extreme rigidity and chaotic unpredictability constitute the general parameters of disturbed family behavior. How much homeostasis and how much morphogenesis is optimum probably varies from family to family and the environment in which they function. It becomes very important, then, for a family therapist to understand a particular family's unique system, the larger system in which it functions, and its specific strengths and to work with its potential areas of weakness. With this in mind, ideas that give us a more specific perspective on family interaction are presented.

INTERACTION PATTERNS

The concept of *interaction pattern* bridges the abstract concepts of systems theory to the specific, concrete world of family life. As people develop relationships, they create patterns or negotiate (overtly or covertly) to change them. Therefore, patterns may be conceived of as rules, implicit or explicit, for who does what, when, where, with whom, and how. Every communication or interaction between two or more people tends to either reinforce or change a given rule. Interaction here means any verbal or nonverbal exchange between at least two people. In a broad sense, therefore, interaction is virtually synonymous with communication.

Levels of Communication: Content and Relationship

When two people communicate, there are at least two levels operating. One is the *content* or *literal level* (what). The other is generally referred to as the *relationship level*. In the process of sending the message, there are clues (tones, gestures, and expressions, etc.) telling how that message is to be taken, and the latter is fundamentally a reflection of the relationship between the two people. Awareness of this metacommunication phenomena, or communication about the communication is due to Bateson (1955). The process (how) used to communicate the content, carries important relationship messages. Bateson's colleagues express the distinction as follows:

> Communication not only conveys information, but at the same time it imposes behavior. The report aspect of a message (verbal content only) conveys information and is, therefore, synonymous in human communication with the *content* of the message. The command aspect, on the other hand, refers to what sort of a message it is to be taken as, and therefore, ultimately to the relationship between the communicants. [Watzlawick, Beavin, and Jackson, 1967, P. 48]

Metacommunication, therefore, constitutes "a comment on the literal content as well as on the nature of the relationship between the persons involved" (Satir, 1967, P. 76). The difference and significance of these two levels can be illustrated. If I meet someone in the corridor and routinely and unenthusiastically utter the words, "Hello, John. How are you?" and then proceed to walk past him without so much as a direct glance, I have "said" quite a bit about my view of that relationship. I do not feel warmly toward John, I do not particularly look forward to being with him, and I have no strong intentions to develop a more intimate relationship with him. There are a host of other possible messages.

Contrast the first interaction with this: I meet John in the corridor and excitedly and enthusiastically say, "Hello, John! How are you?" I give his arm a firm but gentle squeeze and stop to chat with him for a few minutes. Note that the verbal content of the interaction is identical to the first sequence. However, the process is such that a host of very different relationship messages emerge. The tone of my voice, the physical contact, and my spending additional time to chat with John contain the following likely messages: I like John; I feel warmly toward him; I feel at ease with him; I look forward to seeing him; I feel secure with him; I value him; and I probably think that he values and enjoys me, too. Note that none of these messages was verbally expressed, but they were most likely "experienced" by John and me.

The concept is highlighted with a marital illustration. My wife and I are sitting in the family room when the phone rings. I pick up the phone (within my wife's hearing distance) and say, "Oh, hi, Jack . . . What? . . . Friday? Sounds great. We'll be there, I'll guarantee you . . . Who, Bill and Sue? Sure, we'll pick them up along the way: No problem with that." I hang up and tell my wife to what I have committed our time. She overtly acquiesces, although she internally is experiencing the pain of disconfirmation. She chooses not to express her thoughts and feelings about it. Through the process I used, I nonverbally metacommunicated several likely relationship messages: that I call the shots; I count, but my wife's thoughts, feelings, and intentions do not. Her acquiescing to the content of my message and her silence on the relationship issue may be metacommunicating the following messages: My wife does not count herself, and she would rather suffer pain quietly than risk open relationship conflict negotiation. She then becomes coresponsible with me for the creation and the maintenance of that relationship pattern.

This, incidentally, is an excellent illustration of the systemic nature of relationships, namely, that it takes at least two to create and maintain an "arrangement" or implicit relationship rule. Thus, the process of giving and receiving messages becomes an important component of healthy, vital functioning. This is especially significant in the case of a marriage and family system where individuals carry sociopsychological survival value toward each other. Parents, spouses, and siblings are one's most potent survival figures. If I do not get emotional support and consistent self-validation from my spouse, chances are that my self-esteem suffers radically. Of course, a good deal of my self-esteem came and continues to come from my relationships with parents and siblings; hence, the importance of receiving congruent, self-validating messages from members of my family.

Understanding and Congruence

One basic factor in dyadic communication is the ability to understand each other's messages at the content and relationship (metacommunicative) levels. The matching of the message sent and the message received is known as the *shared-meaning process*. When the message sent (at both levels) is congruent with the message received, there is shared meaning. Otherwise, it is either a simple case of basic mismatch of information or the possibility of a double message. At this point, the possible emergence of the *double bind** occurs.

Double messages occur when there is a contradiction between different aspects of the content ("You're really fun when you're stupid") or between the content level and the metacommunicative level. An example of the latter might be a husband who tells his wife that he would like to spend more informal chat time with her and yet becomes glued to the television all evening. A wife says that she would like to improve the frequency and the

---

* We are indebted to the work of the communication theorists, especially from the early Palo Alto, California, group (Bateson, Jackson, Watzlawick, Beavin, Haley, Satir, and their associates.)

quality of her sexual relationship with her husband but repeatedly finds excuses to avoid engaging her husband sexually.
Satir (1967, P. 37) offers the following powerful examples: "(a)
A mother tells her daughter to be 'a little lady.' Yet the first gift
she sends her at a girl's detention home is a set of seven, sexy
different colored brassieres. (b) A father says his son should not
defy him. Yet he also complains that his son does not stand up
to him like a man."

By themselves, double messages do not necessarily constitute
a double bind. The essence of a double bind is: (1) a person is
exposed to a repeated flow of double messages (2) from someone
who has survival value to the person and (3) there is no availability of clarifying or checking out the meanings received,
placing upon him the hopeless task of translating them (the
conflicting messages) into a single way of behaving (Satir, 1967,
P. 36). The double bind, then, creates a context wherein the
relationship becomes confused, unintelligible, subject to many
distortions, and without the ability to resolve this state of confusion.

Role Playing Double Messages

Pair up with someone in your class and mutually agree on what two
family positions you will each role play (such as father and son or brother
and sister, etc.) Proceed, with the agreement that neither one of you may
comment upon how the two of you are talking or relating. For five minutes,
carry on a conversation about an important issue in that relationship. In
the process of doing this, make a concerted effort to send as many double
messages as you possibly can.

At the end of five minutes, begin metacommunicating—talk about how
you talked. Share your subjective experiences to that exercise. Have an
observer of your interaction report upon your communication styles and
describe the double-level messages.

The inability to clarify, to check out, and therefore to achieve
a shared meaning seems to be the most crucial element in the
interaction pattern. In the human condition, double messages are
inevitable. People have different backgrounds, attach a varied
set of meanings to the words and gestures exchanged, and fluc-
tuate in moods. The question then for the therapist and for the

couple or family is not whether double messages exist, but is there present, in the system, the interaction repertoire for clarifying and eventually sharing a meaning? It becomes crucial, then, for the therapist to watch for incongruency of messages, to assess the family's capacity to deal with those incongruencies, and to teach the members various ways of achieving shared meanings. Chapter 7 offers some methods of doing this.

Space: The Quest for Closeness and Distance

The question of social-emotional space is a fascinating and crucial aspect in family dynamics. One of the basic existential quests of the human being, as previously mentioned, is a quest for relatedness, belongingness, and closeness. Yet, in the process of achieving closeness, a person still needs to maintain his or her autonomy and individuality. Life then becomes a struggle to achieve and maintain a delicate balance or rhythm between togetherness and separateness. Since the family is the arena par excellence for living out this balance, the question of social space becomes an important matter for investigation. We believe with Kantor and Lehr (1975) that social space is probably the most important variable in family dynamics. Much of the material in this chapter is designed to provide the reader with answers to the following questions that Kantor and Lehr (1975, P. 7) address in their book: "How does a family set up or maintain its territory? How does it regulate distance among its own members?"

Dyadic Spatial Patterns

In this section, the focus is on closeness-distance patterns in dyadic or two-person relationship systems. Although the discussion is based on the marital relationship, remember that the concepts are applicable to any intimate dyadic relationship. It is likewise important again to emphasize that a two-person system, e.g. the marital relationship, does not operate in a vacuum. It is really a subsystem in a larger relationship context. It is helpful to diagram dyadic spatial patterns in the following way (Fig. 1):°

° We are indebted to Dr. Sherod Miller, Elam Nunnally, and Daniel Wackman for the conceptualization of space in terms of Figure 1. Many of these ideas emerged from numerous personal conversations with Dr. Miller, who

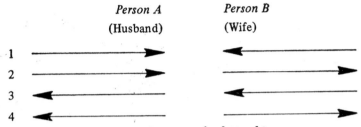

Figure 1. Patterns of relationships.

In Figure 1-1, the arrows depict moments when the husband and wife (or parent and child, or brother and sister, etc.) are enjoying the comfort of their togetherness (funtime, sharing time) or the meaningful productivity of their interaction (supportive behavior or open conflict negotiation). It is generally a way to encounter each other at varying levels of emotional intensity, a time when both husband and wife choose to be there. In Figure 1-4, the arrows represent a situation where both decide to leave the marital space temporarily and engage in independent activity, alone or with other people. Like the first pair, both husband and wife make this a matter of choice, and it is defined as an acceptable avenue of behavior. For example, when the husband or wife chooses to spend time with the children, with friends, with a book, or at work, the system can be depicted as the fourth pair of arrows, provided the other person has also emotionally "let go" of him or her (albeit temporarily).

A healthy marital relationship is thought of as one that is able to wed a satisfactory combination of the first and fourth arrow sets. When the deviation or the quality of the togetherness suffers, one member tends to intensify efforts at restoring the previous homeostatic balance. The same thing happens if the duration or quality of the time apart is threatened. At this point, chances are that the marital relationship moves to a pattern that may be characterized by the second or third pair of arrows. This is generally the way marital difficulty begins or is manifested.

should take major credit for the formulations in this particular section. The most recent statement of this material may be found in Miller, Nunnally, and Wackman (1975). Their discussion includes *leading-following* as a dimension of the diagram. Our discussion is limited to *closeness-distance*.

It is also possible for the couple to adopt a more or less permanent state of emotional apartness. Usually, though, the latter state emerges after many struggles with the second and third patterns.

Figure 1-2 refers to a pattern where the husband is pursuing his wife for more togetherness and where the wife is trying to withdraw or ward off the pursuit. Figure 1-3 is identical to the second, except for the direction of the arrows: It is the wife who is pursuing her husband for more togetherness and the husband who is running away. And here we come to a very interesting systemic quality: The greater the emotional energy invested in the pursuit, the greater the energy invested in withdrawing from that pursuit; and the greater the effort to withdraw, the greater the tendency to pursue. This phenomenon is an example of what Haley has labeled the "first law of human nature" (Haley, 1963). The system then tends to escalate into a vicious circle. The reader is now perhaps beginning to see one of the real payoffs of systems theory: that there is a characteristic visible in the whole (marital relationship) that is not contained in the mere sum of its parts. It further brings to life the concept of systemic responsibility and circular causality. Who is responsible for the escalation, the husband, the wife, or both? Did he withdraw first, which resulted in her pursuit, or was it her pursuit that resulted in his withdrawal? We contend that they are both equally involved and, therefore, equally responsible.

To illustrate the viability and the reality of the concepts just presented, selected highlights of a case with which we worked are offered. The wife is named Joan and the husband, Ted.

CASE ILLUSTRATION: Ted and Joan met each other while students in a university. Ted was known as one of the campus activists at a time when Vietnam was a heated social issue. When Joan spotted Ted, she whispered to a friend, "That's the guy I'm going to marry." She had herself introduced, and within a few days their relationship was defined as a courtship and was immediately sexualized in intercourse. Ted's immediate investment in the relationship was sexual, and it remained so for a couple of years after marriage. Joan, almost from the outset, was using sex as an avenue to pursue Ted emotionally. The courtship lasted about six months. Soon after the marriage, Ted became uncomfortable with Joan's emotional pursuit. Within a year, Ted took a second job, a move apparently designed to be a socially acceptable way to evade Joan's pursuit. In the second year of their marriage, Joan became pregnant. The counseling sessions eventually revealed that part of Joan's motivation to get pregnant at the time she did was to try to hook Ted emotionally back into the relationship, believing that the parent role would serve as a strong link to the marriage.

Soon after the child was born, Ted initiated a separation. Two months later, he was back. Notice that, as soon as enough emotional space was achieved, Ted was willing to move back into the relationship. When adequate emotional space is achieved, the tendency toward togetherness is strengthened. Several months later, Ted wanted another separation. He left, and six months later, he was back again. At the hint of a third separation episode, Joan reacted differently. She indicated then that she had had it and that *she* wanted a divorce. As soon as she indicated termination of her pursuit and her intention to pull out, the direction of Ted's emotional investment changed radically—away from his job and extra-family concerns toward a pursuit of Joan. We have yet to encounter a pursuit as intense and as dedicated as Ted's.

Joan succeeded in getting a separation. Ted went to live with his mother about 60 miles away. Almost every weekend, he pursued Joan, begging her like a small child to have him back and start all over again. For three and one-half years, this erstwhile campus activist did not so much as date a single woman. In fact, so intense was his pursuit that Joan developed a sexual problem as a defense mechanism. She became totally unable to have any erotic feelings for Ted nor for any other male of marriageable status. She experienced erotic attractions only toward men who were much younger than she or who were of a much lower social and educational status. In essence, her erotic feelings were reserved for men with whom there was little possibility of developing an ongoing, intimate relationship. This is a clear illustration of the sensitivity of the human organism toward sociopsychological pressure.

Role Playing Dyadic Patterns

Have two class members play the role of Ted and Joan. Have two therapists interview them in the following situations: (1) when Joan was still pursuing Ted in the early years of the marriage; (2) when Ted was intensely pursuing Joan; and (3) after Ted and Joan developed a comfortable balance between togetherness and separateness.

Watch for the process characteristics of these situations and be able to document your interpretations, as observers, of the dynamics involved.

Had we operated solely out of an individual, intrapersonally oriented approach, it would have been difficult to understand the full interpersonal drama unveiled before our eyes and guts. The marital system contains characteristics that go beyond just what was taking place within Ted and Joan. There were interpersonal forces that emerged in the course of Joan's and Ted's marital relationship that affected their intrapersonal systems. This does not minimize the importance of the intrapersonal, for the person, after all, is still the arena in which relationship influences are "recorded" and felt. It is true to say, however, that it is best to look at both intra- and interpersonal systems to obtain a fuller view of the human condition. For a yet fuller view, of course, the sociocultural system in which the family is embedded must also be analyzed.

Triads: Scapegoating as a Triangular Process

When a dyad is troubled, it often seeks a third point. Concern with the third point diffuses the intensity (when one is being emotionally suffocated) or substitutes for the lack of intensity (when one's partner is withdrawing emotionally). If, for example, the intensity in the husband-wife relationship diminishes to a dissatisfactory level, the wife may seek emotional companionship from her daughter. This lets the husband off the emotional hook; he does not have to be fully responsive to his wife's relationship needs. A triangle is born. What are the apparent payoffs of such a triangle?

One, the marital relationship is maintained, and two, the husband and wife do not have to deal with risky relationship issues. At what price are these benefits achieved? There are fewer chances of achieving a genuine intimacy in each of the three relationships (husband-wife, mother-daughter, and father-daughter). The pressure on the daughter to cross generational boundaries and to act as an adult in the form of a pseudo-spouse or a pseudo-friend to her mother may become so heavy that the daughter could easily show symptomatic behavior in one form or another. She could show excessive dependence on her mother, become psychosomatically ill or delinquent, or perhaps even become psychotic. In any case, the scapegoat (bearer of the family symptom) generally assumes a type of behavior that maintains a given homeostasis. In the example above, daughter eventually "agrees" (usually unconsciously) to her mother's "request" to take responsibility for the mother's emotional nurturance.

Observation of families in clinical settings has resulted in several fascinating ideas about triangular structures in families. Here, for example, are some of Fogarty's conclusions about triangles:

> The three points of these structures are made up of three family members or of two people and an issue—such as drinking—which takes on the significance of a third person. The lines between the points are the pathways used by each member to relate to the other; along them interaction takes place among family members. While two persons may shorten or lengthen the space between them, at no time is there change in the overall area of the triangle. Increased closeness between any two family members results in increased distance from the third member. Movement of persons along the line of the triangle is reactive, often unaware, and without the free use of self-control. *The triangle is a closed system with the sum of the distance between the three members remaining fixed* [italics added]. [P. 43]

Fogarty's observation of the sum of the distance among the three points remaining fixed assumes, of course, that the triangle has not been broken in therapy or through natural morphogenic processes. Although research needs to verify this observation, we have found this concept of fixed distances with variable points useful and applicable in family therapy. Furthermore, it corresponds with the wide belief among family systems theorists that the more disturbed the family, the more rigid its structure. Since triangles are the building blocks of family disturbance, a greater manifestation of homeostatic mechanisms is assumed in disturbed families. The characteristics of being fixed and rigid certainly are representative of homeostasis.

Concentrate for a while on triangles that include mother, father, and child as the three points. In our clinical experience, this trio presents the most common triangle. This is probably so because children are extremely sensitive to the influence of the marital relationship upon their sense of security and development. Parents constitute the most important survival figures in a child's life. Children require the affirmation of parents. Furthermore, a

> child will develop esteem about himself as a sexual person only if both parents validate his sexuality. He must identify with his own sex, yet that very identification must include an acceptance of the other sex. Sexual identification is the result of a three-person learning system. Parents validate a child's sexuality by how they treat him as a small sexual person. But they mainly validate it by serving as models of a functional, gratifying male-female relationship. [Satir, 1967, P. 48]

There is much at stake for the child in the parent's marital relationship. There is, then, little wonder that children often go to extremes to "save" or "take care" of their parents. The authors have encountered children of all ages who take on a variety of symptoms because they sensed that their mother or father needed them to assume a certain role. We recall a sixteen-year-old boy, who, despite previous academic excellence and consistency, suddenly developed a case of school phobia because his mother wanted him to take care of her. There was also the case of the six-year-old girl whose speech deteriorated to the level of a three-year-old because her mother sent covert messages that she wanted her daughter to remain a baby, so she could count on daughter's dependence and not fear losing the third point in the triangle. Her husband was gone most of the time.

James Framo offered a bold hypothesis when, in 1965, he stated that "whenever you have a disturbed child you have a disturbed marriage, although all disturbed marriages do not create disturbed children" (Boszormenyi-Nagy and Framo, 1965, P. 154). We believe that, barring the presence of organicity, Framo's observation is accurate at a high level of confidence. Our clinical experience and, certainly, the family therapy literature support Framo's viewpoint. On the basis of these observations, we believe the triangle offers an excellent explanation for this phenomenon. It means that emotional disturbance in a child is, in the vast majority of cases, intricately related to a triangular structure where mother, father, and child constitute the three points. In cases where a disturbed marriage does not produce a disturbed child, it could be hypothesized that the mother and father have chosen an issue, e.g. drinking, or a nonfamily person, e.g. a mistress or lover, as the third point.

As far as the authors know, the theory of triangles provides the best explanation for some of the findings that have emerged from birth-order research. For example, such research has found that the firstborn manifests the greatest amount of psychological problems, with the last born second in number (Toman, 1975). This is believed to be so because the firstborn is the first child available to the parents for triangulation. Middle children are apparently able to avoid much of the heat along the way, even if they manifest symptoms temporarily. The authors have often anecdotally heard, after the oldest leaves home for marriage, college, or a job, that the second child "is acting just like his older brother." When the second one leaves, the same is said of the third, and so forth until the last one is all who remains. Then, the homeostatic mechanisms get a booster shot because father and mother, probably quite unconsciously, sense the risk of marital breakup, should some easily available third point no longer be there. Folk wisdom has long sensitized people to the joys and dangers of being the baby of the family.

An interesting piece of statistical information was presented in 1975 by the Bureau of Labor and Vital Statistics, which stated that the fastest-rising divorce rate was observed among couples married between twenty and twenty-five years. This period, incidentally, tends to coincide with the launching of the last born. As family size dwindles and as life expectancy increases, increasingly more couples are living beyond the time they launch their last child and thus enter their postparental years. It seems, therefore, that when the last-born children leave, many triangles are broken, and those dyads that are unable to face their person-to-person issues end up in separation or divorce.

Ordinal position then becomes a partial answer to the often intriguing question "Why was this particular child chosen over the others as the scapegoat?" Toman has elaborated upon this concept in his scholarly publication, *Family Constellations,* as have those who espouse the Adlerian psychological viewpoint (Ansbacher and Ansbacher, 1964). Satir (1967, Pp. 33-35) talks about additional factors that may influence this choice. Chance characteristics, such as ugliness, physical deformity, adoption, beauty, intelligence, or striking resemblance to a parent or grandparent, may facilitate the choice. A father, for example, who has strong feelings of occupational inadequacy may pick on his bright son because the latter is a living mirror of his own desires and wishes for competence. The sex or age of the child may also stimulate marital conflicts, as experienced by the daughter or son who reaches a given state of development and pushes for autonomy—an issue that the parents are struggling with in their own relationship.

The importance of the marital subsystem emerges as triangles are discussed. It may be concluded that a healthy, functioning marital relationship is perhaps the best antidote to emotional disturbance in children. Some documentation for this emerged in an innovative study conducted by Murray Bowen and Warren Brodey. They hospitalized the families of five schizophrenic children and observed their behavior intensively. Brodey (1959) writes:

> The striking observation was that when the parents were emotionally close, more invested in each other than either was in the patient, the patient improved. When *either* parent became more emotionally invested in the patient than in the other parent, the patient immediately and automatically regressed. When the parents were emotionally close, they could do no wrong in their "management" of the patient. The patient responded well to firmness, permissiveness, punishment, "talking it out." or any other management approach. When the parents were "emotionally divorced," any and all "management approaches" were equally unsuccessful.

Boundaries and Coalitions

Patterns that take the whole family system into account are now discussed. The family system is composed of three major subsystems: the husband-wife, the parent-child, and the sibling subsystems. Just as it is important for a family to maintain clear boundaries between itself and the rest of society, so too it is important for the subsystems to maintain clear boundaries. The concept of boundaries brings us right back to an aspect of social space—how much togetherness and how much separateness. "The boundaries of a subsystem are the rules defining who participates and how" (Minuchin, 1974, P. 53).*

Boundaries protect the differentiation of the system. If I am a son and a sibling, the family has a different set of expectations of me as a son and of me as a brother to my sister. My personal and interpersonal development depends on clear boundaries existing among the subsystems in my family.

> For proper family functioning, the boundaries of subsystems must be clear. They must be defined well enough to allow subsystem members to carry out their functions without undue interference, but they must allow contact between the members of the subsystem and others. The composition of subsystems organized around family functions is not nearly as significant as the clarity of subsystem boundaries. A parental subsystem that includes a grandmother or a parental child can function quite well, so long as lines of responsibility and authority are clearly drawn. [Minuchin, 1974, P. 54]

Deviation from the clarity of subsystem boundaries can go in one of two directions: (1) enmeshed boundaries and (2) disengaged boundaries. *Enmeshment* refers to the tendency to emphasize togetherness, belongingness, and conformity at the relative expense of separateness and a sense of personal autonomy. Personal and subsystem differentiation become diffuse. *Disengagement,* conversely, refers to the tendency to tighten the boundaries between the subsystems and even between its members so that meaningful interaction between the two or more subsystems becomes increasingly difficult. Separateness and autonomy are emphasized at the relative expense of belongingness and togetherness. Minuchin depicted three boundary patterns (Fig. 2).

It is important to keep in mind that all families possess some degree of enmeshment and disengagement. Furthermore, there

---

* Much of the discussion of boundaries is drawn from Minuchin's ideas.

| Disengaged | Clear Boundaries | Enmeshed |
| (Inappropriately rigid boundaries) | (Normal range) | (Diffuse boundaries) |

Figure 2.   Boundaries found in families.

may be combinations of clear, enmeshed, and disengaged boundaries in the same family. Father may be disengaged from the family (and enmeshed with his job). Mother and daughter may have enmeshed boundaries, while sister and brother maintain fairly clear boundaries.

However, when extreme enmeshment or disengagement develop into chronic states, symptoms in one or more members are likely to appear. Therefore, the model of healthy family functioning at the process level may be shown (assuming a nuclear family system) (Fig. 3).

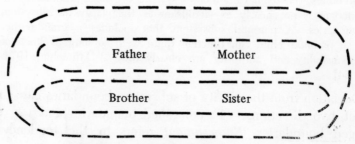

Figure 3.   Healthy family boundaries.

Clarity of boundaries does not mean unavailability; it allows for meaningful communication and movement between one subsystem and another. It also means that the subsystem has the capacity to close ranks temporarily in order to deal with an issue requiring a minimum of interference from other subsystems. For example, father and mother are available to their children for support, education, and play. But when they, as husband and wife, sense the desire for time alone, whether for recreation or for conflict negotiation, they are able to create the social space to perform such a function and to ward off unwarranted demands from the children. The siblings, in turn, are available to their parents. But, hopefully, their social space is respected enough that they are able to develop their own sense of peer cooperation and companionship.

You and Your Parents' Marital Relationship

Write an essay covering your major reactions to your parents' marital relationship. Go as far back as your memory can take you and record your subjective responses as you watched your parents' marital relationship unfold. If you did not observe your parents interact overtly, what were your fantasies and assumptions about their relationship? Be especially attentive to the times you felt triangled in the marital relationship. How did you respond? Did you find yourself getting closer to one or the other, or to neither? Do you see any parallels between your reactions then and your basic reactions to the triangles you might experience in your various social networks currently?

We have found the concept of boundaries tremendously helpful in assessing the strengths and the areas of possible trouble for families. Realizing this, the concept of boundaries is especially valuable to the family therapist in planning therapeutic interventions and goals. This construct enables the understanding of structures beyond dyads or triads. It allows for analysis of the whole family structure, its attempts at working the differentiation of its members, and its attempts at regulating distance and closeness within the family. In one family we saw, for example, there were triplets (sixteen years of age) who blocked the path between the younger male siblings and their parents. Once we spotted this, we were then able to restructure the family system to allow direct access from the younger male siblings to their parents and relieve the triplets from the burden of parentification. *Parentification* refers to an inappropriate assignment of parental roles to a child (*see* Chap. 2).

SUMMARY

In this chapter, we have attempted to give the reader a sense of the family as an interactional system. The basic concepts of systems theory were presented and applied to the family as a social system. The breakthrough of conceiving the family as a complex, adaptive system, as opposed to the previous mechanistic and organismic models, which concentrated simply on homeostasis and neglected morphogenesis, was described. Systems concepts were made specific by the demonstration of interaction patterns as strategies that the system members use to achieve their goals (usually related to the question of space: distance or closeness). The distinction between the content and metacommunicative levels was shown to make the concept of process more intelligible and more meaningful. The last sections offered ways to look at dyadic, triadic, and larger interaction patterns (boundaries).

CHAPTER 2

THE FAMILY AS AN
INTERGENERATIONAL SYSTEM

$\mathbf{A}$LL OF THE MAJOR personality theorists recognize in varying degrees the impact of the family on the developing individual. Just as the personality theorists have documented the familial impact on the developing individual, so have the major counseling theorists referred to the family as a given in the development of pathology and the remedial process. With counseling theorists, the attention given families is primarily etiological in nature and is theoretically viable only for speculative purposes; rarely is the family perceived as an avenue for treatment or intervention. These theorists' ideas seem appropriate in designating the family as a primary source of etiology, but we disagree in placing the family's role in treatment only as a source for developing etiological hypotheses and vicariously "working through" the disorder. Our contention is that the family's power and dynamics have been central in the construction of the identified patient's "problem," and, quite naturally, it is expedient to utilize those same dynamics and power as leverage to promote change in a productive and growth-producing direction.

The family is the primary source from which individuals extract a sense of self or no self, according to two of the leading spokesmen for family therapy, Carl Whitaker and Murray Bowen (Whitaker, 1970). Another strong advocate of family therapy, Salvador Minuchin, has elaborated on the place of the family in the development of an individual's identity. Minuchin (1974, P. 47) states, "In all cultures, the family imprints its members with selfhood. Human experience of identity has two elements: a sense of belonging and a sense of being separate. The laboratory in which these ingredients are mixed and dispensed is the family, the matrix of identity."

The nuclear family is itself in continuous interaction with the larger, extended family system. The two architects of that nuclear family are themselves the product of a family that had and continues to have, an impact on them. This chapter explores the impact of past generations on the present.

MATRIX OF IDENTITY

The matrix of identity introduced in Chapter 1 is expressed graphically in Figure 4 for review and amplification. The idea communicated consists of self-identity stemming from experiencing a sense of belonging to the family group and yet a sense of separateness from the same group. At the core, these constitute perhaps the most fundamental of human experiences. These are forces that members of the previous generations have struggled to work through as functionally as possible for themselves. The

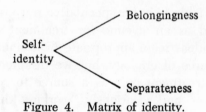

Figure 4.   Matrix of identity.

store of values and interaction patterns the past generations have created have an impact on the ideas and interactions of present generations. Through the continuance of these patterns by the present generation, future generations will continue to be influenced by the reverberations of the previous forces, unless significant changes occur at some point. One way to conceptualize the manifestation of forces around the belongingness-separateness issue is to think in terms of boundaries.

Matrix of Identity Exercise

From your knowledge of your parents' experience in their families of origin, identify their individual development with regard to the matrix of identity. Determine whether there was a functional balance of belongingness or of separateness for them or if there was a significant discrepancy.

Upon completion of this process, do the same, only this time consider your own experience in your family of origin. Once these are completed and continuing to think of the matrix of identity construct, attempt to determine the connections between your parents' experience in their families of origin and your family-of-origin experience.

Impact of Family Boundaries on One's Identity

In Chapter 1, the concept of family boundaries was presented. The family with clear boundaries is capable of providing for its members both a sense of belongingness and separateness. The family characterized by enmeshed boundaries provides an abundance of belongingness but is deficient in providing a sense of separateness. The family with disengaged boundaries provides the sense of separateness, but its members experienced a fuzzy sense of belongingness. Families with either of the two latter boundaries activated results in an incomplete self-identity for the individual.

Accepting Virginia Satir's concept of the parents being the architects of the family, parental significance in determining familial boundaries becomes apparent. The central position of import for the marital dyad has been empirically demonstrated through the work of Lewis and his colleagues (1976). The parents' sense of self-identity determines to a large extent the type of boundaries with which they are comfortable. If they are secure with their self-identity, clear boundaries can be developed. If in their family of origin their self-identity was not crystallized into a functional one, the nuclear family they help to form suffers in various ways. If an individual emanates from a family where a sense of separateness was promoted and belongingness ignored, that person may be prone to developing enmeshed boundaries in his or her future nuclear family to satisfy the felt deficiency. In doing this, the individual is attempting to complete the self, but in the process provides a familial environment for the offspring that results in a low sense of separateness. This pattern is then perpetuated intergenerationally, promulgating fractured and incomplete self-identities. Bell (1962) dramatically illustrated how weak familial boundaries result in a pathological drama that involves several generations.

Another way an individual suffers in a family that does not provide a complete matrix of identity is through being short-changed from learning through modeling or imitation. Modeling, as represented by Bandura (1969), implies that the behavior of one person leads to a similar response by the observing person. If the developing youngster is deprived of the opportunity to observe how a full sense of self-identity can be developed in the family of origin, the chances of implementing a growth-producing process in the future nuclear family are diminished. Again, there is the inevitability of the impact of one generation upon those that follow.

The Intergenerational Connection

Develop a fictional family where the parents have incomplete self-identities as a result of their family-of-origin experiences (one deficient in belongingness and the other deficient in a sense of separateness). Have the family consist of the parents and at least one child. Have individuals assume these roles and portray a situation that presents the family trying to decide what they will do for their vacation. Once the scenario has been completed, discuss issues such as the following: (1) What will be the strongest impact of the child(ren)'s experience in the family of origin on their self-identity? (2) As a therapist, what would your goals be with this family? (3) What might you consider as intervention strategies and techniques to achieve these goals? (4) Considering this family, and the matrix of identity construct, what resistances to treatment might you encounter for what reasons? (5) What might you do to facilitate working therapeutically with the resistances you have identified? (6) What boundaries do you think would best characterize this family prior to the onset of therapy?

The Transgenerational Influence

In recent years, there have been three individuals who have most directly advocated an intergenerational approach to family therapy: Murray Bowen (1966, 1972); Ivan Boszyormenyi-Nagy (1965, 1973); and Geraldine Spark (1974). Although their respective approaches do have idiosyncratic differences, the final outcome seems to be very similar. The designated goal in implementing this approach is to free the present nuclear family by facilitating the parents' movement back to their own families of origin in order to resolve unfinished business with their parents. Through this intergenerational movement, the first two generations are able to benefit from enriched relationships for the remainder of their lives. The third generation, the children, benefit from not being used in a vicarious fashion by their parents to resolve tensions, frustrations, and indebtedness still felt toward the first generation.

Transgenerational movement was exemplified by Murray Bowen at a Groome Child Guidance Center workshop in Washington, D.C., during the fall of 1974. At that time, he commented that the most effective way to help a pressured child serving as a family's identified patient (IP) was to direct the child's parents back to work on the relationship with their parents. His reasoning was that, in most cases, the pressures exerted upon the child by parents come from the parent's unresolved conflicts in their family of origin. By following this procedure, Bowen hopes to disrupt the fusion that is present in the family. This fusion is what Bowen refers to as the *undifferentiated family ego mass* (1966).

An early pioneer of family therapy, Nathan Ackerman, referred to a similar phenomenon, *interlocking pathology in family relationships* (Ackerman, 1956). All of the members of the family are locked together, and one or more of its members are not developing into their own separate person in the group. There is no allowance for what Bowen refers to as *differentiation of self* for the individuals in this type of family (1966). To facilitate this process, Bowen uses a technique and process referred to as the *genogram,* which is detailed later in this chapter and in Chapter 6. The genogram is a process devised to have the parents "map" on paper their extended families and study the resultant product. During this process, the parents are assisted in identifying unresolved conflicts in the family of origin, or what Bowen has referred to as the *extended family emotional field,* which can then be analyzed.

To facilitate transgenerational movement, Bowen works with either one of the parents separately or sees them conjointly. He is not as adamant regarding the presence of both spouses in each session as are other therapists, such as Carl Whitaker (1970). Bowen believes that because the family functions as a system, change in one member of the system brings about changes in the other members to accommodate the initial changes effected by the member involved in therapy. He also elects to work with extended family problems by sending the patient back to the family of origin with very specific assigned homework. The homework assignments are agreed upon by Bowen and the patient prior to implementation. Examples of what may be expected of the patient by homework assignments in this process are documented in an excellent article that portrays Bowen's ideas ("Toward the Differentiation of a Self," 1972).

Karl Menninger has commented that one of the most common scenes he has observed in all of his therapeutic experience is that of parents passing unresolved tensions, frustrations, and hostilities generated with their own parents on to their children (Menninger, 1958). These same children, in turn, pass them on to their children, and the intergenerational process is in gear. With this perspective in mind, it becomes evident how a nuclear family's emotional field (Bowen, 1966) not only affects the present participants, but the succeeding generations as well. One of the most powerful and dynamic works to be completed in this area is the book, *Invisible Loyalties: Reciprocity in Intergenerational Family Therapy,* by Boszormenyi-Nagy* and Spark (1973). In this work they outlined the rationale basic to understanding and doing intergenerational family therapy.

Like Bowen, Nagy and Spark do not limit their focus to a horizontal picture, i.e. the present generation. They also recognize as critical the vertical, or intergenerational, dimension. A movie, *The Outerspace Connection,* explores the vertical dimension of man's historical development and roots as possibly emanating from the influence of beings from another planet. In an analogous sense, we can refer to the "inner space connection" as being the intergenerational connection that accounts for much of each individual's existence.

---

* Other than in references, *Nagy* (pronounced *Naj*) is used in place of the full surname *Boszormenyi-Nagy*.

The Future Generations

Recalling the fictional family developed (P. 36) consider the following:
1. Without intervention, how might these children relate to their future spouse in marriage?
2. Without intervention, how might the children of this family relate to their own children (third generation) as parents?
3. What would be the resulting matrix of identity and personality characteristics of these third-generation children?

Generational Bookkeeping

Nagy and Spark view the basic building block of relationships as being a hierarchical network of obligations. The obligations of primary concern are generally of a covert nature. Relationships are characterized as being held together by a gyroscope that keeps current accounts of the total balance of obligations among the participants. The expectations that relationship participants hold for each other are ever present, and each participant keeps track of the debts and credits. With this in mind, the idea of relationship bookkeeping is understandable.

The notion of obligation is intricately tied up with the family system's role as the source of the matrix of identity, the system of highly interrelated relationships through which the self emerges via interactions that touch upon the core human experiences of belongingness and separateness. Because of the weight that the family relationships carry, a network of corresponding rights and obligations necessarily enter into the expectation of individual members vis-à-vis each other. There is in human systems a force that seeks for justice, fairness, or balance in the accounting of these obligations. "All relationship systems are conservative. Their logic demands that the members' shared investment of care and concern should serve to balance out all injustices and exploitations" (Boszormenyi-Nagy and Spark, 1973, P. 11). By internalizing the group's expectations around the balancing of obligations and rights, members develop a sense of loyalty to the family system. This loyalty is tied to the individual's quest for relatedness and belongingness. Every move toward individuation and emotional growth is a potential and at least implicit threat of disloyalty to the family. It can then be seen that the self, obligations, and loyalty are highly interwoven concepts. Nagy and Spark identify how members of a family behave loyally to the system as a result of external coercion, conscious recognition of interest in membership, consciously recognized feelings of obligation, and unconsciously binding obligation to belong.

Loyalty within one system may be determined by the results of bookkeeping in another system. An example of this is Nagy and Spark's observations that western society may soon be burdened with irresponsible, resentful, and justifiably disloyal citizens. This is explained on the basis of children being born into families where the parents either do not intend, or are emotionally unable, to care for them. The result is that the children feel no sense of obligation and experience no sense of justice, resulting in behavior labeled by the psychodynamic psychologist as *psychopathic*. The psychopathic deviant in this respect is defined as being that person without reason or ability to sense obligations. This perspective then also serves as an explanation of much of human motivation.

Horizontal Bookkeeping

In human relationships, much behavior can be explained on the basis of individuals analyzing their ledgers and manifesting behavior that attempts to balance them. Behavior in relationships from this orientation is then understood in accordance to what individuals feel they owe or have coming to them from these various relationships. Thus, the more the environment is full of love and trust, the more indebted one feels; the less able one is to repay the debt, the more rapidly the debt grows. On the other hand, the more the environment is full of hostility, resentment, and disregard, the more the credits accumulate; the longer this goes unpaid, the greater one's credits grow, not just quantitatively, but probably qualitatively as well.

Bookkeeping Time

Contemplate your family of origin in reference to the concept of relationship accountability. Identify the various members in your family and place their names on separate sheets of paper. For each person develop a list under the word *debts* and *credits*. Under "debts" identify experiences and situations for which you feel indebted to that person. Under "credits" identify experiences and situations for which you believe that person is indebted to you. Proceed now to consider questions such as the following: (1) If these lists were presented to you as a therapist, how would you portray the matrix of identity for this person? (2) Considering the lists as a therapist, how would you hypothesize this person's perception of the relationship boundaries in this person's family of origin? (3) As the therapist, what ideas might you have to facilitate this person's balancing of the relationship ledger in the family of origin?

An example of bookkeeping time is the case of the alcoholic. Imagine a marital dyad that contains an alcoholic husband. If the marital environment is conducive and supportive, it becomes difficult for the alcoholic to justify his disruptive and irresponsible drinking behavior. If the alcoholic can manipulate the spouse into being unloving or nagging, etc., he can then justify, according to his accounting system, the notion that the spouse is indebted and he is deserving of a binge. Although some psychodynamically oriented psychologists recognize this as being masochistic, the alcoholic has achieved the goal of establishing justification for his behavior. Although the justification has been established, it is not without further ramifications.

As alcoholics reflect on their behavior, either consciously or unconsciously, they begin to sense their essential disloyalty and indebtedness for the drinking behavior. They then begin to experience guilt and remorse and resort to more drinking to cope with their sense of disloyalty. They are now involved in an escalating vicious cycle. While this is happening with the alcoholic spouse, the other is simultaneously experiencing a sense of unpaid debt from the alcoholic spouse and feels more justified in nagging and feeling resentful. Assuming the nonalcoholic spouse is female, she now becomes the proverbial martyred wife of the alcoholic, and the two are involved in a destructive systemic relationship. This is a process we have seen and heard about numerous times in our therapy with alcoholics. This brief sketch is an example of analyzing the idea of loyalties and accounting of obligations in a horizontal or single generation.

Vertical Bookkeeping

The vertical, or transgenerational dimension, can be exemplified in the following manner. If my parents provided me with an environment that I interpret as positive and conducive, without allowing me the opportunity for repayment, I in essence become a "debtor." They are the "creditors"; but they block avenues for me to make my relational payments. I am thus indebted. This may result in my attempting to shed debtor status in various ways, among them: not committing myself to other relationships freely and thus avoid feeling disloyal to my familial system; being oversolicitous of my children in an attempt to rid myself of the sensed obligations and indebtedness; and being of a placating and appeasing nature to most in my environment and never acknowledging my own feelings and desires. Another alternative may be one of responding to the smothering sensation I experience by trying to bolt out of the system and rebel in order to receive my freedom, which in essence is only a quasi or superficial freedom. For example, assume I attempt to repay my indebtedness by being oversolicitous of my children. By selecting this procedure, I am also casting my children into a setting similar to what I experienced and creating the potential for perpetuating this relationship pattern into generations beyond the three already involved. As a result, it becomes evident that the undischarged obligation has been passed on, resulting in not allowing the generations to interact with each other in a more open and honest fashion. The "unfinished business" in one generation thus impinges upon and affects the ensuing generations.

Mechanisms Utilized to Facilitate the Bookkeeping Process

In an important book, Stierlin (1974) further elaborates upon the dialectical approach to understanding human behavior as a result of relationships. In his introduction, Stierlin opens with the story of the prodigal son (Luke 15), who returns home after engaging in behavior he reports as sinful, only to be joyously received by his father. The zealous celebration of the prodigal son's arrival by the father then results in the older, more obedient son's irritation. To this story, Stierlin raises the possibility that perhaps the prodigal son in his disobedience was more obedient than his "well-behaved" brother. The implication is that through his disobedience he has satisfied his father's wishes for excitement vicariously. Therefore, by overtly being disobedient, he was covertly obedient and satisfied his father's expectations. Thinking of the concepts of loyalty and obligation, the prodigal son is now the creditor and the father the debtor. Thus, the celebration is explicable under circumstances that, on the surface, seem undeserving of such recognition.

In an attempt to explain what takes place in a creditor-debtor relationship, Stierlin introduces the concepts of centripetal and centrifugal forces in relationships. Centripetal forces imply the tendency to stick together at all costs. The opposite of this is centrifugal force, meaning movement away from each other. He then identifies the three transactional modes of binding, delegating, and expelling to explain how these forces are developed and maintained.

BINDING: Binding is that mode employed by parents to tie their children to themselves and locking them into the "family ghetto" at all cost. Naturally, this is a mode that is utilized when centripetal forces are activated. Although Stierlin emphasizes parent-child relationships in his work, these principles are applicable to any relationship.

In discussing binding, Stierlin conceptualizes the process as potentially being implemented at any of three levels: affective or id binding, cognitive or ego binding, and binding through exploitation of loyalty or superego binding. The following are explanations of each of the binding modes

Affective or id binding is the exploitation of dependency needs with emphasis on regressive gratification. This process results in a fostered dependency to lock the bound individual into the relationship system. *Cognitive binding* is the process of interfering with differentiated self-awareness on the part of the bound individual. This binding is usually facilitated by what R. D. Laing (1965) has referred to as *mystification*. Mystification comprises three steps: (1) attribution—attributing a characteristic or role to an individual that is functional to or for the "attributor"; (2) invalidation—disqualifying any action that is manifested by the individual who is being mystified; and (3) induction—the active recruitment and seduction of the person into finally accepting the attribution as being his existence or at least part of it. Binding through the exploitation of loyalty or superego binding implies inducing excessive breakaway guilt in the bound individual and turning him or her into a lifelong, self-sacrificing member of the relationship system.

DELEGATING: Delegating is the mode employed when the individual is sent out of the system, with a "long leash of loyalty" to hold him in check and complete the mission. To explain the delegating mode, return to the story of the prodigal son and accept the implication of the celebration offered earlier as true. The prodigal son was released with the "leash" of providing his father with vicarious excitement. This amounts to a limited and qualified autonomy at best. This particular mode activates and exemplifies both centripetal and centrifugal forces. The prodigal son was sent out (centrifugal force), but only so far (centripetal).

EXPELLING: The transactional mode of expelling consists of enduring neglect and/or outright rejection of an individual. These individuals naturally are left with a sense of being creditors and are definitely not debtors in the framework of loyalties and obligations. As a result, their behavior toward others may be characterized by a "the world owes me" attitude. It is probably clear that this mode is activating and demonstrative of the centrifugal forces.

Whether it is centrifugal or centripetal forces that are being activated and maintained by the various transactional modes just explained, there are transgenerational implications in the sense of loyalties and obligations.

The child exposed to centripetal forces may respond by exposing his children to centrifugal forces. An example is the youngster caught in centripetal forces, via the affective binding mode, marrying and being emotionally unable to provide emotional support to the offspring. This deficiency then results in the children feeling neglected or exposed to centrifugal forces.

These latter-generation children then expose their children to centripetal forces to provide them with what was missing in their childhood. Again there is evidence of the vicious cycle, or the circular nature of human relationships based on loyalties and obligations in family systems.

Examples of the Impact of Past Generations

Although the examples utilized thus far to illustrate the role of transgenerational or "inner space" connections have been what may be interpreted as every day, the assumption should not be made that dramatic enactment is not witnessed. Many of the family therapy pioneers, such as Ackerman, Jackson, Lidz, Searles, Wynne, and Haley, have elaborated on the role of the family in the development of schizophrenic behavior. These experienced psychotherapists give many demonstrations of the murderous hate existent in schizophrenics for their parents. Simultaneously existent with the hate, there is paradoxically a deep and devoted love present, as testified to by the schizophrenic's willingness to sacrifice themselves for the sake of their parents' psychological well-being. As discussed in Chapter 1, the schizophrenic-identified patient allows the parents to delude themselves into good health. Again, how could the concept of loyalties and obligations of a transgenerational nature play a part here? Assuming that such patterns exist, the following is a preferred explanation.

The parents of a schizophrenic are the product of parental relationships that primarily used the transactional mode of expelling in relating to them. In attempting to give their child (consciously) what they did not receive, they bind the youngster by activating centripetal forces. While consciously doing this with declared good intentions, they unconsciously use the youngster to gain retribution for the debt they feel is due from their parents. The collection that rightfully belongs with their parents is now made through their child, who is unconsciously the parent surrogate, in regard to retribution for a long-felt payment forthcoming. In this case, the payment the schizophrenic provides is that of continuing to provide a source of activation for centripetal forces for the parents. They can now come together and be united out of concern for their psychotic youngster in what Wynne and his associates (1958, Pp. 205-220) refer to as *pseudo-mutual union.*

Boszormenyi-Nagy and Spark (1973) have documented how a married couple may develop problems out of a sense of loyalty to their families of origin. This loyalty to the family of origin may surface in the masked form of impotence, premature ejaculation, physical beatings, and in many other ways. In all cases, the purpose is that of communicating to the original family that one is still loyal and will not make an outside commitment. By engaging in this behavior, the individual who still feels indebted to the family of origin can diminish the experience of "debts owed." Nagy and Spark believe that to some degree all marriages are burdened with the spouses' unsettled accounts of loyalty to their families of origin. The family traitor or scapegoat may be holding the family together by dysfunctional behavior and thus pay off the guilt-burdened debit account.

Carl Whitaker (1970) claims the influence of past generations in the nuclear family is seen in the form of "ghosts" in the therapeutic setting. In working with a nuclear family, the spouses frequently refer to their families of origin and the respective impact on the present relationship either overtly or covertly. Whitaker contends that in order to deal with the "ghosts," an effort should be made by the therapist to get them in, so reality can be worked with and not illusions. Although he does not say this explicitly, it seems that Whitaker attempts to attack loyalty issues by helping the spouses to realize, through therapy with their families of origin that their parents are not "God-like figures," but human beings like themselves. He then discusses how this can be accomplished without grandiose goals, but by being casual and exploring the grandparents' family history and marital relationship in the presence of the spouses involved in therapy. Framo's (1976) rationale and approach to working with the families of origin is similar to Whitaker's.

Levy's classic study of 1943 indicated the presence of the transgenerational influence. His study disclosed the presence of a correlation between an overprotective attitude in mothers and deprivation of love in the mother's own childhood. In this sense, the mother set up a pattern in which she sought to obtain from her children what she had not obtained from her mother. This process could also be explained by using Minuchin's concept of boundaries. The mother comes from a relationship system characterized by disengaged boundaries, resulting in a vacuum being experienced by the mother. This vacuum consists of a deficiency in a sense of belongingness. To compensate for this, she formulates a relationship with her children characterized by enmeshed boundaries. The apparent question then becomes: When does the pattern cease perpetuating itself?

Boszormenyi-Nagy and Spark (1973) refer to a process similar to what Levy identified in regard to how a child can be illegitimately used by parents to satisfy unfulfilled needs. They use the term *parentification.* This refers to the process whereby parents unconsciously attempt to place their child in the position of parenting them. This may come about as a result of the parents perceiving themselves as being in the position of deserving payment. Their ledger is tilted in the direction of their being creditors, and the child, to his detriment, is expected to provide payment. Another explanation is that of the parent attempting to recover the relationships they had with their parents through the child. This latter explanation is regarded as being especially prominent if the spouse fails to gratify this need.

For all of the previously mentioned family therapists, the concern is to assist in the balancing of transgenerational ledgers. The implication naturally is that this is best expedited when the parents of the spouses' families of origin are still alive. When the spouses' parents are dead, the issue of balancing the ledger is not buried with the lost parent but still very much alive. Norman Paul (Paul, 1965, P. 339-345; Grosser, 1967, P. 186-205) has discussed in some detail a process he refers to as *operational mourning,* which can be used to facilitate the process after the death of a spouses' parent. Paul believes that incomplete mourning of the dead individual can result in defenses against further losses and disappointments. Once the "brakes of defenses" are applied, the result is a rigid, homeostatically locked family system with the fear of losses and other disappointments being transmitted to the children.

The implementation of the operational mourning process can help a spouse identify repressed feelings of indebtedness to the lost parent and how they influence the current marital relationship. The affective experience that results from operational mourning can provide for the entire nuclear family the development of greater empathy and understanding of the origins of current relational difficulties. As Paul has stated, this allows the spouses to realize how much the past is not the past. Paul and Grosser's clinical study of fifty families with a schizophrenic member and twenty-five with at least one psychoneurotic member demonstrated vividly how the past was not simply the past. In their study, they discovered that losses that occurred as much as fifty years before investigation were still exercising a stifling effect upon the current family relationships.

Paul's and Grosser's results suggest that, in families with a psychoneurotic member, the loss is usually experienced directly by the patient. In the case of a schizophrenic patient the loss was usually experienced directly by a parent, and the transgenerational influences of the loss seemed directly related to the etiology of the schizophrenia in the patient. This transgenerational communciation from parent to child illustrates what Bowen (1966) refers to as the *family projection process*.

Paul's operational mourning process includes a mourning response induced by directed inquiry about the reactions to actual losses sustained by family members. The therapist encourages the member directly involved to recollect as many details of the original loss as possible to facilitate the grief work. The other family members observe and respond to the feelings generated, which usually results in a powerful empathic experience for all concerned.

Paul's operational mourning process includes a mourning response induced by directed inquiry about the reactions to actual losses sustained by family members. The therapist encourages the member directly involved to recollect as many details of the original loss as possible to facilitate the grief work. The other family members observe and respond to the feelings generated, which usually result in a powerful empathic experience for all concerned.

The Result of Death

This is the report of case data from a family seen by the authors. A family consisting of mother, father, and seventeen-year-old son was referred by a school counselor. The son was failing in school and for all practical purposes seemed to be aimless in motivation and direction. When first seen, the family was characterized by very poor communication between mother and father (disengaged), with mother and son apparently fused (enmeshed) over a number of issues revolving about his being responsible for himself both in and out of the house. It quickly became apparent though, that as mother was expressing her anger over the son's lack of demonstrated responsibility (picking up clothes and bringing in wood, etc.) she would quickly do these things for him. The father remained sullen and detached throughout these chaotic episodes and in therapy.

Through the first six sessions, we concentrated on restructuring by reassigning responsibilities to various roles and both clarifying and changing family rules. This was completed with moderate success and change. In the seventh session, time was devoted to exploration of the families of origin. Both parents indicated their parents had died, and as the mother related this, tears came to her eyes. When reference was made to her tears and how death of loved ones can be painful, she began to sob openly and profusely. Her husband and son became almost motionless at this display, as if they were aware of what was to follow. The mother then began to present an experience with death other than her parents. When her son was three years old, she took him and a nephew of a similar age to the local fair. She placed the two youngsters on one ride, and as she stood watching, she saw her nephew thrown to his death from the machinery. The therapists soon determined that this family had never discussed this incident after the burial of the nephew. The opening of this situation resulted in a powerful empathic experience for all involved. The experience had the effect of releasing energy into their system that had been dammed up for the last fourteen years through their masks of stone and silence. The therapeutic process moved quite rapidly and with much success from the seventh session on. Termination was reached at the end of the fourteenth session.

For further understanding and integration of this experience, attempt to recreate the therapeutic system in the seventh session. Once the various roles have been assigned and prior to beginning, consider the following:

1. As therapist, what type of responses would prove most facilitative to working with the emotion present in this situation?
2. How could the father and son be included in this therapeutic process for the greatest benefit to occur?
3. How could this session be terminated?

We hope that this overview of the primary therapists advocating therapy with extensive consideration given the family of origin is illuminating. As Spark (1974) has identified, the enabling of family members to work with their invisible loyalties and obligations provides for "a rebalancing of time, efforts, or concrete services" to begin to take place within current relationships. The end result of involvement with the families of origin being the release of a new supply of energy for utilization in more creative and productive living in the present by members of the nuclear family under consideration.

CLINICAL APPLICATIONS OF
INTERGENERATIONAL CONCEPTS

As with most elements of therapy, there seem to be times when work with the family of origin is more appropriate than others. By employing this approach, the authors believe a concept of Virginia Satir's can be applied. Her thought is that, if the past can be used to illuminate the present, the person will probably have a good future—if the past is used to contaminate the present, there is probably a bleak future (Satir, Big Sur Recordings).

Appropriateness of an Intergenerational Orientation

The following are signs that indicate the advisability of employing an intergenerational approach: (1) if the parent(s) openly disclose the presence of an unbalanced relationship with their family of origin; (2) if one or both spouses either overtly or covertly bring their family of origin into the therapeutic setting as ghosts; (3) if the therapeutic contract calls specifically for development work; (4) if the therapeutic contract is for premarital counseling; (5) if the therapeutic contract stipulates divorce counseling; and (6) if the therapeutic contract stipulates treating one or more sexual dysfunctions.

UNBALANCED PARENTAL RELATIONSHIPS: Where there is an unbalanced relationship with the parents of one of the spouses, it seems imperative to direct therapeutic time and effort to the intergenerational connections. A case in point was a family seen by the authors at the request of an attorney who had become involved in a child-abuse case. The child was seven years old, and his second grade teacher noticed open wounds on his arm when he entered the school one morning. It was later documented that these wounds were inflicted by his twenty-four-year-old mother the evening before.

The family consisted of a mother, father, and a five-year-old sister, along with the abused youngster. In engaging the family in therapy, it quickly became evident that the battered seven-year-old had been parentified by his parents, especially the mother. She expected her son to provide her with love, support, and reassurance that was beyond the capability of his young years. In exploring the mother's relationships in her family of origin she disclosed how her mother had expected much from her, and she could never quite meet her mother's expectations. Always falling short of meeting the demands, she was met with criticism and frequent physical beatings. Thinking of her life's relationship ledger, it was evident how she experienced herself as the creditor, and placed her firstborn in the position of paying the debt off.

This case illustrates clearly what Steele and Pollock (1968) disclosed as a result of their work with child-abusing parents. In exploring life histories of these parents, they determined that these subjects were exposed to parental demands for responsive behavior and prompt compliance accompanied by sharp criticism. The individuals, as children, responded by not feeling loved and by believing their needs and wishes were unimportant or even wrong. Steele and Pollock found that this pattern of child rearing was transmitted from parent to child, generation after generation, and seems to be culture bound as a result. These abusing parents, feeling unloved and psychologically abandoned by their parents, pass on the experience of being a creditor in the intergenerational relationship ledger. Both Glass (1970) and Reiner and Kaufman (1969) have documented findings similar to Steele and Pollock.

In this family, the husband-wife relationship could be characterized as disengaged, with the husband assuming a peripheral role in the family. This resulted in the son being parentified by the mother to the point of escalation into child abuse. Naturally, the marital relationship was a source of sharp focus during the source of treatment, but this was facilitated through devoting three sessions to exploring the mother's family of origin in the presence of the other three family members. In this sense, the therapists capitalized on Paul's (Paul, 1967; Paul and Grosser, 1965) ideas of operational mourning and helping the other family members to develop empathy and understanding for the mother's experience and current situation. This family was seen for a total of twelve sessions, at which time treatment was terminated, at the agreement of both therapists and the family. The therapists feel comfortable that not only is the family more functional in a healthy sense now, but this will probably be carried on into future generations by their children, in opposition to the dysfunctional pattern that was present.

PARENTS PRESENT IN THERAPY AS "GHOSTS": The second indication for an intergenerational focus is if either of the spouses refer to the families of origin for comparison or contrast. A statement heard many times by those who work with families is "You're/I'm just like my/your father/mother." When this statement is heard by the therapist, it presents a clear transition into an intergenerational focus. Naturally, if the family of origin parent subsystem is available, every effort is made to bring them into the therapeutic milieu. The rationale for this is hydra-headed: (1) this provides an opportunity to confront with reality what otherwise would remain a ghost in the therapeutic endeavor. As comments are made about members of the families of origin, it is difficult for the therapist to work with them and determine what is real and what has been subject to distortion or the mystification process. By having those involved in the current situation, reality contact can be facilitated. (2) Not only are the new participants valuable in the actual treatment session but also outside the setting through engagement in intergenerational homework assignments.

As efforts are made to balance the intergenerational relationship ledger, assignments can be made that all members hear about firsthand. An example is the parent from the nuclear family who, feeling she is a debtor to her parents, can be helped to understand how she can begin to repay her parents. At the same time, the family-of-origin parents can learn to appreciate the necessity for the repayment and allow it without stifling attempts made by their child. Once the ledger is balanced, the now-adult child can begin to interact with others in her environment without the burden of relational debt interference.

Balancing the Relationship Ledger

Have one group serve as a family and construct a scenario that results in one of the parents making an evaluative or comparative statement regarding the other spouse and one of their parents. Have two people identified as co-therapists who will work with this family without forewarning regarding the situation to be presented to them. Consideration should be given to the following by the co-therapists: (1) how to introduce the intergenerational concept to the family, (2) how to emphasize the value of including the extended family into the therapeutic process at this time; and (3) what to encourage them to do regarding getting their parents into therapy. This same role-playing process can be employed with each of the following explanations offered for utilization of an intergenerational orientation.

DEVELOPMENTAL WORK: A third situation for which an intergenerational approach could well be adopted is therapy with a developmental focus. Developmental work implies a situation where the couple or family members feel comfortable with their current relationships but request exploration of ways in which they may improve. A developmental orientation is becoming prominent, as evidenced by the recent rapid expansion of the Association of Couples for Marriage Enrichment, the Minnesota Couples Communication Program, and other groups and organizations in which the primary concern is educational or developmental. In developmental counseling, we believe an intergeneratoinal orientation is valuable. By implementing an intergenerational approach with the use of the genogram (explained on P. 55), a great deal of explorative developmental work can be accomplished. This procedure allows the couple or family to look in great detail at the roots of their current familial relationship dynamics. This understanding can then be employed to better determine what they may want to do with their past and present relationships and how they can accomplish it.

PREMARITAL COUNSELING: The fourth area in which the intergenerational approach is valuable is in premarital counseling. By helping the prospective spouses to do the following, the chances for a vital and healthy marriage are greatly enhanced:

(1) to analyze, if needed, and reconstruct viable person-to-person relationships with their family of origin prior to marriage. The goal is to allow the two individuals to move into their marriage unencumbered with either debts or credits from the family of origin; (2) to develop in the couple an understanding of the rules and processes existent in both families of origin and what it is they may want to bring into their marriage. Naturally, along with the "what," the "how" or the process they are going to utilize to develop their relationship is very important. (3) Along with the relationship focus, both will probably better understand each other as individuals as they gather a more in-depth appreciation for each other's roots. During this process, if at all possible, both families of origin are directly involved in the therapeutic sessions to facilitate the process and allow them to realize their past, present, and future involvement in the soon-to-be-developed nuclear family

DIVORCE COUNSELING: If the therapeutic contract calls for divorce counseling, the authors believe this affords another valuable opportunity for implementing the intergenerational approach. One of the couples seen by the authors for divorce counseling is a good case in point. They came in initially at the request of the family court commissioner as the wife was seeking divorce resulting from the husband's infidelity.

In exploring the families of origin, it became evident that the wife had come from an enmeshed family and the husband from a disengaged family. The wife's family seemed to be attempting to sabotage her marriage from the beginning through derogatory comments about the husband. There also seemed to be superego binding (the loyalty or guilt level) in the sense that the wife's mother continually referred to how she missed the daughter's assistance and involvement. In exploring their marital relationship, it seemed that the wife had found it difficult to commit herself to her husband for fear of being disloyal to her enmeshed family of origin. At the same time, the husband was experiencing himself as a creditor coming from his disengaged family of origin, which resulted in more tension in his marital relationship. As the couple was led to understand the dynamics present between them, they were able to be more objective. They decided to reconcile after a brief therapeutic separation.

By using the intergenerational approach with a couple in divorce counseling, we believe that a far greater understanding can be gained by the couple regarding the relationship they are attempting to dissolve. If the marital relationship ends in dissolution, hopefully the new learnings can be utilized in future relationships they may develop.

SEXUAL DYSFUNCTIONS: The last area to be given attention, regarding an intergenerational approach, is that of treatment in the area of sexual dysfunctions. Most of the current researchers and therapists of sexual dysfunctions refer to the need for attention being devoted to each member's family of origin. Among these are Kaplan (1975), Masters and Johnson (1970), and Hartman and Fithian (1974). The primary concern for attention to the family of origin by the above authors is in exploring the development of sexual attitudes and values in childhood.

The intergenerational approach being advocated adds another dimension. To exemplify this, the following questions are offered: Is the current sexual dysfunction a manifestation of an unbalanced intergenerational relationship ledger? Is one made impotent as a result of loyalty to his family of origin and not wanting to imply commitment or investment in the marital relationship? Is the sexual dysfunction being offered by one of the mates to communicate to their family of origin that their marriage is not as good as their parents? In doing so, the individual is balancing the relationship ledger to pay off the felt indebtedness. Does one spouse demand and expect too much of his or her mate because he or she feels him- or herself to be a creditor in the family of origin? Exploration of the intergenerational impact gives a more holistic perspective to understanding the working with sexual dysfunctions. We believe this orientation leads to understanding sexual expression in the marital relationship more fully with smaller chance of error in intervention based on less than full understanding.

The Genogram

As mentioned earlier, the primary vehicle used in the therapy to implement the intergenerational concept is the genogram. The

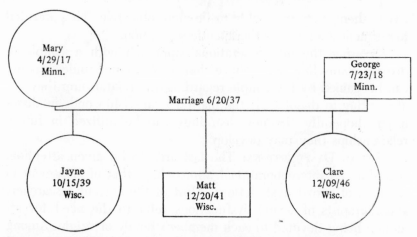

Figure 5. Sample genogram of two generations. If either of the parents were married before or after the marriage represented above, this is also represented graphically. The symbols for that union are placed on the side of the spouse involved and connected with another marriage line. On this marriage line, the date of marriage is indicated along with the date of dissolution and the reason for it. If there were children as a result of that marriage, they are also included symbolically.

genogram components and implementation process are now explained.

Genealogists have for years utilized what is commonly referred to as a "family tree" to delineate a family's ancestry. The authors utilize a similar diagrammatic approach to represent a family in the therapeutic process. For facilitating the development of greater understanding of the family system by the family, the genogram is of central importance. The genogram provides therapeutic analysis of the intergenerational concepts detailed earlier in this chapter (Fig. 5). The process employed is quite simple. We have not encountered anyone who has been unable to complete it after being provided with a simple set of instructions and a large sheet of newsprint. A large piece of paper is needed when it is considered that family membership doubles each generation; in addition at least three or four generations are to be represented.

In the directions, the person constructing the genogram is

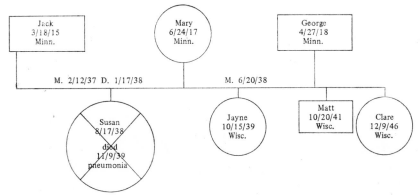

Figure 6. Sample genogram of two generations with more than one marriage.

asked to use symbols, i.e. circles for females and squares for males. He or she is asked first to represent his or her mother and father in the middle of the page toward the bottom. A vertical line is then drawn from each symbol about ½ inch, and these two lines are then connected with a horizontal line to represent the marriage or generational line. A vertical line is then drawn downward from this line for each child that resulted from that marriage. At the end of each of these ½-inch lines, a circle or square (depending on sex) should be placed. The firstborn should be located furthest to the left, followed to the right by each child born thereafter with the last-born child being located furthest to the right. Inside each symbol the name of the individual with their birthdate and state of birth is printed. In Figure 6, a death is represented by placing an X in the appropriate symbol accompanied by the date and reason for death, if known, immediately outside the symbol. Naturally, the symbol for death is frequently seen as the writer of the genogram moves back into generations three and four. In most cases, at least three generations can be represented. When the genogram is assigned, the person is encouraged to search back and represent as many generations as possible. In order to do this, the writer of the genogram usually contacts other family members for information. Many times, this simple process of contacting other family members for information is therapeutic and begins to send "healing ripples" through the family system, in much the same fashion as ripples emanate from the place where a pebble is dropped into a pond. As individuals begin to explore their extended families of origin, the therapist provides guidelines to follow, to facilitate the process. The individuals are directed to pay particular attention to what are referred to as *dynamic events*.

1. Among the dynamic events, naturally the first is that of births. Births take on added significance as consideration is given to spread between siblings and understanding reasons for brief or extensive periods of time between births. Stillbirths and miscarriages are also included, as they can have powerful effects on the family at that time and well into the future.

2. Another dynamic event is family moves. When and where did the family move? For what reason? How and by whom was the decision made? With what effects?

3. Job changes constitute another dynamic event. When was it, or more typically today, when were they made? With what results? What kind of job stress was there and when was it?

4. Family separations also should be considered. When were there separations? For what reasons? For how long? What were the apparent effects?

5. Health and habits comprise an important dynamic event. Who was ill? With what? Who had the major responsibility for caring for the ill person? For how long? What stress resulted? How was stress manifested, if at all? Habits refer to such as alcohol consumption or other abuse of chemicals; eating habits that might result in health problems, i.e. obesity; gambling also constitutes an example of other behavior classifiable as a habit.

6. The dynamic event we refer to as *environmental stress* comprises the following kinds of experiences: exposure of extra-marital affairs; one or both parents in school, requiring baby-sitting for children; impact of religion within the family; and the presence of extremely high or unrealistic expectations.

Construct Your Own Genogram

Following the directions that have been offered for constructing a genogram, complete the process for yourself. Once it is completed, come together with two or three others and share your genograms with one another. Have as your objectives those of allowing others to get to know you better through the process; for you to get to know yourself better as they offer insights gained from exposure to your genogram; and getting to know them better as a result of understanding their origins. Attempt to see what behaviors or attitudes you have perceived in them that seem to relate directly to their experiences in their families of origin.

In the session where the finished genogram is to be used, the rationale for its utilization is again emphasized. After it is explained to those present that the genogram can provide new insights into how the present family functions, the non-genogramic spouse is asked to observe and serve as a co-therapist in a sense. The reason for this is that he or she may have additional insights into the spouse's family as a result of not being as emotionally involved.

Apparent patterns or events that may account for behavior manifested in the present family system are then sought. In doing this, many of the principles mentioned earlier in this chapter should be kept in mind by the therapist. Examples are the types of boundaries present in relationships through the generations, triangulations, mystification, and incomplete mourning, etc. Generally, it is productive to ask the person about how they perceived their parents' relationships, as well as other relationships in the family. During this part of the process, many of the rules of an unidentified nature that govern relationships can be crystallized. Examples of these rules are: only the husband can spend large sums of money; only men can work outside the home; women are responsible for discipline; the husband determines with whom the marital dyad socializes; the oldest male child is the one given the greatest freedom and consideration; and other such unspoken but evident rules. For further comment regarding family rules the reader is referred to an article by Don Jackson (1965), one of the pioneers of the field of family therapy.

After the genogram has been exhausted, it is generally wise to ask the more generic question of, "What similarities do you see in these past generational relationships and your current marital relationships that we have not touched upon?" Our experience has been that quite often, in view of this question, the observing spouse has contributions to make. This question also allows the therapist to begin summarizing and assisting the clients in identifying plans of action for change based on the new insights.

An instrument that has been found to be beneficial and to augment the genogram is the *Family Bond Inventory* (FBI) (Fullmer, 1972). This is presented briefly here and then fully discussed in Chapter 6.

The Family Bond Inventory is a tool designed to facilitate the portrayal of a family in a sociometric sense. To augment the genogram, the individual involved is asked to represent the family on an 8½-by-11 piece of blank typing paper. The individual is instructed to place a circle on the paper for each family member in accordance to how close or distant he or she perceives him- or herself to be from each other family member. This quickly gives the therapist a sense of what alliances were present in the family from this person's point of view, along with the perceived power of each member and other variables. This tool graphically presents the important consideration of emotional distance, as elaborated upon by Kantor and Lehr (1975). To complete an FBI for generations prior to the one or two most familiar to the client, he or she may have to ask someone who experienced the past generation more directly.

SUMMARY

In this chapter, the concepts of inter- or transgenerational influences were considered. An effort was made to communicate in what ways past generations continue to influence present family functioning, even though all members of past generations may be dead. The works of Bowen, Boszormenyi-Nagy, Paul, Spark, Stierlin, and Whitaker were given primary consideration in this exposition. After the establishment of a theoretical orientation, the process and tools for putting the intergenerational concepts into operation in a therapeutic setting were presented. This therapuetic process, as well as a tool (the genogram), was presented in a systematic fashion to facilitate understanding.

Chapter 3 integrates ideas presented in this chapter, along with others, into a global theoretical framework.

CHAPTER 3

A THEORETICAL MODEL FOR
FAMILY FUNCTIONING

T HIS CHAPTER BRINGS TOGETHER the various theoretical strands presented in the first two chapters, adds some other viewpoints, and then ties them together in a coherent theoretical model. The following material provides the therapist with a cognitive map that enables him or her to conceptualize, in broad strokes, the outlines of healthy and disturbed family functioning. The model not only helps in understanding or diagnosing a family's structure and functioning but also in sensitizing the therapist to areas in need of restructuring.

THE ROOTS OF HUMAN MOTIVATION

In the first chapter, we mentioned that the self is inconceivable apart from the social context in which a person is embedded. It was also mentioned that the self is the subjective unit that "carries" and "records" the transactions among the different selves involved in an intimate relationship system. It is important, therefore, to examine some of the major motivational forces that move a person to act or react in certain ways. What are the major life forces?

Classical Psychoanalytic View

Freud offered one of the most influential of answers when, early in his career, he postulated that the basic drives were sexual and self-preservative. He later dropped the drive toward self-preservation and reduced man's major instinctual force to the erotic or sexual drive. Later in his career, pressed by clinical evidence such as that emerging from studies of sadism and masochism, Freud again revised his classification of the basic drives. To the sexual, he added the aggressive drive. The sexual gives rise to the erotic component of human activities and the aggressive to the destructive element. In line with this distinction, Freud postulated two kinds of psychic energy: the *libido* (from the sexual drive) and aggressive energy (from the aggressive drive). Freud also linked the drives to fundamental biological forces, defining a drive as a stimulus of the mind which came from the body (Brenner, 1973).* Freud's view was really, as Dicks (1967) says, a physiological psychology of impulse gratification sufficient perhaps to account for the physical base of sexual attraction but short of the human's search for relationships.

In fairness to Freud, it should be pointed out that he associated the libido concept with object seeking. The concept of "object" in psychoanalytic literature refers to persons or things that are significant in one's psychic life. The phrase *object relations* refers to the individual's attitude and behavior toward such objects. The infant's first contacts with its significant objects, e.g. mother's breast are exclusively self-centered, being concerned simply with the gratifications the object affords. The object is "cathected" at first only when the infant begins to experience need-satisfaction through the object; otherwise, the object is physically nonexistent for the infant. The concept of cathexis, incidentally, "is the amount of psychic energy which is directed toward or attached to the mental representative of a person or thing" (Brenner, 1973, P. 19). Cathexis is a psychological, not a physical, concept, and the greater the energy invested in the object, the more psychologically important it becomes.

Psychoanalysts assume that a *continuing relationship* with an object develops only gradually to the point where, even in the absence of the object, the child maintains an interest in the object. Whereas initially the child may be interested in the mother only when he or she is hungry or uncomfortable, the mother

---

* Our references to psychoanalytic thought are drawn mostly from Brenner's (1973) excellent introductory work on psychoanalysis.

later becomes important on a continuing basis, even apart from those moments of actually receiving pleasure or gratification. One of the important characteristics of the experience of early object relations, according to this view, is a high degree of ambivalence. Feelings of love alternate with feelings of hate; the latter is the result of frustrating experiences involved in episodes when gratifications are not experienced. As the child grows, the conscious feelings toward the object tend to reflect the loving more than the hateful side, the latter becoming more prevalent in the unconscious.

This classical psychoanalytic statement on the drives, owing mostly to Freud's articulation of it, seems to us peripheral to some deeper quests involved in the human experience. On the basis of present evidence, we prefer to state that the human being's fundamental quest is for relationship and for a meaningful individuality within a relationship setting. A self finds meaning *qua* self only when it is grounded in a meaningful relationship with other selves. This latter notion is elaborated upon shortly. The quest for relatedness becomes apparent in the often reported marital dissatisfaction of partners who report having a wonderful sexual relationship, but who are not affirming each other as lovable persons. The same case could be made for children who, despite lavish physical and material gratification, become lonely, withdrawn, or bitterly enraged because of the absence of meaningful affirmative relationships in their families. Bruno Bettelheim has documented this process of interpersonal isolation and the resultant tragedy in children in his powerful book, *The Empty Fortress* (1967).

Fairbairn's Object-Relations Theory

A more appropriate view of object-relations theory was developed by W. R. D. Fairbairn (1954), who elaborated upon the concepts of Freud and Melanie Klein (1948). Some space to a description of Fairbairn's view is given because like Framo (1973),* we believe that the Fairbairnian articulation provides a viable bridge between intrapsychic dynamics and the transac-

---

* Framo's contribution in articulating and extending Fairbairn's thought is immense. This section reflects Framo's integration and elaboration of the material.

tions observed at the interpersonal or system level. To Fairbairn, *the most basic motive of life is a person's need for a satisfying object relationship.* To Freud, the pleasure principle and its related push for instinctual gratification were primary, making the discharge of somatic tensions the basis of human relationships. Fairbairn thinks it is an individual's need for others and the quest to feel needed by them that forms the foundation for social life. To him, instinct is simply a function of the ego—a vehicle for the attainment of a person's object-seeking needs. Pleasure, then, is incidental to this search for relationship. Aggression, in these terms, is a response to frustration in a person's efforts to seek affirmation and satisfaction from the object being sought, not simply to the lack of physical gratification. Libido, then, is not pleasure but object seeking, and the libidinal goal is directed toward satisfactory object relationships.

The process of interacting with one's *significant others*° is a mixture of satisfying and frustrating experiences. Like Freud, Fairbairn saw the developmental process of individual growth as characterized by ambivalent feelings of love and hate. The significant other, e.g. mother or father, sometimes appears accepting and satisfying and sometimes rejecting and frustrating. However, if the family system is such that the child can test the reality of the parent's responses and can recognize the real person of mother, father, brother, or sister, he or she can learn a basic sense of trust in self and in one's significant others and thus develop a tolerance for ambivalent aspects of his or her relationships. In a healthy movement toward developing a positive self-concept and the expectation of generally affirmative reciprocity with significant others, the child is not hampered by unresolved needs of earlier developmental stages. Summarizing the outcomes of this Fairbairnian model of healthy individual development, Dicks (1977) writes:

> The preponderance of secure, loving outcomes of reality-testing and conflict resolution between rage and love creates in the growing individual a reservoir of *relational potential* with the human figures of his little world, by the process of internalization

---

° *Significant others* are referred to as the primary sources of object seeking. Parents, spouses, and siblings are significant others *par excellence,* as seen later in this chapter.

or introjection. The child can make the *good object's* feelings his own, both as self-valuations and as role models. He identifies with them, and they form his inner resources. Through them he learns "how to love as an adult," because he has felt adult love on, and in himself. The child tolerates the struggle of ambivalent feelings within him, and in others, because has experienced the parents' tolerance and mastery of his, and their, anger in a mainly loving way and context. [Pp. 37-38]

Dicks refers to the outcomes of internalizing or introjecting significant others as role models. Children internalize their parents as role models: one as a prototype of male and the other as a prototype of female potentials. The quality and content of these internal role models have consequences for family interaction. Before moving further on this question, what Fairbairn says about unhealthy development is discussed.

As previously mentioned, growing up in a healthy family system is stressful enough. If, however, we add to this setting parents who are unloving and rejecting, the situation becomes much more difficult. The child, especially in early childhood, cannot escape the "social field," which is primarily the family. Parents are so significant to children's survival as a physical and psychological being that they cannot give up their parents externally and, even less so, internally. In this situation, a person retains many unresolved needs—a quest for relatedness invested with profoundly ambivalent feelings of love and hate. The child then handles these frustrations and hurts by internalizing the loved-hated parent in a desperate attempt to control the object or significant other in the inner world of the psyche. The loved-hated parent is repressed and retained as an introject, thus becoming within the psyche a psychological representative of the external object, e.g. the parent. Keep in mind that it is not the feelings as such that are internalized but the emotional relationship between the self and some significant other. *The internal objects become subidentities, becoming part of the personality structure.* When this occurs with one's primary significant others (parents), a person's relational capacities become subject to many distortions. One hears, for example, about a husband or wife who has an apparently unquenchable demand for love and attention. No matter what the spouse does, it is always suspect and "never enough."

When the experience with a person's primary relations is basically rejecting and unaffirmative, Fairbairn hypothesizes that a *splitting* of the introject (internalized emotional relationship) occurs. This bad, unsatisfying internal object is split into (1) an element characterized by an unrequited love-need (*libidinal ego*) and (2) an element characterized by the dangerous, hateful, enraged aspects of the relationship with the rejecting primary object (*antilibidinal ego*). In the libidinal ego are the covert tendencies for extreme dependency and a frighteningly strong wish for tenderness and being loved. In contrast, the antilibidinal ego carries the covert tendencies toward hating and destroying the primary object. Thus, these "bad internal objects" are at war with each other, consuming much of the psychic energy the central ego (the initially integrated self) needs for reality testing and for its efforts to invest in external relationships. The extent to which the central ego is split into bad internal objects depends on how early in a person's development the splitting occurs. The more severe the rejection and the earlier the splitting, the more detrimental the effects are on a person's internal capacities.

The Social Roots of Madness: Laing's Viewpoint

R. D. Laing, the noted British existential psychiatrist, claims that individuals interact in social contexts based on facades and games where the most important rule is never to be aware that there is a game going on. Henceforth, it is paramount to fulfill social role expectations rather than discovering and retaining one's "true selves." The net effect is as Laing (1967, P. 58) says: "By the time the new human being is 15 or so, we are left with a being like ourselves, a half-crazed creature more or less adjusted to a mad world. This is normality."

From the perspective of internalized objects, Laing seems to be describing the emergent split between an individual's "true inner self" and "false outer self," which is experienced with great insecurity. Furthermore, the psychotic breakdown occurs when the split cannot be maintained any longer. Laing's implication is that "madness" serves as a pathway for the individual's recovering his sense of wholeness and unity.

We join Laing's thesis from the perspective that the experience of severe rejection by primary objects, particularly during childhood, leads to a splitting of the central ego into disharmonious internal objects. One way to leave this situation is to go mad—with the hope that the maladaptive dichotomy will dissolve and the world will be consequently experienced as harmonious and whole.

Severe and early splitting results in a tendency to subjectively distort many aspects of a person's relationships with his intimates. As Framo (1973, P. 275) writes, "Life situations in outer reality are not only unconsciously interpreted in the light of the inner object world, resulting in distorted expectations of other people, but *active, unconscious attempts are made to force and change close relationships into fitting the internal role models.*"

The Drive for Consistency

Many psychologists have focused on developing theories concerned with the drive for consistency. These theories claim that individuals seek harmonious relations with the world and are accordingly motivated to ignore or change perceptions that may lead to disequilibrium. Leon Festinger's (1962) *cognitive dissonance theory* is perhaps the most developed of these approaches. For example, one is experiencing dissonance between an overt behavior ("I am reading a book I chose") and a covert belief ("This book is boring"). Since one's private belief is less anchored to external reality, it will probably change. ("Actually, this book is fascinating—I'm learning a lot.")

Similarly, people unconsciously hold strong internal role models that are often imposed upon the world to avert conflict. A common example is this: Fathers often want their sons to become athletic superstars and establish an internal cognitive map that perceives their sons' behavior from that framework, so that all rewards to the son for his athletic pursuits reinforce the father's world view. However, all punishments also reinforce father's world view, since they are regarded as representing situations where the external situation was not appropriate for the son's athletic talents. This type of internalized world map filters perceived data so that they affirm one's inner map. Bandler and Grinder (1976) have made extensive efforts to represent how an individual develops cognitive maps to perceive his or her world. They make a strong case that the person's map is not his or her territory, but rather his or her representation of it. To what extent do internal maps of the world force and change the world to be consistent? How pervasive is this phenomena? What determines whether one's internalized map is maladaptive or healthy? Who determines?

The Fairbairnian formulation is useful because it helps to explain some puzzling interactional phenomena. For example, how do some people function well in non-intimate settings, such as at work or in social settings, but remain painfully infantile in their intimate relationships (Framo, 1973)? Thus, the tendency for love and closeness can be expressed in a public setting, while the tendency for hate and destruction can be expressed in an intimate setting, such as family life. This formulation also clarifies some of the intrapsychic forces that lead people to create double binds for themselves and for others.

Congruent or Incongruent Patterns of Internalized Objects?

From internalized-objects theory, we can view ourselves as carrying various sets of prescribed roles and relationships that fit particular social settings. Each pattern of internalized objects is therefore context dependent. Several social contexts are presented below. Think of your inner map that prescribes how you interact in each given setting and compare it with the patterns which emerge from other settings.

You and your spouse (or partner) in an intimate setting.
You and your parent(s) reflecting over the past.
You and the local mechanic at the gas station.
You and your dentist during dental care.
You and your boss during salary negotiation.
You and an unknown member of the opposite sex during a casual encounter.
You and a clergy person in liturgical service.
Our many masks represent the sets of patterns or internalized objects lodged inside our minds. Can they be congruent? Should they? Why or why not?

Individuality in a Context of Relatedness

Fairbairn stressed the point that a person's quest for relatedness is the most fundamental motive of life. In his articulation, he implied but slightly understressed the importance of a person's search for a meaningful individuality—an experience of one's sense of separateness and apartness. It is not possible to have a meaningful relationship with a significant other without a healthy sense of one's individuality. Thus, it might be said that in emphasizing relationship, Fairbairn implied and included a person's search for individuality in his formulation of the basic life force. However, we think that this aspect bears clearer expression.

The relationship-individuality concepts were juxtaposed when, in Chapter 1, identity was defined as being composed of two paradoxically related and inseparable human forces: belonging-ness and separateness. We also linked these two basic human experiences to the types of family boundaries that a person is subjected to in his family of origin. At this point, the aspect of individuality is briefly detailed.

Inspired by existential thought, especially through the works of Martin Buber (1965), Ivan Boszormenyi-Nagy (1967) offers a sharp articulation of the subject. He conceives the self as an integral part of relationships in which the self is defined and which the self in turn defines:

> Relating has an active and a passive aspect. The other is needed because I want to perceive him as the "ground" against which my person becomes distinguishable as a figure. I want to make him an object for myself as subject; I may want him as an object for my instinctual strivings, for my identity delineation, and for my security needs. In other words, being a self obliges me to express myself and I actually become an entity in the process of expressing myself to another entity. Sensory deprivation amounts to expressive deprivation; it is object deprivation as well as deprivation of the meaning of the self. [Pp. 58-59]

The search for identity and relationship then constitutes in current thinking the most fundamental basis of human motivation. This quest for self and other is what makes the human person a social being—a conscious organism with a need and a capacity for entering and forming human relationships.

Navaho Medicine: Treating the Relationship, Not the Disease

Dicks (1961) depicts Navahoes as viewing sickness as a sign of dis-harmony with nature. Each individual is considered to be a significant part of the whole universe, and whenever the universe becomes imbal-anced, the imbalance manifests itself in sickness. Since all individuals are interrelated in this pattern of life, Navaho medicine concerns itself with not only restoring the health of the sick person but restoring universal harmony in the family and in many members of the tribe who have become out of alignment with nature.

We find this to be a dramatic example of family therapy's underlying attitude. It also supports Ackerman's assertion that although family therapy is relatively new, family healing has a history.

The Special Meaning of the Family

In our discussion so far, we have referred to "primary objects" and "significant others." In our view, the family is the arena par excellence that contains these primary or significant others. Although the theoretical ideas presented above have applicability and meaning in nonfamily relationships, such as friends and work associates, they apply above all to family relationships. The latter represent the prototype of all our other relationships; their impact and meaning is unique in our lives in the formative years and later.

Family Reels

Laing (1972, P. 45) asserts that "the internalized family ('family') which is constructed during childhood, represents the embodiment of relations and operations between elements and sets of elements." The elements may be any objects, introjected or external. The "family" provides patterns habitually used to ascribe relations between objects. These patterns consequently shape our reality images.

Laing (P. 17) comments, "The 'family' mapped onto the family, or carried over to other situations, is no simple set of introjected objects, but more a matrix for dramas, patterns of space-time sequences to be enacted. As a reel of a film, all elements are co-present preset to unfold in sequence in time as a film on the screen. The reel is the internal family." Hence, Laing's "family reels" are analogous to series of cognitive templates that pattern experience in filterlike fashion.

The central influence of the family is shared by no other relationship in existence. *My* sense of belonging and separateness are intricately woven in the interactions *I* have had with my family. This psychosocial bond, moreover, is imbued with a genetic relatedness that is external and that links people to a genetic chain that spans the whole history of the human species. The sense of reciprocal loyalty and indebtedness that binds family members are nowhere duplicated, except perhaps in the form of projection or transference. As Boszormenyi-Nagy so beautifully says, "If I help any suffering human being, I am likely to enter into a genuine I-Thou dialogue with him. If, however, he happens to be my son, he constitutes, in addition, a unique counterpart of my existential realm; he is irreplacable with any other human being."

Fusion and Mental Telepathy

Murray Bowen sees all families as periodically experiencing some sense of fusion or "stuck-togetherness," particularly when stress and tension are at high levels. Members of extremely fused families may even come to know the feelings, fantasies, and dreams experienced by other members—signifying what are typically labeled *paranormal events*. It might be said that such conditions represent mental telepathy where interpsychic communication takes place. When have you experienced such a telepathic event with a significant person in your lifestream? Did it occur in the context of a highly stressful and tense time in your relationship? Is fusion always maladaptive?

BASIC CONCEPTS FOR UNDERSTANDING DISTURBED FAMILY FUNCTIONING

The work of family theorists and therapists cited in this section point to certain system characteristics that seem to be highly correlated with the production of disturbed relationships and with family members who have a low level of self-differentiation. Many of the seminal concepts developed by pioneers in the field of family therapy that are useful for understanding the family interaction of clinically symptomatic families are introduced and integrated.

Fusion and Differentiation in the Family

To better conceive of the idea of maintaining one's individuality while maintaining one's relatedness to some significant other, we borrow the concept of fusion from Murray Bowen (1966). This concept is helpful in defining the level of differentiation and the level of undifferentiation in the self. *Fusion* refers to the self being emotionally merged with the self of another significant person. For example, a husband comes home and reports to his wife that his boss is angry with him. After a brief description of the problem and as the interaction proceeds, the wife suddenly shows some sign that she is more upset about husband's problem than the husband is himself. One then begins to wonder whether she is able to define that particular issue as primarily his or primarily her problem. The husband becomes uneasy because he is having a hard time demarcating his own boundaries, i.e. having a hard time defining what is his and what is his wife's domain. She may end up telling him what to do or what to say about the problem, thus violating his own sense of autonomy. If he cooperates with her attempt to fuse into him in this particular issue, then he becomes coresponsible for the fusion.

Back to Your Roots

Plot your family tree or genogram (see Chap. 2), including all generations of which you are aware. For each individual, think about how you see your internalized relationship in terms of the degree of belongingness, separateness, loyalty, and indebtedness.

Write your first impression for each and then respond to how you see each member viewing their relationship with their spouse and others, including yourself. Examine this map for patterns—both within and between generations. Do you emerge as a part within this whole system? How has this system functioned as the matrix of your identity?

This conceptualization is based on a basic distinction between the self and pseudo-self. The self refers to the ability of the person to maintain an "I" position. That is, I own or I have my own thoughts, my own feelings, my own intentions and my own plans of action, and that I can maintain this position despite pressure from another person to change my thoughts, my feelings, or my actions. It does not preclude my openness to feedback from outside sources. I can listen to other's expression of thought, feeling, and action, but I can evaluate them on my own terms and principles, and in fact act on my own judgment about those feelings and ideas. The pseudo-self, on the other hand, is that part of me which is subject to change in order to accommodate my own thoughts, feelings, and actions to fit somebody else's perception or somebody's wish. That is one side of the pseudo-self. The other side of the pseudo-self is one that looks more like blaming, attacking, or rebelling. In essence, these two aspects of the pseudo-self are similar, since the blamer, the attacker, or the rebel is still fused in the sense that he is simply reacting to somebody else's conception and does not have his own "I" position from which to operate.

SELF-DIFFERENTIATION SCALE: In order to give some conceptual handle on levels of differentiation in self, Bowen (1966) developed what he termed a *differentiation of self scale*, which ranges from 0 to 100. Zero represents an absence of basic self, no "I" position, a rare phenomenon in reality, and 100 represents a person who has total command of him- or herself, i.e. who has total basic self and no pseudo-self. The latter as well is in reality a fiction, because no one is totally differentiated, as far as documentation to date indicates. From 0 to 50, the lower half of the scale, includes the range of people who are governed basically by their feelings, who have little energy left for self-determined, goal-directed activities, and are therefore subject to the whims and the ups and downs of their human moods. The upper half of the scale, from 51 to 100, represents the range of people who are increasingly higher in their level of basic self and much lower in the level of the pseudo-self. There is more autonomy and less fusion with significant others, and therefore, less energy is expended in maintaining the self against potential sources of fusion. There is, in addition, more energy for goal-directed, self-determined activity. It is important to remember that some degree of fusion is present in all levels of functioning below 100. Those individuals above 60 on Bowen's scale constitute a small percentage of people.

The basic value of Bowen's scale is to give a conceptual map for looking at levels of differentiation—for conceptualizing levels of self-differentiation. One indicator for gauging a person's level of differentiation is to detect the percentage of decisions made by persons on the basis of their own thought and judgment about a certain situation, integrated naturally with their own feelings, but not dominated simply by feelings. Bowen claims that the higher one is on the scale, the greater the incidence of decisions based on thinking rather than feeling. We would rather state it this way: The higher the one is on the scale, the greater the degree of integration between thought, feeling, intention, and action. The higher one is on the scale, the more self-directed activity one can engage in and the less one's propensity for being caught in emotional fusions with other people.

Self-Actualizers and Bowen's Differentiation of Self Scale

Abraham Maslow (1970) carried out a long-term study of self-actualized people—those "who have developed or are developing to the full stature of which they are capable" (P. 150). Some of the self-actualizers examined were historical cases, and others were personal acquaintances. One of his conclusions was that "the dichotomy between selfishness and unselfishness disappears altogether in healthy people because in principle every act is both selfish and unselfish" (P. 179). Furthermore, he observed that "the most socially identified people are themselves also the most individualistic people." We think that his description of self-actualized people closely identifies with Bowen's notion of the highly differentiated individual. Do you find those whom you evaluate as self-actualized also highly differentiated? Think about historical and contemporary cases, famous and infamous, dyads, groups, and cultures. Where do you rate yourself and your significant others?

It is important to note that the concepts of self-differentiation and fusion are quite related to Minuchin's concept of the family boundaries; namely clear, disengaged, and enmeshed. A person who has a high level of self-differentiation probably comes from a family who has clear boundaries. A person who comes from an enmeshed family and is therefore overtly caught up in the family emotional system would be what might be termed *overtly fused*. This person tends to stress the belongingness, relatedness, and togetherness aspects of human striving. This is exemplified by the people who, although adult chronologically, are nevertheless unable to venture on their own, get married, or get a job, and are in fact caught up by the family system, performing such roles as taking care of mother or the family business or some other role.

The person from disengaged boundaries, on the other hand, coincides with what is called *covert fusion*. This is the person who claims independence from his family of origin, who mocks people who are close to their families, who brags about his ability to make independent judgments but who, in most cases, feels alienated. What is really happening is that the fusion that person feels toward his family is so strong, so potent, that no chance is given to the family for overt fusion. In our experiences with college aged people, the anecdote about the student who, having been away from home for several months, yearns to go back is often heard. Once home, it is not long before the "need" to leave strikes. For this person, only short family visits are tolerable because longer visits result in overt fusion. Individuals in this case find their sense of self threatened and potentially annihilated by visits home that are too lengthy. In either case (overt or covert fusion), the dynamic is that of being stuck to what Bowen calls the undifferentiated family ego mass, the family within which the family member is fused or merged. Usually, there is one dominant member in that family ego mass who portrays, at least overtly, some kind of dominance over the lives of the other family members.

Pseudo-mutuality and Pseudo-hostility

Note that Bowen's concept of fusion, overt or covert, and self-differentiation parallel quite strongly our contention that the basic motive of life is to establish identity and relatedness. Bowen uses different terms and perhaps a different metaphor, but his thought bears striking resemblance to the model of belongingness and separateness. The concept of pseudo-mutuality developed by Lyman Wynne and his associates (1958) extends the hypothesis. Wynne starts with the assumption that the human being's basic motives are a search for personal identity and a need to relate to others. He defines identity very much like Bowen, and he assumes that identity is a product of one's own family relationships. Family experience in some cases strengthens the basic self and in other cases weakens it. The problem then for Wynne et al. is how one can structure a person's strivings for relationship and for a meaningful identity. He talks about three basic relational alternatives found in families: (1) pseudo-mutuality, (2) mutuality, and (3) nonmutuality.

Pseudo-mutuality resembles the kind of interaction that would emerge if two persons with a low level of self or a high level of pseudo-self were to interact in an intimate basis. These two people would typically be emphatic about experiencing togetherness, to the detriment of identity. The search for togetherness or for relatedness is so strong that self-identity is sacrificed for some semblance of relatedness. In the process, of course, the senses of togetherness and self-identity suffer. This is how Wynne and his associates (1958) described the concept of pseudo-mutuality:

> In pseudo-mutuality emotional investment is directed more toward maintaining the *sense* of reciprocal fulfillment of expectations than towards accurately perceiving changing expectations. Thus, the new expectations are left unexplored, and the old expectations and roles, even though outgrown, and inappropriate in one sense, continue to serve as the structure for the relation. . . . In pseudo-mutuality, the subjective tension aroused by the divergence or independence of expectations including the open affirmation of a sense of personal identity, is experienced not as merely disrupting that particular transaction but as possibly demolishing the entire relation. [P. 209]

In contrast to pseudo-mutuality, a relationship characterized by *genuine mutuality* reflects the willingness to recognize and explore differences that may lead to an expanded knowledge of the relationship and of the self and others in that relationship. In this kind of relationship, differences are not interpreted as a threat to the ongoing relationship, but rather as welcome avenues to new levels of understanding.

Cox's Theology of Juxtaposition: Growth Amidst Differences

Harvey Cox (1969), a Harvard theologian, has proposed a "theology of juxtaposition" that suggests that "the contradiction we feel between what is and what has been should not be overcome by finding someway to negate the tradition. . . . Juxtaposition sees the disrelation between the inherited symbol and present situation not as a lamentable conflict to be resolved but as a piquant cacophony to be preserved" (P. 131-132). This world view accordingly demonstrates the attitude that the experience of differences may induce growth or new experience. What implications does such an attitude have for interpersonal relationships?

The third alternative, *nonmutuality,* simply refers to no ongoing intimate relationship and no contact for developing a set of mutually agreed-upon expectations. It is similar to the kind of relationship that a customer develops with a saleswoman for a specific task and no more.

Later on, Wynne brought out a twin concept to pseudo-mutuality, which he called *pseudo-hostility*. This refers to a preoccupation to maintain relatedness by enduring and continuous bickering and turmoil. Quarreling and turmoil are ways to maintain a relationship without opening up the possibility of genuinely expressing some of the tender, deep relationship feelings involved. Expression of positive feelings, as well as opening up areas of conflict, bring in the twin threat of being fused overtly or being totally alienated because of conflict. Therefore, as a way to bypass this threat, a pseudo-hostile relation maintains a negative environment that in a way preserves the relationship at a certain level. Notice the similarity between the dynamic involved in pseudo-mutuality and pseudo-hostility. Both have the same goal of maintaining relatedness without losing the self. In pseudo-mutuality, the fear is of being rejected, and so a number of placating adaptive kinds of behaviors emerge, whereas in pseudo-hostility, the fear is toward being overtly fused and consumed by the other, and therefore the intent becomes to create conflict.

Self-Differentiation and Family Interaction

In Bowen's conceptions, as well is in Wynne's formulation, it is interesting to note how the interaction structure that emerges is closely related to the intrapersonal dynamics that members bring into a relationship and how in turn the relationship maintains the kind of intrapersonal dynamic involved. Bowen's thought is extended to the level of interaction. He asks the question: In what areas are symptoms expressed in the family? He lists three major categories: (1) the marital conflict, (2) dysfunction in the spouses, and (3) projection to one or more children. The degrees of undifferentiation in the family members are absorbed by one or more of these three aspects. Most families use a combination of these three within which to absorb their levels of undifferentiation.

In light of this framework, marital conflict is seen as arising when one spouse refuses to give in to the other's attempt at fusion or when an adaptive spouse refuses to continue adapting or placating. Bowen has observed that in spousal fusion, one member develops a position that controls the interaction of the relationship and the other submits or adapts. Both are involved in the fusion; the expression of the fusion is different. Still, co-responsibility in the system dynamics is illustrated. Usually it is the adaptive one who becomes the candidate for dysfunction (for symptomatic behavior), whether psychosomatically or emotionally. In systemic fashion, the dominant spouse gains from the submissive one greater strength and a higher level of apparent functioning. The greater the overfunction of one spouse, the greater the underfunctioning of the other. Often, the dominant spouse is unaware of the dynamics of this borrowing from the submissive spouse; therefore, he or she conceives of the spouse as the weaker one and in need of leadership and care. Where one spouse decides to adapt or submit, dysfunction is found in one spouse and overfunction in the other.

Where one or both spouses refuse to submit to the fusion, then marital conflict arises in the form of bickering, much like the pseudo-hostile concept of Lyman Wynne. Dysfunction in one spouse can absorb much of the undifferentiation in other areas of the family and thus protect the other members of the family from showing symptoms. This explains the phenomenon, quite often observed, where one spouse seems to be functioning at a high level of productivity, but the other spouse shows all signs of underproductivity, withdrawal, and even inability to cope with day-to-day tasks.

Family Projection Process

The third area where symptoms are manifested occurs as a result of projecting the apparent level of undifferentiation onto the children. To some extent, this projection occurs in all families. The degree to which it occurs determines the severity of the symptoms portrayed by children. In Bowen's as well as in our experience, the most common clinical pattern is that where the mother projects her sense of immaturity or undifferentiation to one child while the other children are free of any obvious dysfunctions. The father is usually disengaged from the family. The process of projecting one's level of immaturity or undifferentiation on to a third person, in this case the child, is known as *scapegoating*. Because the scapegoat is the one most strongly fused with the family, he or she becomes overtly or covertly the most attached to the family emotional system and the one who most likely ends up with a lower level of differentiation. The children who are peripheral to this basic family projection process emerge with a basic level of differentiation that is higher than that of their parents.

At this point, Bowen's concept of self-differentiation, is associated with fusion to the object-relations theory presented earlier. Note that the children represent, to the parents, valued or feared expectations, based on their own parental introjects. Quite often, roles are assigned to children on the basis of parents' own unresolved introjects. For example, the process of parentification, which implies assigning to a child a parental role, may be the result of unconscious motivation by parents to assign to a child the task of nurturing or caring for them (libidinal wishes). The result of parentificaton is that the child who is parentified carries the burden of responsibility for the parent, a burden that is generally too heavy for a young child to carry. Furthermore, it blurs the generational boundaries between parent and child and therefore does not allow the child to develop a sense of identity as a growing child. The child becomes an adult prematurely. One of the child's identity needs is to be a child, to depend, and to be nurtured for a time, until he or she is strong enough and adult enough to carry more of the weight of this responsibility.

Another way that the projection process occurs is by connecting with the antilibidinal ego. The anger and the rage toward one's parent, which is carried in the "bad parent" introject, is acted out on one of the children. In the form of an unconscious wish for revenge, parents often engage in the phenomenon of child abuse, as well as other lesser forms of parental cruelty directed toward children. The projection process takes on varied forms and goes through different channels.

In Chapter 2, Laing's mystification process of role assignment was discussed. Mystification is a process that involves three different aspects: (1) attribution of a certain role, (2) disqualification of any attempt by the child not to assume that role, and (3) induction, meaning, the child has finally accepted that role and plays the part. The projection process is exemplified by a parent who projects to the child the wish for behaviorally acting upon the parent's sexual or aggressive fantasies. The child then accepts this role definition and goes out into the world and becomes, for example, a "Don Juan" in an attempt to act out the parent's wishes. The child's behavior, then, is a good illustration of what Bowen means by pseudo-self. The child does not really wish to act out in a sexually loose way but acts on the basis of parental delegation and to that extent loses his or her real self.

The family projection process is carried down through different generations. The triangled child, the major object of the projection, develops a lower level of self-differentiation and chooses a mate at about the same level of self-differentiation. This new couple in turn produces children, one of whom will be triangled and will become the object of the projection process. The child who becomes the object in the projection process develops a yet lower level of self-differentiation than his or her parents and in turn will marry someone of the same level of self-differentiation, and so on.

A downward spiraling of self-differentiation reaches the point where, eventually after several generations, one or another of the future children becomes psychotic. This accounts for the observation that, from this perspective, several generations are required to produce a schizophrenic. The siblings who are not the primary object of the projection process generally develop a level of self-differentation higher than their parents and choose mates of an equal level of self-differentation. They create an upward spiral, or at least they carry the potential to do so. However, we think it is important to point out that the other children are caught in this family system as well and that they absorb some of the undifferentiation in the family ego mass. These other children are in reality in quite a vulnerable situation, in the sense that the object of projection could switch from one child to another.

The switch, incidentally, is what often happens when an individual therapist treats a child apart from the nuclear family. If the therapy is "successful," the child who was initially the object of the projection may be able to escape from it; this means that another member of the nuclear family becomes the object of projection, assuming that the rest of the system has not really changed radically. Unwittingly, then. the individual therapist could be sucked into supporting the family myth of labeling that individual as the sick one. It is our judgment that, in most cases, the success story of individual therapy is translated into a painful story in another member of the nuclear family.

A concise but poignant example of this is Strean's (1970) analysis of the famous Freudian case of "Little Hans." Strean discusses Hans's treatment, as conducted by his father, which resulted in the eventual elimination of his stifling phobia of horses. Shortly after Hans's "cure," his father and mother divorced. Several years later, Freud saw Hans as a nineteen-year-old young adult and reported that he was still free of his phobia. Hans was still living alone; his father had remarried and lived in a different city, as did his mother. Could it not be said that Hans's crippling phobia had a functional role in the total family context, and by not giving accord to the symptom as an indication of family stress, "the battle was won at the expense of the war?" We wonder how many other "successes" in individual therapy have resulted in similar dynamics.

Another consideration is that of the impact of family homeostasis on the individual being treated by a therapist with an individual orientation. If the client begins to experience change as a result of individual therapy, the family as a system has two options: (1) to change with the disturbance expressed through another family member; or (2) the family amplifies the homeostatic forces to move the identified patient back to assuming his functional role of being dysfunctional.

What function does the projection process serve in the family? Framo (1973) answers this:

the function of recapturing the symbolically retained old love objects who have their representation in current real family members, thus delaying the pain of loss and mourning. Object possession, perhaps the chief motive underlying irrational role assignment, helps prevent individuation which can result in the catastrophe of separation, the old dread of abandonment, and facing the fact that one has irretrievably lost one's mother or father. [P. 279]

Schism and Skew

To bring more light to the concept of family projection process, some of the research and conceptual formulations developed by Theodore Lidz and his associates (1965) are analyzed. Like Minuchin and Bowen, Lidz puts a great deal of importance on the ability of husband and wife to create what he calls a *parental coalition,* that is, developing, in Minuchin's terms, a clear husband-wife subsystem within a family. By so doing, the parents are able to create clear generational boundaries—a situation that helps the children to maintain their own identity within the sibling subsystem. Lidz believes that the child needs a same-sex member with whom to identify and an opposite-sex member who is seen as desirable. When the husband-wife relationship is characterized by mutuality, the child is able to achieve the task of identification. If it is characterized by pseudo-mutuality, the child cannot achieve this. Following the work of Parsons and Bales (1955), Lidz postulated the importance of parents following sex-linked roles. Like Parsons and Bales, he identified the father as being the instrumental leader and the mother as the expressive or affectional leader. Instrumental roles are defined as those that are task and goal oriented and therefore carry a meaning external to the relationship. The expressive roles are tied up with the expressing of affection between the members of the family.

Although Parsons and Bales and Lidz, later on, are correct in saying that traditional roles tended to follow the instrumental-expressive dichotomy, their pointing to these as necessarily bound up with sex roles is a mistake. It is a view that is too culture bound. We consider the essence to be *gender identity;* that a male feels male and a female feels female. These gender identities need not be bound with specific social cultural tasks that change continually. Women today, for example, are becoming much more involved in playing the breadwinner role, which is instrumental, but it does not take away from their femininity. Men, too, can engage in expressive roles without detracting from their masculinity.

Lidz, however, was right in saying that a healthy husband-wife relationship is crucial for good family functioning. When the husband-wife relationship is disturbed, then problems emerge in the family. His findings indicate that the marital relationship becomes disturbed in two basic directions: (1) The marriage can be characterized by *schism*, a relationship marked by failure to achieve mutuality, with a consequent outbreak of unresolved conflict. The result, then, is a chronic state of marital separation at the emotional level. This tension is eventually transmitted or projected upon the children. (2) The marriage relationship may be characterized by *marital skew*, a relationship where one member is strong, overfunctioning, and therefore dominant, and the other member is weak and underfunctioning and generally submissive. Note the parallel beween these two categories and the first two areas of symptom formation outlined by Bowen. Lidz concluded that either one of these marital structures can create an environment in the family where the tensions are projected onto the children. The family environment created is characterized by irrationality and the lack of a logical, rational basis for communication. The children in this context cannot make sense of their environment and thus of their own identities.

It is at this point that the concept of triangle again helps in understanding the projection process. Bowen was one of the first theorists to conceptualize the emotional system in terms of triangles. He claims that the triangle is the smallest stable relationship system, the molecule of the emotional system. When a two-person system is unstable or under stress, it tends to seek a third point and thus forms a triangle. Whatever the source of discomfort in the dyad, whether it is too intense a togetherness, or the lack of it, the person who first feels the discomfort tends to bring in a third person and thus shifts the tension from the dyad to the third person. This is done in such a way that the twosome is now able to talk about the third person and avoid each other. Thus, when the husband-wife relationship becomes troubled, it becomes convenient to zero in on one of the children, defocusing the husband-wife problem and yet maintaining the relationship at some level. When there are more than three people in a family system, then a series of interlocking triangles typically arises. Generally, though, one triangle becomes the primary one around which the other more peripheral triangles are interlocked. In therapy, it becomes important to identify the primary triangle and change it. Following the concept of inter-relationships, by changing the primary triangle, the other peripheral interlocking triangles undergo a compensatory change, perhaps therapeutically.

What Causes Family Dysfunction?

In answering the question of causation of family dysfunction, it is important to avoid linear causal thinking, where one member is defined as the stimulus and the other as the response. We think it is important to think cybernetically. This thinking involves the feedback model of causality where a circular process is involved. The so-called cause was really an effect of a prior cause. What was initially defined as an effect becomes the cause of a yet later event. In essence, there is the notion of the vital interrelationship of system members. Every member, therefore, is jointly responsible or coresponsible for all the family events, because family roles are reciprocal. For example, one cannot have a master without a willing slave, barring physical coercion. One also cannot be dominant without a submissive or adaptive person. In this light, Haley (1967, P. 23) states "It seems doubtful that the 'cause' can be sought in the behavior of any single individual or even that of a set of parents. The pattern undoubtedly is passed down over many generations. However, the pattern must also be continually reinforced if it is to continue. At a minimum, two people, each of different generations, must cooperate to perpetuate it."

Haley's last statement again highlights the multigenerational perspective. It is insufficient merely to state that a wife attempted a coalition with her son because of marital dissatisfaction. There is a prior question. What influenced the marital dissatisfaction? What kept the couple from maintaining the parental coalition and from working through their conflict within the dyad? The wife's action may be motivated by the implications of disloyalty to her parents, should she become emotionally involved with her husband. She triangles her son in order to avoid the guilt of disloyalty. Thus, cause is really a "statement about regularity in larger networks" (Haley, 1967, P. 24).

Haley's comment about patterns needing to be reinforced in

the present family system, if they are to continue, is extremely important. The past is not just past because it feeds into the present system. That is why Bowen is able to say "Go to your past and change it." Furthermore, Haley's comment adds much more light on the nature of therapeutic change, for it points out the need for the present system to change if real changes are to occur. It is not sufficient simply to change past thoughts about childhood events. This emphasis also lends much hope to the process of therapy, because there is a handle on the present system, and if that system can change significantly, then members of that system can change correspondingly. People are not tied by a certain kind of deterministic force which, because of the unchangeable past, binds them to an unchangeable present or future. However, it is important to keep in mind that, when talking about the present system, more than just the nuclear family is included. The present system includes the extended family and, eventually, the larger community and society.

FAMILY DEVELOPMENT

The dynamics in the family of origin can illuminate many of the forces at work in the present system, as seen earlier, but not everything can be accounted for by a look at the dynamics in the family of origin. It is true that people seek partners at about the same level of self-differentiation and that the choice is motivated by complementary needs and that these needs are shaped by forces at work in the family of origin. There are, however, other factors involved. One factor is exemplified in the concept called *emergence*. This is the idea that when two or more people engage in an intimate, ongoing relationship, they create unique behavioral patterns that are irreducible to just the individual members. This idea is clearly outlined in Chapter 1, when, in discussing the concept of systems, it was stated that the whole is more than just the sum of its parts. Many of the major behavioral patterns people in intimate relationships develop are clearly attributable to, or shaped by, forces in the family of origin. Others, however, are unique to a marriage or a family. Therefore, it is important to study the specific rules and behavioral patterns that particular families create. Again, Chapter 1 offered many of the concepts that aid in the understanding of interaction patterns.

Another factor involved is what might be called simply *situational idiosyncrasies*. These refer to the events in particular geographic and social milieus that impinge on the family. For example, the impact of economic, political, religious, and educational systems contribute to the strength and weakness of the family. Another factor in family dynamics involves the concept of the family's development over time. Just as the individual has his or her own developmental cycle, so the family has its unique developmental life cycle. It is important to understand the tasks and expectations with which families are faced as they move from one stage to another. Particularly important in this regard is understanding of the dynamics of transitional phases in the family life cycle. These are the phases when the organization changes significantly; these are the periods of great stress. Some of the major transition phases in the course of the family life cycle are outlined.

Stages of Family Development

Because social systems are open to change in response to environmental factors, the process of change (morphogenic forces) becomes of theoretical and practical interest to the therapist. The major works of the eminent sociologist Reuben Hill have been devoted to the development of a framework to study periods of intense and significant change in the course of the family's life cycle. Hill's theoretical and empirical studies, as well as the works that were inspired by his thoughts, have made it clear that families experience sudden developmental changes over time. Symptoms often appear at these periods of transition. *Symptoms are often signs of a family's inability to make the move successfully.*

Rather than falling into a trap of interpreting all stress as pathological or as signs of disturbance, it is important to point out that all families, no matter how healthy, undergo some level of disorganization as they move from one stage to the next. The more important question is the family's ability to recover and to successfully move to the next stage. There are certain developmental tasks that families are faced with at the start of a new stage. The manner in which families deal with these tasks influences present and future functioning. In support of this, Haley (1973, Pp. 24-25) writes, "Symptoms appear when there is a dislocation or interruption in the unfolding life cycle of the family or other natural group. The symptom is a signal that a family has difficulty getting past a stage in the life cycle."

How is the concept of *stage* defined? What constitutes movement from one stage to another? Simply stated, movement from one stage to the next occurs when role relationships among family members undergo significant restructuring. At these stages of dramatic reorganization of role relationships, the family is believed to be in the process of coping with new developmental tasks at the family and individual levels. The push to move to a redefinition of roles can come from internal or external sources. When, for example, two people previously engaged are married, their expectations of each other change drastically; the changes involve their economic, domestic, and sexual expectations.

The concepts of life cycle stages and family and individual developmental tasks blend compatibly with the current emphasis on morphogenic processes. At those disjunctions in the life cycle when the family members are confronted with new developmental tasks, previous patterns of interaction may become inadequate. Deviation-amplifying processes (positive feedback loops) take over to move the system to a new level of reorganization. Assuming the desired level is reached, homeostasis or deviation-counteracting forces reassert themselves to maintain another stage of temporary, relative stability. Timing is crucial in this framework, for either premature change or delayed adaptation could lead to undesired behavior among family members.

The criteria that family developmental theorists have used for determining stages have predominantly been geared around normal or expected changes in the life span of the average nuclear family in western culture. Actually, it is the researcher's particular interest that determines which criteria are employed. If one were simply interested in measuring the family's adaptation to temporary or permanent loss, one would choose those points at which these events have occurred: death, divorce, sickness, launching of children, and so forth.

To date, major efforts have been spent on delineating normal or expected changes; for example, marriage, birth of a child, changes in age and school placement of the child, the children leaving home, and the retirement of the breadwinners. These are theoretically (with increasing empirical support) the periods in the life cycle when significant reorganization of role relationships occurs. The framework used to categorize family life cycles in several stages attempts to demarcate those points or blocks in the life cycle at which a significant reordering of the family role relationships have occurred.

In an effort to develop a scheme to represent meaningful stages in the family life cycle, it must be remembered that the family as a social system is in constant change. Therefore, theoretically, just about every day in the life cycle of the family represents a stage. We wish however to present a scheme of developmental stages that captures significant periods of change. This enables one to look for points in the life cycle where symptoms may occur perhaps more than at any other time. One way to do this is to look at the "normal" or "expected" changes that families go through in the course of the life cycle. In light of these expected changes, the criteria most often used are the following: (1) family size or changes in the number of positions in the family, (2) changes in the age and school placement of the oldest child, and (3) changes in occupational status of the breadwinners. Together, these criteria give us the often used eight stages in the family life cycle as Evelyn Duvall (1971) has presented them:

Stage 1. Married couples (without children)

Stage 2. Childbearing families (oldest child from birth to thirty-six months)

Stage 3. Families with preschool children (oldest child three to six years)

Stage 4. Families with schoolchildren (oldest child six to thirteen years)

Stage 5. Families with teenagers (oldest child thirteen to twenty years)

Stage 6. Families as launching centers (first child leaving to last child's leaving home)

Stage 7. Middle-aged parents (empty nest to retirement of spouses)

Stages 8. Aging family (retirement to death of both spouses)

The above scheme was developed with marriage as the beginning point in time. The period of courtship is another significant stage, and therefore the therapist ought to have that in mind. Courtship is the stage in which two people are beginning to make a decision about forming their own system. The dynamics involved in their families of origin begin to work. They are deciding whether the two families are going to be married. The marriage is the uniting of more than just two individuals. It is the uniting of the two families. Even at this stage, couples are already trying to develop and implement their communication system, power structure, and modes of expressing affection. The way in which they deal with these tasks of courtship has some impact on the manner in which they deal with those same tasks in marriage.

The point of marriage is particularly significant because couples are faced with the task of establishing their identity as a couple. This involves moving away from their families of origin, a move that involves a significant shift in family loyalties. It is interesting to note that the highest divorce rate occurs in the first two to three years of marriage. Apparently many couples have a difficult time reconciling their loyalties to their new family of procreation with their family of origin. The birth of a child changes the system from a one-relationship nuclear system to a three-relationship system. To the husband-wife roles are added the parental roles; much more now is demanded of the parents, physically, financially, and emotionally. Parenthood can stress the marital relationship, especially if the marital relationship has not received strong bonding.

Note that the family with an infant is of a qualitatively different system than the family of a preschooler or a school-age child or a teenager. As children grow, they revise their expectations toward their parents. Parents too revise their expectations of their children. The system then must find ways to cope with these developmental pressures. The teenage period is particularly crucial. It is similar to the time of marriage, in the sense that loyalties, belongingness, and separation forces begin to emerge at dramatic rates. Teenagers are thinking of launching their own careers in marriage and in occupations. If the children have been triangled, then the launching stage becomes a particularly frightening one for both child and parent. It is at this point that the marital relationship must be strong enough to remain its own subsystem and therefore allow the children to move ahead.

When all the children have been launched, the husband and wife are again alone. If triangling took place, this stage becomes vulnerable to separation and divorce. In fact, recent statistics have shown that couples married between twenty to twenty-five years have been showing the fastest-rising rates of divorce. If the marital relationship has remained strong and well bonded, couples experience a tremendous rise in satisfaction. The retirement stage has been, so far, more traumatic for the husband than the wife. However, as women take greater participation in the labor force, retirement will increasingly become an equally significant event in the lives of women. Widowhood, involving the death of one's spouse, is obviously a time of great loss and one that requires a significant adjustment on the part of the individual, especially in western culture. Widowhood may spell the end of a person's marriage, but it does not end her family life. She still has ties to her own extended family, either of origin or of procreation.

Note that the life-cycle scheme presented above details only those changes that are normal or expected in almost every family. There are, however, other less predictable situational changes that are no less significant in the life of a family. For example, physical illness on the part of one member can shift the role relationships in a family system. As the mother becomes seriously ill, who then takes over her role? What kind of changes does her illness bring about in the family system? Mental illness is another factor. There are occurrences such as premature death, divorce, job loss, and moving from one place to another. All of these events bring about shifts in the family role-relationship system. They result in processes of adaptation, disorganization, and re-organization. The family developmental framework makes it clear to the therapist that the family system is rarely, if ever, static. It is a social system subject to many situational and predictable changes. Hence, a family system that is unable to muster the forces for adaption tends to be vulnerable to symptom formation. The alert family therapist often looks for correlations between symptomatic manifestations and shifts in the family life cycle. He or she can determine the kinds of specific tasks with which the family is dealing, where they failed, and with what tasks they need to rework.

WHAT CONSTITUTES A "HEALTHY" FAMILY?

What then constitutes a healthy family? In contrast, how can one conceptualize the breakdown of family function? As the family is a system and the development of the individual within that system was viewed, one characteristic came forth repeatedly. That is, a healthy family is one that is able to provide homeostatic and morphogenic forces in a judicious, meaningful way: The family is able to provide some stability and order and also the ability to adapt to the inevitable changes that occur in the life span of the family.

It seems that the structure needed to accomplish a balance between order and change is one where the subsystem boundaries are clear, rather than typically disengaged or typically enmeshed. As the works of Bowen, Minuchin, Wynne, and Lidz indicate, the clearness of boundaries is especially crucial in the husband-wife subsystem. If the husband-wife subsystem is unclear (enmeshed or disengaged), then the family structure becomes subject to the development of interlocking triangles, the projection process, and the blurring of generational boundaries. All of these impede a child's ability to develop a meaningful relatedness and self-identity. To us, clear boundaries are indicative of clear communication patterns. The healthy family is characterized by honest, direct, person-to-person communication, thus bypassing the path of triangling a third person.

If some stability is present with availability for change, and if boundaries are clear, characterized by clear communication patterns, then it follows that the family is most likely to be successful in fulfilling the individual and family developmental tasks throughout the life cycle. Such a family is able to develop genuine mutuality in their relationships, to affirm each other as individuals without fear of discovering differences and without fear that differences might spell rejection. It is not similarity or common knowledge that makes a good relationship, but the ability of the relationship or the system to deal with differences, for there will always be differences.

SUMMARY

This chapter brought together the various constructs presented in Chapters 1 and 2 and integrated them with some additional viewpoints. The chapter began with a discussion of the basis (roots) of human motivation. Classical psychoanalysis (essentially Freudian) pointed to the sexual and aggressive drives as most fundamental—the basis for object seeking and for social life. This was primarily a biologically based view, a perspective where psychological processes were seen as manifestations of the drive to discharge somatic tensions (the pleasure principle). Fairbairn's object relations, as elaborated by Dicks and Framo, was then introduced as a more appropriate view of human motivation. According to Fairbairn, the basic motive of life is a person's need for a satisfying object relationship. He believed the foundation of social life was the individual's need for others and his quest to be needed by them. The internalization of the significant other is characterized by ambivalence (love-hate), conceptualized as *splitting* of the introject (internalized emotional relationship). This view provides a bridge between intra- and interpersonal dynamics. We then highlighted the importance of individuality in a context of relatedness and pointed out the unique meaning of the family system in this quest for relatedness and individuality.

Basic concepts for understanding interaction in dysfunctional families were presented. The following concepts were covered: fusion, differentiation, pseudo-mutuality, pseudo-hostility, non-mutuality, the family projection process, triangle, intergenerational linkages, and schism and skew. A plea for multi-causal, nonlinear, and intergenerational thinking in answering the question of what causes family dysfunction was made.

Family development theory was introduced as a way of viewing the developmental stages of the family unit. A conceptual framework for demarcating family stages was introduced. It was noted that symptoms are often signs of a family's inability to move from one stage to the next.

A delineation of empirically discovered characteristics that constitute a well-functioning or "healthy" family concluded this chapter. They are: (1) a good balance between homeostatic and morphogenic processes; (2) clear subsystem boundaries; (3) strong marital subsystems; (4) clear, honest, direct person-to-person communication; and (5) maintenance of generational boundaries.

CHAPTER 4

A MODEL FOR THE THERAPEUTIC
RELATIONSHIP IN FAMILY THERAPY

Perhaps the best way to talk about the function and role of the family therapist is to ask the question, What is family therapy? In his overview of the field of marital and family therapy, David Olson (1970) writes that any intervention focusing on the family system instead of the individuals in that system can be considered family therapy. Gerald Zuk (1971, P. 65) defines family therapy: "It is the technique that explores and attempts to shift the balance of pathogenic relating among family so that new forms of relating become possible." In each definition, the primary goal is effecting change in the relationship between two or more family members. The client is the family, not just one member of that family. These views assume that the family is indeed a system of highly interrelated individuals such that a change in one part brings about compensatory changes in another part of the system.

Although the majority of family therapists prefer to work with at least two or more members of the family, the *number* of people in the therapy room is not the essence. *Who* is present may be strategic and, in fact, is something to be considered as part of the therapeutic strategy. What is of the essence is the intervention process that *seeks to change the family patterns of relating.* Murray Bowen, for instance, often elects to work with one member, in the hope that through strategic changes in that person's manner of relating to others, the entire family will change. Therapists may quarrel about the effectiveness of such an approach, but this style is by definition still a form of family therapy. What makes it so is the intent to change strategic patterns in the family relationship system, albeit through an individual member.

95

THE THERAPEUTIC SYSTEM

As soon as a therapist and family agree to work together in therapy, a new system emerges: the therapeutic system. This is the family vis-à-vis the therapist. This event is not trivial. First, the step to seek counseling brings into the family's consciousness the realization that they, or at least one member of the family, need help. In a society where rugged individualism is a cultural ideal, this realization is often a rude awakening. Second, in a viable therapeutic system, the therapist is allowed to enter the family boundaries temporarily; the family has to accommodate to the "newcomer." Third, even outside the therapeutic hour, the therapist's position and influence are felt in a "ghostlike" fashion. Family conversations are often punctuated by phrases such as "As Dr. Corrales said," or "Dr. Barnard won't like that."

Forming the therapeutic system is crucial to the therapeutic process. Until the family relaxes its social boundaries enough to give the therapist the privilege of making catalytic moves toward change, efforts at restructuring the family are probably going to be met with resistance or abandonment. However, it is important for therapists to make clear in their own minds the distinction between (1) the family system and (2) the therapeutic system. The family system, of course, is the primary unit that seeks therapeutic help; it is usually composed of a husband and wife, as well as extensions, combinations, or remnants of these positions. The therapeutic system is the temporary relationship unit composed of the therapist, on one hand, and the family system on the other. The therapist and family strive for clear subsystem boundaries, with access from one subsystem to another and also with a clear sense of delineation as to the individuals' primary units of identification. The ideal therapeutic system may be diagrammed (Fig. 7).

GROWTH IN THERAPY

Implicit in the concept of the *"therapeutic system"* is the assumption that it exists *primarily* for the sake of the family; that is, for the purpose of creating contexts for positive change in the family system. The term *primarily* is emphasized because of the

Figure 7. The therapeutic system.

desire to communicate an important secondary function of the therapeutic system: the therapist's growth. Therapeutic progress is extremely limited when the therapist is not open to personal growth. Generally, one good indicator for the level of progress in therapy is the therapist's own sense of growth.

Carl Whitaker (1970) captures this discussion about the focus of change in the phrase *the battle for bilaterality.* Who changes, the therapist or client? Whitaker's response is that it is important for both to change. We agree, because therapists who are not open to change and to their own personal dynamics (1) may block out certain aspects of the family's experience, (2) may be less able to empathize, (3) may be paralyzed by fear, or (4) may unconsciously sabotage the family's efforts to grow. Consequences (1) and (2) are closely related. If I am not open to looking at a painful struggle in my own life, I may not want to recognize those same struggles in my clients. Thus, my *own* defenses have blocked my ability to recognize, to understand, and, hence, to empathize.

Consequences (3) and (4) are somewhat related. When confronted by a situation in therapy that reminds me of my own pain and inadequacies, I may experience fear, guilt, hurt, anger, or any combination of these reactions. Inability to cope with these feelings may blunt my capacity to join and to restructure processes that may be at the very core of therapeutic change. Or I might, out of jealousy or vindictiveness, unconsciously sabotage their efforts to move beyond the cutting edge of real change. It might be too painful for me to watch my clients develop relationships healthier than my own. If, for instance, I have feelings of severe inadequacy about my own assertiveness in my own marriage, I may resent a husband's obvious movement toward achieving a facility for being assertive in his own marriage. At the same time, I may exhibit placating behavior toward a wife who strikes me as dominant or controlling because her behavior touches my fear of strong women.

ROLES OF THE THERAPIST

Given that family therapy is an intervention strategy for changing dysfunctional family relationships, what specifically does the therapist do to create the context and the catalytic forces for change? The different roles that family therapists are often called upon to play are briefly conceptualized. Chapters 5 and 6 are devoted to the specific application of these roles.

The therapist engages in such a multiplicity of behaviors that it is difficult to catalog the repertoire of actions and reactions. It is best to attempt a presentation of clusters of characteristic behaviors that, in our judgment, represent the most therapeutic modes of relating to clients.* Our treatment builds upon, but is not limited to Howells's treatment. In fact, there are differences in a few of the behaviors considered desirable, notably in the therapist's willingness to challenge, confront, amplify conflict, and even "manipulate" the family.

Supporting—Empathizing—Accepting—Absolving

Supporting, empathizing, accepting, and absolving charac-teristics not only enable the therapist to join a family and to create rapport and support; they also are very human and humane responses to human misery. Showing warmth, love, tolerance, and acceptance builds the esteem of family members. These behaviors presuppose in the therapist the ability to tolerate and accept, without condescension, a wide range of human short-comings, a capacity to love and value the human being because he or she *is*. It is this capacity that allows the therapist to be an observer of human failings. "Embarrassing, belittling, hurtful

---

* This section owes much to Howells's (1975, Pp. 275-281) list of desirable characteristics in a therapist's personality and behavioral repertoire.

attitudes and experiences are exposed within the family discussion. The toleration of the therapist removes the sting from all these experiences; in particular, guilt is relieved" (Howells, 1975, P. 278). This ability to accept and to give emotionally depends upon therapists' experiences of giving and receiving affection and affirmation in their own relationships.

Assessing—Diagnosing—Comprehending

In addition to affective competence, the effective family therapist is able to conceptualize the massize data presented in a family session. The therapist should be equipped with concepts, theories, and, above all, a methodology for sifting through the data, all of which help to begin forming a diagnostic map of the family as a whole, of the various subsystems, and coalitions, and of the intrapersonal structure of the individual members. The first three chapters of this book are good examples of the kind of conceptual-theoretical repertoire that a therapist might have. Therapists should be encouraged to be sensitive (1) to data they gather through their senses and (2) to their own inner reactions to what they are sensing.

Personal Sensing

Form groups of about five to seven members. Share incidents in your recent relationship experience during which you became particularly uncomfortable. Your gut feelings were telling you something about the interpersonal system you were in at the moment. What were your feelings telling you about the situation? About the part you contributed to it? About the part the other or others were contributing to it? Relate the discussion to the "diagnostic messages" that your inner reactions can produce while in the role of therapist.

Therapy seeks to facilitate change in the present family structure. Therapy really seeks the answer to the question "So what?" So what if the father is disengaged and so what if the mother is enmeshed with a daughter who is showing psychosomatic symptoms? In practice the diagnostic process is not just a prelude to therapy but is in fact the *beginning* of the therapy process. In our experience with a wide range of counselors, however, diagnosis is quite often implicitly taken as the *end of therapy*. It is one thing to understand the problem and to share the insight with clients and quite another to actually catalyze the needed changes. In summary, although diagnosis is an important part of the therapeutic process, it is not sufficient and should be considered simply as the starting point and the background for the "guts" of the therapeutic encounter.

Organizing—Leading

Being a family therapist involves administrative roles. These aspects begin with the first contact, usually by phone, and play a crucial role in influencing the later stages of therapy. The therapist's ability to organize the therapeutic system, especially in terms of who is at the initial session, has much to say about who is going to win the "battle for structure." The battle for structure involves the issue of who is in charge of shaping the therapeutic structure. We agree with Whitaker (Haley and Hoffman, 1967) that this is a battle the therapist must win immediately. Our view is that the therapist is the organizer and leader of the therapy hour. However, it is the kind of leadership that enables family members to take initiative for their own growth. The family therapist must be an expert in creating contexts that facilitate the family's coming to terms with certain issues. If the therapist believes it is important for the husband and wife to deal with issues related to their respective families of origin, the therapist organizes a meeting with the relevant family members. Family members, like children relating to their parents, often test to determine whether the therapist is strong enough to maintain the leadership role, despite their efforts to avoid the process of change. Family members need to experience the sense that the therapist is strong enough to maintain a sense of integrity. Only then are they free enough to share their deepest feelings.

Teaching—Coaching

There are times when teaching is an effective therapeutic tool. Our therapy often includes didactic sessions; such constructs as how families operate, how triangles are formed, and so forth are often covered. Clients often report that the most beneficial sessions were those that involved didactic presentations. Typically, such remarks are accepted as genuine expressions from clients, and their assessment is not challenged. However, our assumption is that those didactic sessions would not have become therapeutic without the affective work that preceded or accompanied them.

The image of coaching is an appropriate metaphor for the family therapist. The coach, as such, is part of the team but does not actually participate in the game. The therapist is part of the therapeutic system but apart from the family system, the "players." The coach offers information and strategies that the players can utilize for developing a more effective game plan, as does the therapist. Carl Whitaker (Personal communication, 6/74) delights in comparing the family to a baseball team where players occupy certain positions and roles. If, for instance, the third baseman is off to field a bunt, the shortstop covers third base. The analogy is appropriate, for family members are in a structure where certain positions are "required." If the family scapegoat leaves (through marriage, work, school, or hospitalization), someone tends to take his place, or the system tends to work its way towards the scapegoat's new setting, applying its impact by remote control. It is not always accidental that a daughter develops marital problems so her family can continue worrying about her.

The therapist, as coach and teacher, can introduce new rules—rules designed to insure the experience of belongingness and of separateness. Information about communication frameworks and skills can be taught and practiced in sessions with the family. It is crucial, however, to relate such didactic material to the specific set of dynamics involved in that particular family.

Reflecting—Mirroring—Revealing

The family therapist is often a mirror to the family, reflecting to the family a picture of their interactions. There is no denying the subjective nature of this mirroring process, for the therapist's pictures are determined by a peculiar emotional and conceptual set of lenses. Even the most nondirective of client-centered therapists gives selective "uh-hum" responses that influence the clients' pictures of themselves. There is a time for being nondirective, but there is also great value for therapists in sharing thoughts, feelings, and intentions about the clients with whom they are interacting.

The therapist, then, is a feedback expert, mirroring and revealing to the family aspects of their family system that may be escaping their present awareness. Particular adeptness is required in relating the content of the communication to its process dimension. Behind much storytelling lies numerous interaction patterns that influence the deep affective responses of family members. When to reveal or share these impressions is difficult to determine, except to provide some general guidelines. Some therapists prefer to restructure a family pattern before mirroring it to the family. This is built on the assumption that it is better to go from affect to thought, instead of vice versa. There are those who, like rational emotive therapists (Ellis, 1961), prefer to go to thought first and let affective feelings follow. Still others prefer to let family members discover their interaction patterns for themselves.

Mediating—Conciliating

The family therapist often engages in mediating between two or more camps to an issue. Therapists may find themselves orchestrating the family's efforts to (1) identify an issue, (2) clarify members' sharing of perceptions and reactions to the issue, and (3) negotiate new alternatives for handling that issue. This process often involves directing the traffic of the interaction, toning down the overfunctioning members by creating an interaction vacuum for them to fill in, and minimizing digressions from the core issue. As conciliator, the therapist is able to create a constructive atmosphere where even strong feelings of hurt and hostility can be shared in a productive and healing manner. Pain and hurt are inevitable in the process of family growth, but not despair. The therapist, then, without assuming omnipotence and overresponsibility, strives to create a climate of hope and security, even in the face of apparent hopelessness. Since it is assumed that "where there is breath," there is hope and the capacity to love, families who make the effort to work therapeutically usually find the ray of hope that keeps them coming back to therapy.

Modeling—Being—Self-Disclosing

One of the most important aspects of family therapy is the family's encounter with the person of the therapist. If the therapist is secure and well differentiated, the family will eventually experience the satisfaction and freedom of interacting with a person who is transparent, who is self-responsible, and whose personal boundaries are clear. The family's sense of freedom comes from the therapist's refusal (1) to be sucked into a triangle, (2) to diminish him- or herself as a person, and (3) to either run away or become overinvolved in a situation that is clearly the family's own business. The family is thus freed to try out a whole range of new behaviors without fear that the therapist will be hurt, angry, shocked or judgmental. The likelihood of the therapist becoming a significant model for the family is increased as movement is made in the direction of becoming a "significant other" to the family. Family members are exposed to a different role model, different from the behavioral set they experienced in their own families. The more models people are exposed to, the better, for it increases their behavioral repertoire, which in turn increases their chances of acting more flexibly.

The courage to be oneself in therapy is not just good technique. It helps in building rapport and in generating the caring that allows the therapist to "give a damn" about the family. It also helps in maintaining a close enough contact with the therapist's own guts to "hear" the emotional reactions to the family and to employ those reactions as diagnostic indicators and as energy sources.

Catalyzing—Releasing—Amplifying

The healing power resides in the family system, not in the therapist. What the therapist can contribute is the catalytic stimulus that releases the healing forces. If the family system was powerful enough to create personal stress in one or more members, then it is also powerful enough to heal and to revitalize those members. We have frequently been amazed by the depth of the love and caring the family members possess for each other, as soon as it is clear to them that the open expression of that love does not result in further hurt and devastation to the self and family. This is true even among the most troubled families. It is important for the therapist to remember this.

It is also important for the therapist to realize that the family is eminently strong and that family members have been living with their pain for years. If this is added to the idea that there are probably no real family secrets,* the conclusion is reached that feelings of overprotectiveness on the part of the therapist are usually inappropriate. This is especially true in family therapy (in contrast to individual therapy), where the transference phenomena are primarily experienced within the family system itself and much less between the client and therapist. Therapists often give themselves much more power than they actually have. Such an attitude muzzles the therapists from acting on spontaneous hunches and gut reactions, leaving them in a state of mild paralysis or continuous editing of their own behavior.

As a catalytic agent, the therapist moves from a position of strength toward a territory of strength. The therapist pokes, nudges, needles, and coaxes the family system out of its homeostatic rigidity, trusting the system to regroup and find a more comfortable and flexible balance. When a glimmer of disagreement among family members is perceived, the therapist amplifies the family's awareness of the disagreement to the point where it is difficult to deny the reality. The family is then faced with the issue of confronting differences, rather than sweeping them under the rug.

Challenging—Confronting—Directing—Reframing

The distinction between catalyzing and challenging is often a grey area, difficult to pinpoint operationally. The *therapist-as-*

---

* This is especially true in regard to matters involving feelings and attitudes between family members. For example, although a child may not have the facts about his father's extramarital affair, he probably knows that father is unhappy and that mother is jealous, down on herself, and depressed. It seems that in many families the only secret is that there are no secrets.

catalyst can be portrayed as staying primarily at the periphery of the family system and giving it a nudge or "throwing a pebble" into it and then witnessing the scene as an interested bystander. The *therapist-as-challenger*, on the other hand, momentarily jumps into the middle of the action and assumes a central role as either a mover or an opposer of an action. The therapist may contradict what a family or a member says, offer a new viewpoint for the family or a member to consider, defend one family member against another, and even demand that certain behaviors occur as a matter of living up to a therapeutic contract. It is important that the therapist realizes that in challenging behavior, one is still in the role of therapist and not as a family member. As therapist, the emotional investment is different: The investment is in being an effective therapeutic instrument, not in fashioning personal emotional survival. With this attitude, it becomes easier to avoid overresponsibility and to accept a family's refusal to continue working in therapy. Even the best of therapists are confronted by the unfortunate reality of a family's decision to back out at the threshold of change.

The family therapist often acts like a social engineer or foreman in directing the construction of new pathways in the family interaction structure. Because old pathways have created ruts that produce movements toward paths of least resistance, the therapist often needs to be directive about the flow of the interaction traffic. If, for instance, the therapist instructs husband and wife to talk to each other about a certain issue and the couple continue to funnel statements through the therapist, the latter might say "Talk to her, not to me." The therapist might stop the action, turn their chairs in order to effect better eye contact, and restate the intention that the couple talk to each other, substituting "you" for "he" and "she." Furthermore, if a son, listening to the conversation of his parents, suddenly interrupts at a time when the therapist is directing the mother and father to open their channels of communication, the therapist could verbally or nonverbally (e.g. with a hand gesture) stop the son. This may have to be done repeatedly, for only then may the old path be less firmly rooted and the new path established.

Reframing is the process of redefining a client's view of a certain event, usually toward a more positive or flexible direction. If a wife says, "I don't know why he (husband) gets so angry when I talk to my mother on the phone." Reframing may take the following form: "I can appreciate your discomfort at your husband's reaction because I sense that you do love your mother very much. But, you know, I was struck by the thought that your husband must really love you very deeply and, perhaps sensing that you're slipping away from him, he is desperately grabbing on to whatever he can in order to hang on to you." Reframing could be a way of catalyzing if offered indirectly from a more peripheral position, or it could be offered more directly to the client as a position about which the therapist is strongly convinced. For example, "Did you ever think that her nagging behavior meant that perhaps she really cares for you?" (This is peripheral.) Or, "It's quite clear to me that her nagging behavior means she cares deeply about you—otherwise she wouldn't give a hoot!" (This is direct.)

The nine categories of therapist behaviors are arbitrarily grouped, since in actual practice it is difficult to define the therapist's behaviors categorically. More likely, the behavior contains several characteristics, with perhaps one being more dominant in a specific instance. An overview of these characteristics quickly gives the reader a sense that our view of effective family therapy contains elements of both directive and nondirective therapy. There are territories where a therapist is best advised to be directive and those where the best advice is to be nondirective.

Effecting Change

The variables that actually contribute to change in therapy are numerous. Those variables to be discussed now seem especially crucial while working with families. These constructs are occasionally referred to as administrative issues of therapy, and appropriately so. Without due consideration given to these constructs, the therapeutic journey is probably going to be rough and less often successful.

The Battle for Structure

Whitaker claims that therapy always begins with a structural fight—a fight over who controls the context of therapy. He claims that this is a battle that the therapist must win as soon as possible, usually with the first telephone conversation. The therapist is the process expert from whom the family members seek help. It is important to have leverage over factors that are important for therapeutic effectiveness. Among the most important factors are (1) who is to be present in therapy and (2) who decides how the therapy hour is to be handled. Families often test to determine whether the therapist has the guts to be authentic and the strength to withstand their manipulations to prevent change. This testing behavior is much like that of a preadolescent who wants to be reassured that if self-control is lost, his parents can be firm enough to take over. Then, within this umbrella of trust, the adolescent begins to take initiative toward more constructive behavior.

It is helpful to keep in mind that families enter therapy with ambivalent feelings. They are hurting very much, desirous of change, and yet afraid that change may mean the loss of what little they have in terms of acceptance, affirmation, and identity. They come in half convinced of therapy and half scared. If they sense that the therapist means business, families are more likely to bring in the affect and the energy they need to achieve therapeutic change. At this point, some families abandon the therapist and shop for one who is willing to play simply a supportive role, to be a listening board for their frustrations. If the family members sense that they can manipulate the therapist to shape the therapy hour according to their own fancies, several things can happen:

1. The family may soon abandon the therapist.
2. The family members split into their usual factions or coalitions and begin to play the therapist against each other, just as they do at home. Mother may come to tell the therapist how bad her husband is and how much her children love her. She telephones to say she would like therapy but that her husband is not interested. If the therapist gives in at this point,

a coalition is formed with mother against father. Winning the battle for structure involves the therapist's taking command of the situation and informing the woman about the best conditions for beginning the therapy.

There are many content issues around which the family can stage the battle for structure. In family therapy the most common issue—and perhaps the most crucial—is *who* will be present for therapy. Other issues might be whether or not there will be a co-therapist, whether or not taping will be allowed, and whether a family member can have a private session with the therapist. There are many other issues brought up, but perhaps the following case will give a picture of the range of possible areas.

We once saw a couple and their seventeen-year-old son, whom the parents perceived as being rebellious, disrespectful, and irresponsible. Since the referral source already had contact with one of us (Corrales), the mother seemed to have already developed a transference for Corrales. Since the family lived 150 miles away, the referral person was depended upon to inform the family about some of the expectations; one of them was the fact of co-therapy. Unfortunately or fortunately, this item was not relayed.

The first thing mother said was, "Why is he [Barnard] here?" After that was explained we sat down, and before we could even get comfortable, mother says to Barnard, "If you're going to smoke and chew gum at the same time, I'm leaving the room." This was her way of saying that she did not want Barnard in the room and that she wanted only Corrales there. Barnard responded, "The smoking I can understand [snuffs cigarette out] but I have a dry-mouth problem, so I'll keep on chewing." Thus, Barnard acceded to a socially acceptable request (smoking) but refused to have the mother run his personal habits (chewing gum). Before we could start another trend of thought, the mother looked at the tape recorder and asked, "Are you bugging us?" We responded, "Yes. We find it helpful in our work with families." Toward the middle, the mother came up with another brilliant idea. She suggested, "How about if I see you [Corrales] separately and my husband can see you

[Barnard] separately? That way the therapy can be more effective." We refused. Curiously enough, in that last ploy, she didn't even mention her son, the focus of the family problem. Mother, as spokeswoman of the family, was apparently given and/or assumed the task of shaping the therapy structure according to the family's wishes. Needless to say, she assumed the task with great vigor. Had we given in to her demands, we would have lost the forum for effective therapy, for we recognized the importance of the threesome getting a sense of their unity and their interconnectedness. The co-therapy team would have lost its "we-ness" vis-à-vis the "they-ness" of the family. Speaking about a couple and their son, Whitaker captures the essence of what we were up against:

> The son is dealing with parents and the parents are dealing with the son. I deal with the threesome, with the bigger unit, as though I weren't concerned with its components. This is the unit that they use to make war with. When there's trouble, they split and play one off against the other. I was trouble, and they would try to use me against each other too. But I refuse to get drawn in this level. They have a common enemy, rather than a person they can use to side with. It becomes a battle between them and me, rather than between themselves. [Haley and Hoffman, 1967, Pp. 269-270]

The Battle for Initiative

The battle for structure revolves around the question of who controls the process of therapy. The battle for initiative, on the other hand, revolves around the question of who controls the clients' lives. The therapist, paradoxically, aims to win the battle for structure to insure that the family members win the battle for initiative. If the therapists have control of the therapy structure, they can then set the rules about who is to take the initiative. If the family members can manipulate the therapist, they can sit back and relax. This point is crucial in effective therapy, because the thin but strong demarcation line between healthy and dysfunctioning families is the latter's unwillingness to assume responsibility for their own behavior. The heart of the therapeutic struggle involves crossing the threshold of responsibility, when the family can at least tell the therapist,

"We don't need you around anymore; we can make it on our own now."

The battle for initiative involves many large and small aspects of the therapeutic process. It may be played around the issue of whose responsibility it is to bring up important issues during the therapy hour. Our view on this matter is that the therapist initially stimulates issues of interaction but should fairly quickly pass that responsibility on to the family. It may also involve a family member asking the therapist to tell another family member about the anger one feels for the other. The cliché of helping someone help themself is appropriate to this discussion. In a strange way, the family must reach the point of defeating the therapist's tendency to play God and Savior. Ultimately the family must take credit for the healing and the growth they accomplish. It is only fair, because for the most part, this map or model fits the territory better than the reverse situation.

Until therapists can accept their own impotence, they will find it difficult to allow the family to accept and take charge of their potencies. That is why in one sense, doing therapy is an unselfish task, although it need not be totally altruistic. Therapists collect fees. Perhaps more important, however, therapists also collect experiences that can expand their own selves and spur them on to growth. Without this bilateral aspect of growth, the therapist may find the letting go of clients difficult.

The family therapist must also find a way to upset the usual pattern of relating in a family and then set up a situation where family members are able to take the *initiative* toward a new way of relating. This is the heart of change: the family's willingness to assume responsibility for their lives. Haley (1963, 1967) suggests that setting up therapeutic paradoxes eventually forces a family to take the initiative for their behavior, yet the behavior is in the direction determined by the therapist. Jackson (1957, 1968), in a similar vein, spoke about upsetting the system enough to break its homeostasis and then leaving the family to regroup on its own initiative. By judicious siding with or against the different coalitions, by relabeling, by amplifying the deviation, or by use of other restructuring devices (*see* Chap. 6), the therapist can unbalance the family to the point where the family must make some kind of a move—perhaps toward a higher level of functioning.

The Role of Transference in Change

Where does transference fit in the entire schema of change? As a psychoanalytic concept, *transference* refers to the process through which a patient projects onto the therapist qualities of someone from the patient's past. Since the patients' parents are the most important persons in their lives, they often endow the therapist with the qualities and powers that children attribute to their parents.

In a systems approach to family therapy, transference phenomena are significantly watered down because a number of the person's significant others are present. It is best for the therapist, as a rule, to stay out of the transference phenomenon. If a son wants to parentify the therapist, the latter can redirect the son's efforts toward his real father, who is present. If a father tries to parentify the therapist, the latter, by hooking up the father with the son, reminds father of his role as father, thus making it difficult for him to play a child to the therapist. Therefore, the transference phenomenon can be made to bounce back and forth *within* the family and keep it out of the interchange *between* family and the therapist for the most part.

One could, of course, speak of the family as using tactics of a child vis-à-vis the therapist, e.g. expecting the therapist to solve problems for them or testing the therapist's limits. There is value in comparing the relationship between therapist and family as moving from a parent-child to adult-adult. However, successful family therapy portrays a situation where most of the energy takes place among family members themselves. Otherwise, the situation is comparable to describing someone doing individual therapy with a family.

Transference, in the psychoanalytic schema, plays a vital role not simply in explaining a client's behavior, but also as a causal explanation of therapeutic change. As the transference strengthens, clients regress increasingly, since they project upon the analyst unconscious ideas, feelings, and strivings rooted in their childhood experiences. Therapeutic change presumably is the result of the in-depth self-understanding that proceeds out of the entire process. Fairbairn departs from this explanation of the cause of therapeutic change. Fairbairn's (1954) object-relations theory, discussed previously, views the ego as the center of the personality reaching out to objects for support. In contrast to the Freudian view of change, he sees therapeutic change as the result of a client's experience of good object relations in the process of therapy. Except for joining, emotional ties between the family and the therapist are secondary to the core processes involved in therapeutic change. Joining is the anesthesia, but restructuring is the surgery. In fact, "staying out of the transference" eventually becomes a necessary ingredient in the process of change. It is the therapist's way of saying "Your primary relationships are within your family system; I refuse to be dragged in as a third point in the triangle."

CO-THERAPY

Co-therapy refers to the process of individual, group, or family treatment by two or more therapists at the same time and place. For clarity in discussion, the term *single therapy* is used to refer to a situation where only one therapist is present. Family therapists differ in their preferences in respect to engaging in single therapy or in co-therapy. The following discussion presents a range of positive and negative aspects involved in doing co-therapy, in contrast to single therapy.

Advantages of Co-therapy

Co-therapy gives the team members a chance to share and to check out their perceptions and reactions. This process usually leads to greater accuracy in diagnosis, wider and deeper understanding of the family dynamics, and wiser choices of therapeutic strategies (Rubinstein and Weiner, 1967). Even the most experienced of family therapists can benefit from such a dialogue, simply because family dynamics are so complicated that they are rarely, if ever, fully comprehended. One could say that there exists in co-therapy a built-in mechanism for supervision.

Co-therapy also gives the opportunity for greater *role flexibility*. As one member confronts, the other can play a more supportive role, or vice versa. This allows the team the capability of joining and restructuring at the same time. Or, as one member becomes temporarily involved "inside" the family system, the other can stay outside to preserve objectivity and to make sure that clear boundaries in the therapeutic system are maintained. It also allows for different levels of activity or passivity. We have often commented to each other how nice it is to be able to "rest" occasionally as the other takes the major role in processing a family issue. The "rest" is valuable not only in and of itself but also as a way to observe the family more carefully from the periphery, without momentarily worrying about what to do next.

The team members can support each other through difficult moments in and out of the therapy session. When a family issue elicits difficult personal reactions in one therapist, the other can help process those reactions either in the session itself or later. The co-therapists are then able to model the qualities of a healthy relationship. The therapists can show that they can disagree, differ, support, negotiate, nurture, and ventilate a range of feelings in a well-differentiated manner.

By sharing the responsibility for conducting therapy, the therapists are able to experience greater security. They can check each other's tendencies to be over- or underresponsible. They can also check each other's need to be needed—an attitude and a feeling that could hinder a family's willingness to terminate the therapeutic relationship. Disturbed families have a great capacity for evoking anxiety in people who relate to them in various capacities, the therapist not excluded. Having a co-therapist allows one to verify or modify reality contact.

Paradoxically, two therapists (symbolic of the parental couple) are able to arouse transference phenomena from the family more easily than the position of the single therapist, and they also provide greater leverage in avoiding being sucked into such projections. Because of role flexibility, the therapist who is the object of the transference can shift gears and nullify the projection while the other supports the member or members involved. Because of the emotional closeness that usually develops between the co-therapy team, countertransference phenomena are more easily checked.

Because the co-therapy team represents a "they" instead of a "her" or a "him," the boundaries of the therapeutic system are more readily kept clear. The single therapist stands a greater chance of being drawn into the family boundaries. In addition, co-therapy facilitates a family member's expression of negative feelings toward one member while expressing positive feelings to the other.

Disadvantages of Co-therapy

Although our experience suggests that a well-functioning co-therapy team is a much more effective therapeutic instrument than a well-functioning single therapist, the reader should not believe that co-therapy is without its potential flaws. Rubinstein and Weiner (1976) write about two major pitfalls in the concepts of splitting and dissociation. *Splitting* refers to a situation where the "team members become separated from a common viewpoint or from a coordinated strategy, or disagree about the goals of either a single session or the long-term strategy" (Rubinstein and Weiner, 1967, P. 212). *Dissociation,* on the other hand, refers to a lack of coordination between the therapists, with a consequent failure to support each other on strategies and goals. In splitting, the therapists are in conflict about something; in dissociation, they are on individual paths.

Differences in therapeutic approaches and goals could hinder the effectiveness of the co-therapy team, especially if the differences are major. But there are always differences, even among those trained in the same school of therapy. The question of how to deal with such differences remains, no matter what the circumstances. Whether or not the team continues and to what extent it is effective depends on the team member's willingness to pursue co-therapy and to work out mutually supportive ways to cope with those differences.

Newness and differences present issues that may or may not be transitory. There are more fundamental matters that determine the success or failure of the co-therapy team. The most basic obstructive qualities to co-therapy effectiveness seem to be (1) lack of trust, (2) inflexibility, and (3) narcissistic competitiveness. These three basic negative factors are closely related. Lack of trust in the other person's ability and integrity may, of course, be a well-placed judgment. In such a case, the most honest response is to termniate the co-therapy relationship. When lack of trust arises as a matter of projection or unchecked assumptions, it is often combined with an egotistical need to appear better in the eyes of the other and of the family. In the same vein, rigidity or inflexibility is often rooted in narcissistic attachment to one's ways, which, at a deeper level, belies a fearful, untrusting, anxious ego.

Competitiveness easily leads to splitting. One direction of the split could take the form of territoriality: "This is *my* family, not yours." Such an attitude often leads to scapegoating of one co-therapist by the other and by the family. The scapegoating is usually motivated by the therapist's need to be one-up, or by the scapegoat's need to be one-down for whatever reason.

Despite the possible potential flaws involved in the co-therapy situation, we view it as the preferred mode of therapy, provided that the conditions are right. The most important condition is, of course, one's personal preference. If single therapy is one's preferred mode, then it becomes that individual's best mode. Assuming that co-therapy is one's preferred mode, then the most important conditions are trust, flexibility, and openness. These are the qualities associated with a well-differentiated personality. This section closes with a quotation from Gus Napier regarding his perception of co-therapy. Dr. Napier and Carl Whitaker engage in co-therapy frequently as they practice in Madison, Wisconsin.

> Co-therapy is a complicated relationship, much like marriage. You have a contract that binds the two of you to trying to help the family, and you must evolve a relationship that includes room for both individuals to be themselves, yet provides some kind of overall synchrony. The formal professional background of the two therapists seems to be relatively unimportant. It is important that the therapists like each other and that each bring a complementary interpersonal skill to the relationship—one who can be humorous, for example, while the other is more serious and logical. It is also

useful if the therapists grew up in families with different dynamics. This heterogeneous history provides a buffer against either therapist's becoming overinvolved with the family. [Napier and Whitaker, 1978, P. 285]

SUMMARY

In this chapter, a theoretical model for the therapeutic relationship was presented. In so doing, effort was directed at responding to several fundamental questions: What is family therapy? What does the competent family therapist do? What makes the family change?

Family therapy was defined as an intervention strategy focusing primarily on a change in the family relationship system. A distinction was made between the family system and therapeutic system, the latter including the therapist. While highlighting the importance of the therapist's own growth in the therapeutic process, the primary emphasis on the client's growth was identified as the main task of therapy. This was followed by a presentation of the major roles of the therapist and the role of transference in the context of family therapy. The chapter concluded with a view of the dynamics involved in doing cotherapy, implying its superiority over single therapy, provided the inclination and proper conditions exist.

CHAPTER 5

THE THERAPEUTIC PROCESS AND RELATED CONCERNS

THIS CHAPTER PRESENTS concepts specifically related to both the process and mechanics of conducting family therapy sessions. As the reader moves through this chapter, a greater appreciation will be gained for what is required from the therapist in facilitating an effective therapeutic venture. Many of the concepts presented in previous chapters are woven operationally into this chapter.

BEFORE THE FIRST SESSION

The therapeutic process actually begins before the family is ever seen. Usually the initial contact is made with the therapist by telephone. This initial contact is extremely important with regard to the "battle for structure" and its impact on future contacts. At this point of initial contact, it is imporant to indicate who should be in attendance at the first session. We believe, as does Whitaker (1970), that as many members of the family, both nuclear and extended, as possible should be brought in for the first session. Whitaker is so adamant about this point that, if the person making the contact refuses to agree to total family involvement, he encourages them to seek help elsewhere. We, in all cases, insist on the total nuclear family (acknowledging realities given, such as a son overseas, etc.) being in attendance at the first session and make a strong effort to involve the extended family as well. The reason for the acute emphasis on as many family members as possible being present for the first session is the acknowledgment of the systemic etiological nature of most human problems. By having as much of the system present in the therapeutic setting as possible a more thorough understanding can be achieved in order to facilitate goal setting and determining intervention strategies. A similar ecological point of view is also stressed by Aponte (1976) in his work at the Philadelphia Child Guidance Clinic.

Most frequently, the mother makes the initial phone call. It is not unusual for the mother or whoever makes the initial contact, to attempt to see the therapist alone for one session "just to explain the situation." The authors believe it can be counterproductive to allow this to happen. If this request is granted, it seems obvious that when the entire family finally gathers with the therapist they will assume the mother already has an alliance and will be guarded in their self-disclosures to the therapist. Whitaker (1970) refers to this situation as "the therapist as mother-in-law." As soon as the therapist sees an individual alone, in a symbolic fashion, he becomes the client's "mother." Assuming the therapist is the "mother" to the client, when the remaining members of the family venture into therapy, the therapist becomes the symbolic "mother-in-law" to them. It is as though the "real" relationship is with the individual with whom initial contact was established and the others now have a "pretend" relationship with the therapist. This danger can be best eliminated by not allowing it to develop.

Often we are confronted by those in clinic settings with the question of "What if our secretary makes appointments for us?" Through a small investment of time, most secretaries can be trained to determine what types of presenting problems are going to suggest family involvement in the therapeutic process. When the secretary makes this determination, a tentative appointment can be made with the caller, and the secretary indicates that the therapist will be returning the call to gather further details. When the therapist returns the call, the battle for structure revolving about who should be in attendance at the first session can be conducted.

The process of informing the mother that the entire family is desired for the first session usually results in some apprehension on her part. Examples of this apprehension are, "I don't think my husband will come in" and "What I have to say cannot be said in front of the children." An effective way to deal with the former concern is to emphasize the importance of the father's role in the family and to encourage her to have him call for a further explanation of the therapy and afford him a chance for clarification of his concerns. By engaging in this practice, the therapist can begin to establish a person-to-person relationship with the father and engage in the practice of affirming him as an individual who is important to the family system. Many times, this effort to invalidate the attribution (Laing, 1965) that has been ascribed to the father is not only facilitative to getting him into therapy, but also therapeutic. It is therapeutic in the sense that the father is being defined in a metacommunicative fashion by the therapist that may be very different from what his role has been and the importance that is concomitant with that role. In regard to the often-heard latter concern of the caller, a brief statement of how the children are probably already aware of what she perceives as a secret or, if not aware of the specific concern, aware that there is a concern in the family, is usually sufficient. The explanation also contains a point that children's fantasies regarding a concern are usually far more severe than what exists in reality.

Once the contract is clear in regard to those who should be in attendance at the first session, the issue of time and fees should be negotiated. Time is an issue that may be used by the family to try to eliminate certain members from attending a session. The therapist may be told that the children cannot attend due to school or father cannot attend due to work. At this point, the therapist should be resolute in stating the presence of all members is vital, and if therapy and change in the family is thought of as being important, arrangements can be made. This mild confrontation covers both the battle for structure, as the therapist indicates what is needed for therapy to progress, and the battle for initiative, as the family is forced to demonstrate a commitment to therapy before the first session. The authors' experience has been such that they have never had the schools deny an excuse to a child for attendance at family therapy sessions. Experience with fathers rearranging work schedules is similar to what Bell (1975) reports. Fathers have demonstrated an amazing willingness and flexibility in scheduling once they are assured their presence is vital for the sake of the family. The issue of fees seems to be handled most effectively matter-of-factly. Brief notice made of frequency of billing and payment procedures is sufficient in most cases. If there is a policy established regarding payment for missed sessions, this should also be explained. The authors' policy is such that if the cancellation is not received at least twenty-four hours prior to the appointment, the clients are billed.

The Initial Contact

Role play the situation wherein one person is the family therapist and another assumes the role of "contact person" for a family via a phone conversation. Try to consider as many as possible of the elements just mentioned. Once the role-played situation is complete, discuss and have others portray the same situation. Try to be honest in criticizing one another to derive the greatest benefit from the experience.

INITIAL SESSION

The initial session is extremely vital to the entire therapeutic process. This session is the only time that the therapist and family are strangers to each other. This provides the therapist the opportunity to observe directly how the family system relates to those outside the family. This relates to the permeability of the family boundaries and results in the beginning formulations of the therapist's construction of a family map. The initial manner in which the family seats itself can be used diagnostically in regard to the presence of alliances, coalitions, and other distance and power phenomena present in the family.

A valuable idea for the therapist to keep in mind upon initial contact with the family is the nonverbal affect of those present. Therapists may decide to respond to the affect communicated initially or simply note it in their awareness. An example of this is a statement such as, "By the looks on your faces, it appears there's considerable sadness" (anger, frustration, etc.). This decision must be based on the therapist's own clinical judgment and awareness of the consequences. Examples of possible consequences are that the family feels affirmed and empathized with; the family feels their life space has been invaded and becomes defensive; or a family rule was broken by identifying affect, especially if a specific individual is identified, resulting in amplified cautiousness. These examples will alert the potential family therapist to the kinds of considerations that need to be acknowledged while interacting with families initially.

Once the introductions are completed, the following format has proven facilitative in the initial session. The family is reinforced by the therapist for their apparent commitment and concern for the family, as evidenced by their presence in the session. This is meant as reinforcement and also to begin "joining" the family and to commence with the process of induction into therapy. This process is analogous to the medical setting, in that prior to surgery the physician administers an anesthetic. In family therapy, the joining procedure can be viewed as the anesthetic that is administered prior to the attempt to restructure, which is the counterpart of surgery. The introduction continues with an explanation of the process, such as, "All of us will be working to try and make your family a group you are *more* pleased to be with."

The initial session is the appropriate time to indicate that the therapy will be helping the family change what they want (battle for structure), but that they will have to be responsible for doing the work to bring about change (battle for initiative), and there is no magic that will create family change without work on their part. An explanation is also offered at this point regarding how the entire family is here this time, and it may stay this way, or specific subsystems may be seen alone and others may be given a temporary "day off." Once the therapist has completed this introduction, the movement into the family begins.

The First Few Minutes

Establish a fictional family consisting of a mother, father, and two or more children. Identify someone to fill the role of therapist and initiate the process involved in the first portion of the initial session. Pay particular attention to nonverbal affect, seating arrangements, how the family resists or accepts joining tactics employed by the therapist, in what fashion the battles for structure and initiative surface, and in what way the family develops an understanding of what family therapy is.

An initial interview process that is similar to what Satir (1967) has described seems to be the most appropriate point to begin the therapy. This part of the initial session is referred to as the *sensing interview*. The assumption is made that mother is probably most familiar with the family dynamics, followed by the identified patient (IP), if one is present in the family. Because of the critical roles these two individuals play in the family drama, they are not asked to comment on the family until the others have spoken first. The rationale for this is that their statements, especially the mother's, may skew what the other family members would declare. The youngest child is spoken with first. By moving to the "baby," an attempt is made to increase efforts to join the family. Usually the youngest in the family is the one who is looked upon most favorably by most, if not all, family members. Considering this, the youngest child is perceived as a good entrance to the inside of the family. The general question presented is, "What is it like living in this family for you?" Beyond this, we explore what each member values about the family, along with what they perceive as being worthy of change to benefit the family. From the youngest child, the therapist moves up through the ordinal positions until the oldest child is reached with the exception of skipping the "identified patient." The next to be spoken to is the father, followed by the IP, and finally, the mother.

Frequently, there is a need to monitor the efforts of some members to qualify or "clarify" what another member is saying. An example is the mother responding to one of her children's initial comments by saying, "That's not the way it is!" At this time, a comment such as the following is usually sufficient: "I appreciate your interest, but he's got the floor now; your time is coming." This type of comment communicates to the family members that individuals are acknowledged as important here and recognizes each one as having individual boundaries within the larger family system. This procedure also begins to establish ground rules for how "we" function here, or more technically, relates directly to the battle for structure. This move can also be defined as a joining procedure, in that it communicates to the family that the therapist is capable of introducing structure into what they may be perceiving as a chaotic family system. If members of the extended family are present, such as grandparents, they are asked to speak first, followed by members of the nuclear family. We begin with the members of the father's extended family first, followed by the mother's extended family. This decision is based on clinical experience, which suggests that the mother's family of origin is generally more involved in the family constellation than is the father's. Thus, an attempt is made to start the interview as far from the assumed core (mother) of the family dynamics as possible.

Upon completion of this interviewing process, the next step is that of arriving at therapeutic goals and finalizing the contract. As a result of hearing members present their concerns about the family's functioning and what they would like to change, goals can be identified for the therapeutic contract period. As Ferber and Ranz (1972), among others, have indicated, the identification of goals with the family is as facilitative to the success of the therapeutic system in family work as it is in working with individuals. Feldman (1976) has stated this strongly:

> In many ways, the most important initial task for the family therapist is goal-setting. Unfortunately, this process is often not carried out. In too many instances family therapists (especially beginning family therapists) start to "intervene" before having formulated (in conjunction with the family) a clear set of goals for the therapy. As a consequence, the therapy often gets bogged down, meanders aimlessly, or is precipitously terminated.

Once the goals are defined as behaviorally specific as possible, it is wise to suggest a definite number of sessions be agreed upon in an effort to achieve the goals. If the family identifies a number of treatment goals, it is wise to concentrate on only one or two for the initial contract period. This is done in an effort to insure success initially and also with the idea in mind that if one change in the system can be achieved, others probably will result from it. An explanation follows pointing out that at the end of this contract period we (the therapeutic system) will evaluate the progress and decide about either termination or continued involvement. The following seems to be accomplished by having an agreement regarding how many sessions will define the life of the therapeutic system: assuring the presence of a commitment to the process by all participants; preventing dawdling by the clients as a result of believing an endless amount of time is available; and providing another criterion for measuring progress. The authors are in agreement with Weakland and others (1974) in believing the initial contract should not exceed ten sessions. The average number of sessions agreed to after goal setting in our clinical practice has been from six to eight.

The initial session is ended on the same note that it was begun. Acknowledgment of their apparent concern and commitment to this family group is again offered. At this time, the acknowledgment is volunteered for the same reasons as it was initially.

Beginning to Work

With the same family (perhaps different role players) and therapist as utilized before (P. 120) continue the initial session to a point of closure. Pay particular attention, as observers, to the processes of moving through the family via the sensing interview, arriving at treatment goals and the treatment contract, and how the session is terminated.

MIDDLE PHASE

The process of the initial session of most family therapy work is the most predictable of all sessions. This is especially true of the therapist who espouses the process presented here. Naturally, the content for each family is idiosyncratic to that family, but the way in which that information is achieved is predictable. Once beyond the first session, the flow is definitely different from family to family. What happens after the first session is what becomes the test of the family therapist's knowledge, sensitivity, and creativity. If the therapist is unable to communicate therapeutic competence to the family during this process, the probability of being allowed into the "family circle" is diminished, as is the potential for effectiveness. Waskow's (1963) study has empirically demonstrated the importance of the counselor communicating competence to the client. This thought also seems to have been captured by Belson (1975, P. 27) when he said, "Nevertheless, I'm now convinced that in the beginning of marriage [family] counseling it is important to have the couple believe in me—not to believe that I'm omnipotent, but that I can do the job. They are in trouble and usually riddled with resentments. By the time they call me, they are desperate. What they don't need is weakness or self-doubt on my part."

The basic concept of communicating therapeutic competence appears to be the hallmark of Milton Erickson's therapeutic techniques, which have been documented as highly effective. Acknowledging Erickson's role as one of the world's leading hypnotic advocates and practitioners, it is understandable that he would emphasize this component of therapeutic communication. Practitioners of hypnosis recognize one of the most vital elements in determining effectiveness is their belief that they are effective. If individuals do not believe that they can induce a hypnotic trance in another, chances are indeed slim that they ever will. In this sense, family therapists who do not believe in themselves and/or who are unable to communicate belief in their own effectiveness probably will not experience much success in family therapy. Naturally, the clients are continually evaluating the effectiveness of their therapist from the first moment of contact, if not before, but the test comes in the middle phase of family therapy.

Others have attempted to identify phases of the therapeutic process. We believe there are three phases capable of being specifically identified. These phases are (1) the initial phase—the first session; (2) the middle phase—all sessions that transpire after the initial session and before the termination session; and (3) the terminal phase—the last session.

The middle phase of therapy is that portion where the bulk of the work takes place. At this point, goals have been established and work transpires to facilitate the family's progress toward attaining them. The focus of this phase may vary, but the emphasis is always toward the attainment of the identified goals. In family therapy, a concern that is presented often is that of the parent-child conflict. Assuming one of the major treatment goals revolves about this issue, the middle phase of therapy naturally is concerned with changing the current relationship patterns. The therapist must now determine the most expedient and effective means of accomplishing this. The type of decision the therapist would make with this family in the middle phase of treatment is caught in this quote from Haley (1976, P. 135): "The typical situation is an over intense parent-child dyad that alternately includes and excludes the other parent. When the sequence is seen in this way, the therapist can select among different approaches. He can enter the family through different doors, either through the father-child relationship, the mother-child relationship, or through the mother-father relationship."

John Howells (1975) has identified a good scheme for identifying the foci which family therapy may take during the middle phase. He labels the three foci of therapy as antecedental, actuality, and anticipatory. *Antecedental* he identifies as "therapy concerned with the resolution of events that occurred in the past. These are antecedental events, hence 'antecedental' therapy" (p. 267). The material identified in Chapter 2 of this book exemplifies antecedental therapy. *Actuality focus* is "therapy concerned with the resolution of events in the present. These are present events, actual, hence 'actuality' therapy" (p. 267). In this element of therapy, the bulk of the work is centered throughout the middle phase. Considering much of the work of family therapy is focused on the process of the family system, it becomes essential to have a "now" or "actuality" focus. Foley and Dyer (1974) have identified eight situations that show process elements characterizing an actuality focus and appearing worthy of intervention. These are:

1. Each family member assumes a special role in the family system, i.e. when labeling takes place.
2. One family member speaks for another, i.e. the family has a role of "family spokesman."
3. Playing the game "If it weren't for them" is noted.
4. Playing the game "If it weren't for you" is noted.
5. A family member invokes the laws of immutable nature.
6. The family adopts the mañana attitude.
7. Nonverbal clues giving permission to speak or refrain from speaking are noted.
8. Discrepancies of feelings, words, or actions are noted.

By making observations and reporting them to the family for processing, the therapist is not only intervening in the "now," but also training the family in how to observe its own process. In this sense, the intervention takes on an educational flavor in conjunction with the present therapeutic impact. The last focus defined by Howells (1975, P. 267) is what he labels *anticipatory*. This means "therapy concerned with the resolution of events that occur in the future. These are anticipatory events, hence 'anticipatory' therapy." This is a focus that is especially prominent toward the end of the middle phase and in the termination interview. Toward the end of the middle phase appears to be an appropriate time to introduce the intergenerational focus. For the most part, the crisis that motivated the family is probably reduced and a strong family orientation is developed by this time. As a result of this consideration, this is discovered to be an appropriate place to begin exploring the parents' families of origin, if this has not been started already. Freeman (1976) has commented on this issue in the following fashion:

> At this middle stage the therapist might need to be very active, asking questions which stimulate the family to identify those subsystems within the intrafamilial and extra-familial networks that could be worked on. Discussing relationships with extended kin can help identify important areas of work. . . .
> As mentioned previously, it might be crucial during the middle stage for the therapist to introduce new issues to the family. Systems theory teaches that there is a need to have new information entering the system to help the system learn more about itself and its connections with the outside world. [P. 267]

This scheme is all-inclusive and appropriate for identifying categories of material that may be found in family therapy sessions.

The remainder of this book deals specifically with both the content usually worked with in the middle phase of family therapy, as well as intervention techniques appropriate for utilization. Considering that many examples are given regarding content and process elements of the middle phase of family therapy in these future chapters, this section is closed with a discussion of a therapeutic variable that is given much attention in the literature.

Transference and Countertransference

Transference and *countertransference* are concepts that have been discussed and related to family therapy as sources of potential disruption, if not total destruction, of the therapeutic process (Boas, 1962). These terms are appropriate to the psychoanalytic scene from which they originated, but not as potentially damaging for active family therapy, as advocated in this book. We agree with Skynner (1976), who states that in family therapy the activity, spontaneity, and directness of the therapist inhibits the development of transference in the therapeutic setting. In the psychoanalytic setting, it seems appropriate to believe that the patient will project some past introject onto the passive, reflective therapist that now must be worked with in the therapeutic setting. In family therapy, the interaction is directed back to the participants and that is where the interaction is focused, with the therapist outside monitoring and directing. Objects for transferential material are present and alive and can be worked with directly. The opportunity for corrective feedback is ever present and concrete, minimizing the potential for distortion through therapist countertransference, as may happen in individual therapy.

When viewed in this manner, the concern that family therapy dilutes the potential for development of transference material is a moot point. In family therapy, the need for developing a transference is not necessary, as the individuals are present and can be worked with directly.

The countertransference issue can also be dealt with directly by the therapist. If one begins to experience feelings toward a family member that are reminiscent of feelings experienced in relation to a person in the past, one can discuss them directly and therapeutically. If, for instance, the male therapist begins to experience the adult female as his mother, he can report this to the family and document for what reasons he is perceiving her as his mother. The group present can then process whether they ever experience her in a similar fashion and in what context. In this sense, the countertransference material takes on the clothes of corrective feedback for the family. With most of the family therapy movement relying heavily on interpersonal-systemic-behavior-experiential models, this concept of dealing with what has been labeled *counter-transference feelings* is most prominent. From this perspective, counter-transference, as well as transference material, is dealt with directly, *in vivo*, allowing the therapist to continue to deal with the battles for structure and initiative. Naturally, the middle phase is out of necessity directly related to the battle for initiative and reminding the family that they determine the degree of change that will take place.

Countertransference

Imagine you are the therapist sitting with a family consisting of a forty-one-year-old mother who appears extremely depressed and hopeless; a forty-four-year-old father who is autocratic and bigoted; a seventeen-year-old son who appears downtrodden and similar in appearance to his mother; a thirteen-year-old daughter who seems Pollyannaish in her overt attitudes and behavior; and a nine-year-old set of twin boys, one of whom appears similar to the oldest son and the other like his sister.

As you consider this group and yourself, who would you be most likely to develop a positive countertransference with, for what reasons, and how might you bring that into the session and use it therapeutically? Now, do the same as you consider the one with whom you would be most likely to develop a negative countertransference. Write your responses on paper and then discuss them with a group of your peers and share perceptions.

TERMINATION PHASE

The end of the therapeutic journey in family therapy seems to be less troublesome for all participants than what seems to be the case in other therapeutic modalities. Fitzgerald (1973) has the following to say as an explanation for this observation:

The couple are heavily transferred to each other, and the transferences to the therapist are, therefore, diluted. In this form of therapy, regression is kept to a minimum by focusing on problem solving in the here-and-now, using the past mainly for understanding the present, and conducting therapy sessions at intervals of one week. (On occasion, when the going is particularly rough, a couple may be granted an extra interview.) [Pp. 87-88]

Although recognizing termination in family therapy as being

less traumatic than is characteristic of other forms of therapy, it is no less important. Gerald Zuk has described a role appropriate for the family therapist and labeled it the *celebrant role.* The idea is that there are appropriate times to join in a celebration with the family regarding what they have accomplished. Rather than having termination perceived as rejection, it is important to identify the termination process as a commencement or "graduation." In the truest sense of the word, it is analogous to school graduation, as all have experienced it. People acquire new competencies and insights and then graduate with the understanding that there is still much to be learned, but hopefully they now know how to learn what is needed for future encounters. What better explanation is there of an effective therapeutic process? A final outcome goal of treatment is not just of remediation or crisis intervention, but also of a preventive nature. Through exposure to the therapeutic process there are presumably transferences of not just the content or skills acquired, but also the process to which the couple or family was exposed and that they can employ on their own.

The graduation process can also be related to the process of individuation from one's family of origin. A new system, the therapeutic system, has been developed, and the various participants of that system are now moving out into new activities. This analogy of individuation for the family is quite easy to recognize, but it is also present for the therapist. Hopefully, therapists are strong enough and have enough outside support that they do not become enmeshed and dependent upon the family developing a dependency. With this in mind, it becomes evident that both the therapist and family must be able to take a stable "I" stance and be comfortable with their identity. As Martin Buber (1965) has suggested, "If I am I because you are you, and you are you because I am I, then I am not I and you are not you; but if I am I because I am I, and you are you because you are you, then I am I and you are you and we can talk." What could be added to this in the form of a postscript is that not only can we talk, but we can meet intimately and we can part comfortably without split loyalties.

Termination may come about as a result of three factors: (1) end of the number of sessions contracted; (2) the couple or family decide they want out; or (3) the therapist decides it is time to terminate. Regardless of what precipitates the client's movement out of direct therapy, the process to be identified now seems to facilitate the exit. This process allows all participants of the therapeutic system an opportunity for input and giving feedback. The seven elements of the termination process are now identified and explained.

1. Ask the family to review what has taken place for them as a result of therapy. Each member present is asked to identify two or three things they have learned about themselves, another family member, or their relationships. Specifically, the concern is with changes they are able to report as having taken place during the time they were involved in therapy. The reason for taking this step has been summarized concisely by Fitzgerald (1973, P. 94): "My purpose in asking for a review is twofold. I like to find out what they regard as having been significant, at least on a conscious level, rather than taking it for granted that I know what has been meaningful to the couple. I believe also that the lively discussion that ensues when I invite them to search their memories for material reinforces, and emphasizes, and underlines what they have learned."

2. Upon completion of the family's overview, the therapist provides the family with perceptions of their changes. Most frequently, the family has identified quite thoroughly the changes that have occurred. Considering this, the therapist is encouraged to endorse and reinforce their statements, as well as make whatever additions are evident, but were not mentioned by the family.

3. A crucial step, the family is recognized for the initiative they have demonstrated in creating the changes that are now evident. The reason this step is deserving of separate emphasis is twofold: (a) for reinforcement of the idea that the initiative for change must come from them. This reinforces what the therapist has been indicating throughout the therapeutic process and establishes that mental set for them, should they decide to reenter therapy at some later date. (b) This step also provides

encouragement and a subtle suggestion regarding change beyond therapy. The suggestion is that they must continue to act in order to maintain and advance post-therapeutic change.

4. Consult with the family regarding what changes they would like to engage in beyond the therapeutic setting. Naturally, this step also includes how they can maintain changes already achieved. Along with the identification of what they are desirous of changing, the "how" of facilitating the change is also explored.

5. Upon completion of the family exploring potential sources of internal change, the therapist offers suggestions for the family's consideration. A common suggestion at this stage is encouragement regarding either starting or continuing exploration of the extended family and the reciprocal impact present for the participants.

6. This step is vital; allowing the family to leave without split loyalties. All of the preceding steps are designed to facilitate this item, but this step is a final reinforcement. The goal is to avoid the family believing they are letting the therapist down by no longer needing him or her. As the therapist discloses encouragement and respect for the family's changes and reassurance of their ability to continue to change beyond the therapeutic setting, the statement at the metalevel is one of pleasure regarding their change and independence.

7. The final step consists of the very pragmatic issue of asking family members for feedback regarding the therapeutic process. What happened that seemed to be counterproductive? What do they think could have been done to quicken the changes being made?

Termination Interview

Using the same fictional family as already developed on pages 120 and 124, perhaps with different role players, portray the termination process as just outlined.

We are strong advocates of the "checkup" concept for couples and families. The annual physical checkup has seemed to gain wide acceptance by the North American public. In the same sense, a checkup for relationship functioning seems to be equally important. This seems to be especially cogent when one considers the way in which relationship dysfunction can be easily manifested in somatic symptoms (Grinker, 1973). When considered in this fashion, one can see that the annual physical checkup may be detecting symptoms of relationship dysfunction, but treated as a physiological problem. Because of these considerations, we routinely schedule a checkup with the couple or family for some designated date in the future. Establishing a specific appointment time seems to be more functional. This time period gives the family sufficient time to practice and facilitate the development of learnings acquired while in therapy. During this same time period, there are usually stresses placed upon family systems that are a test of the family's efficiency in integrating these learnings.

This checkup visit also facilitates the completion of outcome research by the therapist in question. The therapist now has exposure to a couple or family who has completed a specified number of sessions and can engage in post-testing to determine the effectiveness of the therapeutic process. This process can quite easily provide feedback to all participants that can be utilized for their evaluation. Not only does this research benefit those currently involved in the therapeutic system, but also those that may decide to enter therapy in the future.

Outcome research takes many forms, as pointed out by Winer (1972):

> Some effort and concern in research is reflected in the development and use of indexes such as: frequency of talking (Drechsler and Shapiro, 1963), order of talking (Haley, 1964), amount of interaction (Sigal, Rakoff and Ekstein, 1967), silence (Ferreira and others, 1966), decision making (Ferreira, 1963), and pattern of interaction (Coughlin and Wimberger, 1968) of family members. There are those who have developed and used some aspects of projective technique (Elbert, *et al.*, 1964) (Bradt, 1968) and those who use a variety of other approaches (Wallace and Fogelson, 1965) (Goodrich and Boomer, 1963). [P. 236]

Recognizing the many avenues available for studying families and the effectiveness of intervention with families, the decision regarding variables and tools to be utilized becomes the decision of the individual therapist-researcher. As Gurman (1975) has suggested, the most widely accepted position among clinicians today is that marital and family problems are primarily the result of disturbed and ineffective patterns of communication. As a result of this apparent truth, increasingly more marriage and family therapy outcome research is primarily investigating variables related to communication within the system. Recognizing this as the case for researchers today, it still remains the decision of the individual conducting the research to determine what will be explored. For the individual who wants to engage in couple or family research, it may be worthwhile to refer to the Cromwell, Olson, and Fournier work (Olson, 1976) along with Fischer's (1976) article to assess what instruments, standardized and otherwise, are available to facilitate the research.

OTHER RELEVANT TREATMENT CONCERNS

Variables the authors have discovered to be vital to the therapeutic process with families are now discussed. The variables referred to are referral sources, previous therapists and their involvement with the family, and confidentiality. Through the utilization of proper discretion and therapeutic judgment with these variables, we have found them to be as facilitative to the therapeutic process as they are potentially dangerous when proper consideration is not accorded them.

Referral Sources

In marriage or family therapy, many clients come to the therapist as a result of a referral. As marriage and family therapy has gained more recognition as a specific orientation, referrals from other professionals and institutions have become more common. The more traditional procedure that has been followed with the referral source has been getting a release of information form signed by the clients and then receiving past records from the referring person or institution. These authors believe a vital resource for facilitating movement of the therapeutic system has been lost in this process.

Our contention is that, whenever possible, the referring party should be brought in for at least the first session with the new clients. Upon completion of the first session, all members of the therapeutic system can together decide upon the future involvement and role of the referring party. By involving the person who made the referral in the first session, the following is accomplished: (1) There is facilitation of communication of information regarding past involvement with as little distortion as possible. (2) There is clarification of the role the referring person had and possibly will continue to have with the family—this may eliminate redundancy and facilitate a better understanding of the system referred. (3) There is a metacommunication to the family of hope, as evidenced by all those involved with them attempting to work together for their welfare. (4) By becoming familiar with individuals or institutions involved with the family, the therapist becomes more familiar with the family's network and has a greater potential for activating agents in the family network to facilitate therapy. (5) This process goes to great lengths to develop better relationships with referral sources. By allowing those from the outside into the therapeutic setting, an openness is being communicated to them. This perceived openness by referral sources encourages them to reciprocate with more openness than that which seems to be usual. Naturally, the end result of improved communication between referral sources and the family therapist seems to be to the advantage of the group of primary concern, the family.

An example of the value of incorporating the referral person into the first session might crystallize the above ideas. One of us received a referral from a local county social service agency, and the referral person was invited in for the first session. A couple was referred as a result of having all six of their children removed from their home and placed in foster care as a result of child abuse.

The mother had been hospitalized at various times in her life for what was diagnosed as schizophrenia. The husband was sixty-eight years old, more than twenty years his wife's senior, and a domineering and manipulative individual. They were referred to explore their relationship and to develop an understanding of the reasons for the child abuse. After a three-month period, the social service agency would then reevaluate their suitability for returning the children. Upon entering the room for the first session, the husband immediately moved into a hostile attack of the therapist for removing the children from the home and speculating obscenely about what their intentions were.

As a result of the presence of the referring individual, the role of the therapist was able to be clarified. The couple was now able to realize that the therapist was there for their benefit and not as an adversary. The therapeutic contract was agreed to and proceeded satisfactorily for the agreed-upon period of time. We are convinced, considering the clients involved, that, had the referral source been absent from this session, to engage in therapy with this couple would have been extremely difficult, if not impossible.

Previous Therapists

On occasion, the marriage and the family therapist has clients enter therapy with another individual. At times, we have initiated therapy with families and have had them inform us that they are just finishing or leaving therapy with another therapist. We believe it is imperative to explore with them their reason for exiting therapy and now entering with us and concur with Whitaker (1970), who states that the clients should be sent back to the therapist they are attempting to escape at this time. Assuming there are no variables, such as a change in geographic locations as an explanation for their exit, the probability of our receiving their negative transference from the past therapist is great. This process is similar to divorce. The spouse who re-marries immediately after the divorce will probably find him- or herself in a relationship similar, if not identical, to the one he or she was attempting to escape. Considering this point, it seems most facilitative for all participants to encourage the clients to return to the previous therapist and resolve their difficulties directly. If, for whatever reason this step is impossible, it is essential to communicate to the clients this concern for the benefit of the about-to-be-developed therapeutic system.

Another concern in regard to previous therapeutic involve-ment of the clients is the danger of them using past therapists for leverage in therapy. The clients may indicate that therapist A told them this was the reason for the way they are, or this is what they should do to remedy their situation. This ploy by the clients can become an effective tool in preventing the current therapist from winning the battle for structure (*see* Chap. 4) in the therapeutic setting. By citing the previous therapist, the current therapist is thus disarmed, and the potential for effectiveness is probably diminished.

With this in mind, it seems imperative that when the therapist becomes aware of clients employing this technique, it should be defused as quickly as possible. We believe the most effective way to contend with this is to reexplain to the clients that the therapist determines what should happen in this therapy, based on his or her professional competence. At this point, it is wise to acknowledge there are various ways of perceiving and resolving human dysfunction, and in this situation, the therapist's orientation is utilized.

In the case where a couple or family is being seen that has one or more members being seen by another therapist individually, the need for communication among the therapeutic systems is imperative. Without this communication, the possibility of the various therapeutic systems being counterproductive is always evident. If at all possible, it is valuable for the therapeutic systems to meet for at least one session simultaneously to explore the goals of each, as well as to establish communication channels between the systems.

Confidentiality

The issue of confidentiality with either couples or families is the same as any other situation when more than one individual is involved. There is no way that the therapist can insure that what is said is kept within the confines of the therapeutic system. Therapists can indicate that they will keep confidential the information that is produced as a result of therapy, but cannot speak for the others. The most ethical stance the therapist can take is to inform all participants that the issue of confidentiality is individually determined by each member present.

SUMMARY

This chapter presented information relevant to the progression of therapy. The various stages of therapy were discussed, along with their idiosyncratic concerns. Upon completion of the discussion of the therapeutic stages, other variables relative to successful therapy such as the following were explored: the role of checkup sessions; the place of outcome research in marriage and family therapy; the importance of referral sources in therapy and their most facilitative role; issues regarding the role of therapists with whom the clients have previously been involved; and finally, the issue of confidentiality in marriage and family therapy.

CHAPTER 6

THERAPEUTIC INTERVENTION
TECHNIQUES AND ADJUNCTS

THE PRECEDING CHAPTERS have been primarily designed to present the theory and process of family therapy. This chapter discusses ideas regarding potential techniques for intervention in working with a family. Some of the ideas are our original contributions, and many are ideas that have been initially described elsewhere. In all of these cases, we have direct experience in utilizing the techniques and have selected them because of the resultant success experienced. Note, though, that it is not simply awareness of how to mechanically implement a technique that is important. Of equal importance are variables such as a theoretical base from which the techniques are delivered, timing, the particular therapeutic situation, developmental considerations of the family of concern, and other such elements.

We contend that resolution of these concerns must flow from one's own sensitivity and experience: Is this the right time in therapy to utilize this technique? Is the therapeutic situation appropriate to utilize this technique? Is the family such that it could benefit from this technique? Answers to questions such as the following comprise that element of therapy that is more of an art than a science.

The science element of family therapy comprises a knowledge of both the therapy and process involved, as previously presented. Without this knowledge, the therapeutic process is, in all probability, not going to be successful. With this knowledge, success is not guaranteed, but the probability of success is greatly enhanced. It is analogous to the person sitting in front of a large pipe organ, who randomly presses the keys and manipulates the pedals to make music, but ends up with noise. The skilled musician, knowledgeable of theory and practice, sits in front of the same instrument and through application produces beautiful music. In the same way, the knowledgeable family therapist, with practice, can facilitate the production of music by the family to replace the noise they are currently manufacturing. Without theory as a base, the therapist is like a table-tennis ball in an air chamber thrown about at random and only occasionally hitting the hole and being propelled outward. The therapist functioning with integrated theory is able to direct himself and the therapeutic process in a purposeful and productive fashion without having to rely on chance or trial and error.

With these prefatory comments made and hopefully digested by the reader, techniques and adjuncts to therapy are presented. The first group of methods to be discussed is what are referred to as *didactic aids*.

DIDACTIC AIDS

Didactic aids are those methods that concentrate on presenting a cognitive map to the family. A *cognitive map* is a theoretical model that can be used in conceptualizing an abstract element of family dynamics. In employing a didactic method, the therapist appears to be playing a teacher role. In presenting didactic methods, the authors use either a blackboard or prepared handout on 8½ by 11 paper to present graphically many of the following ideas. The authors experience has been that judicial use of cognitive maps seems to expedite change for many families. A map seems to give the family members a sense of direction, an ability to channel their energy toward more clearly defined goals. An appropriate analogy is that of the family setting out on a motor trip to a part of the country they have never visited before. Without a map, they may still reach their destination, but not without undue irritation and frustration. In the same sense, the family who sets out on a trip to become more functional can do so with less irritation, frustration, and potential damaging expenditure with the aid of a map.

Boundaries

The didactic method of presenting the concept of boundaries to a family is the first discussed. To activate this tool, the family has the concept of boundaries, as articulated in Chapter 1, presented to them. The goal of this process is to help them better understand the relationship boundaries present in their group. To facilitate the internalization of this concept, each family member is asked to indicate which of the boundaries they would identify to describe the relationships they have with various members and other subsystems in the family. After this step has been completed, the members can usually identify in what fashion they would like to attempt to restructure the boundaries to allow more comfortable and healthy family functioning. If they experience difficulty in identifying the "how" of changing boundaries in their family, the therapist can be a consultant to them on this point. Whitaker (1970) discusses concretely how he has utilized this concept to facilitate the therapeutic process. He refers to the issue being considered here as the *struggle for territory* and how he helps the couple define their own territories in the relationship. The goal is to provide the couple relief from distress and to increase their ability to progress in successful therapy.

Scapegoating and Triangulation

Scapegoating and triangulation constitute another successfully used didactic method. In presenting these concepts, a diagram such as that found in Figure 8 has been found to be helpful.

The explanation is given of how two people in conflict many times involve a third party to serve as a distraction from their relationship problems. After deluding themselves into thinking

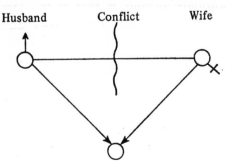

Figure 8. Triangulation.

there is no problem between them, but rather with them and another, they proceed to live out the "lie." The third party in this sense becomes the scapegoat. Naturally, a convenient source for identifying a scapegoat for a marital dyad is the sibling subsystem. Most frequently, it seems that the firstborn child is the one selected. The scapegoated individual may become either a source of irritation (rebellious, engage in antisocial acts, etc.) or of great pride and vicarious satisfaction (extraordinary achievment in athletics, academics, etc.). We believe this construct is probably the source of the best explanation for why firstborn children consistently achieve greater success than occupants of other ordinal positions and also most frequently manifest emotional problems.

After an explanation of these concepts to illustrate what is happening in the family, the marital dyad can hopefully more fully accept and "own" the conflict residing between them. This concept can be used to instill "healthy guilt" in the parents, to serve as a motivation for efforts to change their relationships and eliminate the need for a scapegoat (Boszormenyi-Nagy and Spark, 1973).

Matrix of Identity

The matrix of identity as presented in Chapter 2 (*see* Fig. 4) is another useful concept for didactic presentation. The first step consists of explaining the importance of feelings of belongingness and separateness for individuals in a family in order to develop an adequate self identity. Following this, the various members are asked to evaluate their own sense of belongingness and separateness within the family and in what ways, if any, achievement of these elements is interfered with in the family process. This method then is a source of diagnostic information and simultaneously is a stimulus to the family for exploring its own process.

Communication Principles

We frequently present communication skills and associated concepts in a didactic format. The process employed to present communication concepts is elaborated upon in Chapter 7. We believe that by devoting an entire chapter to communication concepts and principles, the prominence attached to them in working with families is implicit.

The Genogram

Another frequently used method that is appropriately classified as a didactic method is the genogram. This process has been thoroughly presented in Chapter 2.

Didactic Aids

In a small group of five to eight members, establish family roles to portray a family in therapy. Set the scene so that one of the didactic aids is appropriate for use with the family. Whoever is designated as the therapist then implements the particular aid with the family. Once it is completed, take time for processing the exercise. Switch roles and have another of the group members assume the role of therapist and implement another of the aids with a family.

TECHNIQUES RELATED TO SOCIAL AND EMOTIONAL DISTANCE

Techniques designed to work with social and emotional distance manifested in family relationships will now be analyzed. Social and emotional distance, in this case, refers to actual distance manifested in relationships geographically or perceived emotional "closeness" or "distance" experienced by family members in relating to each other. This concept has been elucidated on by others in articulate and convincing writings (Minuchin, 1974; Kantor and Lehr, 1975). The following techniques are designed with due consideration for the role that distance plays in all relationships and how it can be managed therapeutically.

Joining

Joining is all the movements therapists may make that communicate to the family that they understand and are empathetic with the family system and its component elements. Through affiliation with the family, therapists become more confident in believing their spontaneous responses are more syntonic with that system. Examples of joining are the therapists communicating to a family member how they have had a similar experience, feeling, etc.; mirroring a client's body positioning; various verbal reinforcement of appropriate behavior manifested by various family members of the family as a total system; acknowledgment of affect demonstrated without confirming verbalizations from the system; and the therapist utilizing the same vocabulary or expressing interests similar to the family or a specific member.

Peck (1973) discusses the idea of "having a thing" with a member of a marital dyad in treatment with him. He accepts that the development of a relationship with one of the partners regarding an element of mutual interest that is a consistent and natural part of treatment. Peck believes that eventually this point of relatedness leads to an insight into the dynamics of the marital relationship. He (p. 63) says, "The idea of having a thing simply means that there is a point of contact between me and one partner. This interface often seems completely irrelevant. However, God and the unconscious willing, this movement leads into the couple and their struggles."

The goal is to facilitate the therapist's movement into the family system to ease both understanding and effectiveness. By effectively using joining techniques, the therapist can greatly enhance chances of successful intervention. As Minuchin (1974, P. 125) states, "Joining techniques may not always advance the family toward the therapeutic goals, but they are successful when they ensure that the family returns for the next session." Minuchin believes that effective utilization of joining strategies can also speed the early phases of therapy and facilitate treatment.

Restructuring

Restructuring techniques, as defined by Minuchin (1974, P. 138) are "the therapeutic interventions that confront and challenge a family in the attempt to force a therapeutic change. . . . In restructuring, he [therapist] functions like the director as well as an actor" For a family therapist to restructure, it is essential that a conceptualization of the family as it currently is, be gathered. Once the current family map is identified and goals have been specified, restructuring can begin. Examples of restructuring are emphasizing differences present among the family members of a highly enmeshed system; joining in a coalition or alliance in the family to increase stress that can then be used as motivation by facilitating the recognition of a need to change by the family; disrupting pathogenic triangles to begin to develop person-to-person relationships; and assigning homework to be completed between sessions, such as two normally alienated, members talking with each other five minutes per day in order to establish a new transactional pattern in the family. As has been mentioned previously, these are only examples, and many of the suggestions to follow could appropriately be classified as restructuring techniques. This category has been included because of our conviction regarding its desirability and efficacy in working with families.

Family Sculpting

Family sculpting can be an extremely powerful and efficacious technique when working with the family that seems to have a rule that eliminates verbalization of "how it is" in the family. This technique facilitates the expression of each family member's experience in a single visual representation.

One family member is asked to imagine the other members as malleable putty and to place them in spatial and postural relation to one another. In the process, each member's total physical being can be shaped in whatever way desired in relation to the others to express relationships, feelings, and what might have been just vague verbal impressions. The sculptor then shapes and places him- or herself in relation to the rest. Each member has a chance to be a sculptor. In this sense, the picture presented in many cases is worth more than the figurative "one thousand words." Just as this technique is effective with the family lacking in verbal skills, it can be very effective with the highly verbal family. By relying upon physical communication, many of the intellectualizations and other verbal defenses can be circumvented.

This technique can be used diagnostically to develop a picture or map of the family, as well as in an evaluative fashion. After having each member portray how they see the family members in relation to each other now, they portray how they would (like) the family to be. Once this "ideal" is represented, periodic reference can be made to it to determine how successful the therapy is in moving toward the desired goal.

An important element of this as a technique is the therapeutic processing that transpires following its completion. This entails arriving at the family's impressions of how various members presently perceive relationships in the system and what they might do to bring about change. We have found this technique facilitative, as have others (Satir, 1967; Papp et al., 1973).

Sculpting

Form into groups of five to eight and practice sculpting. Sculpt each other as individuals, depending upon what your first perceptions are. Once you have verbally processed this exercise, develop a simulated family from your group and implement the sculpting process. Process this exercise with special attention devoted to the type of information this exercise may have brought into the therapeutic system and how it could be used. Once completed, someone in the group may want to volunteer to sculpt their own "re-created" family in the group. To do this, a group member assigns various group members roles from their own family and then portrays the family by sculpting. From this process, the group members who played the family roles can attempt to describe to the sculptor how they perceive the family. You will find that you can do the same type of enactment for each of the following techniques with equal benefit.

Family Sociogram

The family sociogram is a technique with similarities to family sculpting in both process and outcome goals. The technique involves asking the family members to locate themselves in the therapy room according to how they perceive themselves in relation to the other family members. They are encouraged to use the entire room, and naturally the larger the room, the more amplified the relations appear. With this technique, the alliances, coalitions, triangles, boundaries, and other dimensions of the family become apparent. The major difference between the family sociogram and sculpting is that the latter involves shaping of the individual, as well as distance between individuals. The former concentrates only on distance and location in the room.

The processing of the material manifested through utilization of this technique should take place immediately upon its completion. We have found that effective processing of this technique means asking everyone to discuss the sociogram's ramifications for the family while all members maintain their placement in the room. This practice facilitates a fuller integration of the material extracted as a result of the technique. A secondary aspect of this technique is to have various members place the other family members in the room according to how they would like the family to be. By doing this, not only is the "actual" family picture portrayed, but the "ideal" is also made available for consideration.

Marital Sociogram

The marital sociogram employs nonverbal methodologies to depict each spouse's experience of self in relation to the other in the relationship. Although this technique is discussed here as appropriate for the marital relationship, it can be used with any two-member subsystem of the family. To implement this technique, one spouse is placed in a specific location and asked to remain stationary. The other spouse is then placed directly opposite that one and asked to begin moving slowly toward the stationary spouse until he or she finds a distance that is comfortable. The roles are then reversed and the experience processed. This technique adequately demonstrates for the therapeutic system the quantity of distance (symbolic of emotional distance) each spouse is desirous of in the relationship. The means for arriving at a mutually agreed upon "distance" in the relationship is a natural outcome of this technique.

Rolling Chairs

If chairs with casters on the bottom are available, another useful technique for illustrating emotional distance is possible. Each of the members of the therapeutic system are asked to take advantage of the mobility offered by the chairs during the therapy session. If they find themselves feeling close to another member, they are encouraged to roll over next to that person or, if experiencing a sensation of distance, to roll away from the individual involved. The only limitation imposed is that all participants stay in the emotional field, implying that everyone stays in the room where therapy is taking place. Naturally, if participants leave the room, the technique becomes counter-productive in that it negates the possibility of observable inter-action. This technique can be valuable and can bring new energy into the therapeutic system to facilitate the work of the family and the therapist.

SPECIFIC RELATED TECHNIQUES

Contracting

Contracting is an important technique that has been widely covered in the professional literature (Ferber and Ranz, 1972; Tharp and Wetzel, 1969; Whitaker, 1969; Rappaport and Harrell, 1975; and Sager, 1976). This technique elicits as clearly as possible from the couple or family what they want to change. Along with what they want to accomplish, agreements are made regarding what each will do to facilitate what is agreed upon. Not only does this make the goals explicit, but also the process for reaching the goals becomes more discernable.

As Sager (1976) has clearly stated, there appear to be three levels of contracts with which couples enter a marital relation-ship. He identifies the conscious and verbalized level, the con-scious but not verbalized, and the level that is beyond aware-ness. "Clarifying contracts" is vital to helping both couples and families initiate change in their systems. Couples and families can usually identify problems in the first two levels of con-tractual arrangements, but to work at the level that is beyond awareness requires the therapists' interpretations and work with the couples' families of origin either directly or indirectly (*see* Chap. 2).

Sager (1976) has developed an elaborate profile for examining the contracts that are governing relationships. His process examines such variables as expectations, psychological and biological needs, defenses utilized, and role analysis. Familiarity with Sager's work is advantageous, even though one may not choose to incorporate it exactly and completely, in developing a cognitive map for examining relationship contracts. Although there are other means of employing somewhat similar techniques, such as the script analysis of the transactional analyst or the life-style analysis of the Individual psychologist, Sager's work appears to be the most appropriate for facilitating change within the marital and family relationships.

Sager (1976) has made the following statement relative to couples, but we believe it is equally appropriate for families as well:

> The concept of exploring individual marriage contracts helps to familiarize each marital partner with his own and his spouse's needs and willingness to give and to point out troublesome aspects of the relationship; couples are usually highly receptive to this way of structuring their problems. The technique is particularly valuable in conjoint sessions. Communication is facilitated, and spouses are better able to understand themselves, each other, and their relationship, when the terms of their contracts are revealed. The reasons for their unhappiness, apparently irrational behavior, and bickering or bitterness then become clear. Once they gain some understanding of the contractual disappointments each has suffered, marital partners often feel less helpless and are able to seek more realistic and effective solutions to their problems. [P. 8]

By utilizing the contract technique, the family therapist comes one step closer to winning what has been labeled the *battle for initiative.* This is the common dilemma regarding who is to do the work necessary to induce change within the family system. Some families believe the therapist can magically, or otherwise, do what is needed, and no initiative is required of them. By implementing the use of a *written* contract in the therapy process, the efforts required for change to be manifested are made explicit to all involved in the therapeutic system.

Homework Assignments

Task assignments, or homework, is another technique that we value highly. On the average, the couple or family is seen once a week for one hour. This leaves another 167 hours in the week that could be used therapeutically if tapped by the therapist. Assigning tasks is an effective way of providing continuity of the therapeutic work and of emphasizing client initiative. Naturally, the task assigned is generally based upon the material being worked with in the therapeutic setting and, as a result, usually varies from session to session. The assignment is thus determined by the knowledge and perceptiveness of the therapist. Examples of assignments are: completion of a genogram (*see* Chap. 2); listening to the audio recording of the just completed session prior to the next one; having the usually passive member of the parent subsystem make certain decisions during the week ensuing; and assigning certain responsibilities necessary for household functioning to specific members. A valuable collection of other exercises appropriate for use as homework assignments can be found in a recent book by David Knox (1975). This book is a collection of behaviorally oriented exercises.

Haley (1976) discusses the value and importance of directives or assignments in his form of treatment. He identifies three primary purposes for his use of directives that are consonant with our beliefs and experience: (1) Directives are a way of making changes happen. Considering that the main goal of therapy is to help people behave differently and have different subjective experiences, directives to facilitate change seem appropriate. (2) By directing people what to do, the therapist becomes involved in the therapy. The directive intensifies the therapy by asking the family to complete a task during the week and thus "remaining" with them throughout that period to the next session. (3) Finally, the family's reaction to the directive provides valuable information to the therapist regarding family rules, roles, boundaries, and other variables. Haley, in the same source, makes a strong case that

> everything done in therapy can be seen as directive. If an individual or a family in an interview is talking about something and the therapist says, "Tell me more about that," he is giving a directive.

If the therapist only nods his head and smiles encouraging them to continue, that is also a directive. If someone says something the therapist does not like, he can tell the person not to say that anymore—and that is telling him what to do. If the therapist turns his body away from the person and frowns, he is also telling the person that he should not say that sort of thing. [P. 50]

Not only does the assigning of homework place the initiative for change with the family, but it emphasizes to them the process nature of change. The family is able to see that change involves more than a one-hour commitment once a week.

Home Visits

Venturing into the environment of the family by holding a session in the home is a powerful technique and one we have found especially valuable at times when the therapeutic process seems bogged down. This technique has been elaborated on elsewhere by Donald Bloch (1973). Implementation of this technique allows the therapist to view the "homeground" of the family and determine what effect the physical environment has on the interactions of the family members. Many times, the number of insights that one can gain by conducting at least one session in the family's home is surprising. A pertinent example is the family we once saw that consisted of the parents and six children. The presenting problem centered around the two youngest children, who were perceived as being in opposition to the rest of the family. During the home visit, we noticed that in the dining area, there was a table with six chairs and a smaller table in the corner with two stools. The parents indicated that the two younger boys had always eaten there in order to prevent "discomfort" at the main table, which could only seat six "comfortably." This situation symbolically portrayed the boundaries in this family and how these boundaries subtly indicated that the boys were being defined as "excess baggage."

Dreams

Dreams can be used very effectively in the family therapy process. The authors have used dreams therapeutically with an entire family, but concur with Goldberg (1974) in his identification of goals that can be accomplished by utilizing dreams with couples: "These include: (a) improvement of communications between the couple; (b) expansion of the awareness that each spouse has both of self and of the other; and (c) correction of mistaken perceptions that each spouse harbors concerning the other."

On many occasions, dreams are spontaneously volunteered, at which time they can benefit those present. If not voluntarily presented, the therapist can encourage the family members to keep a pencil and paper next to their bed to record dream memories for discussion with the family. An important ground rule for utilization of this technique is that the goal is for the dreamer to report reactions, feelings, and associations resultant from the dream and not for the other members to play "psychoanalyst." Dreams can be a vehicle for self-disclosure and gaining new insights or recalling insights that may have been forgotten. This is another technique that can be effectively employed to introduce new energy into the therapeutic and family system and enhance empathic understanding for all involved.

One-way Mirrors

One-way mirrors, when available, can be used effectively. Having a family member or a subsystem of the family behind the glass affords them the opportunity to observe the interactions of the remaining subsystem(s), perhaps for the first time. For example, the parents can sit out and observe their children's interaction, as well as watch the therapist modeling effective interpersonal skills with the child subsystem. This technique is not only advantageous for the family, but for the therapist as well. By removing one or more subsystems and placing them on the other side of the mirror, he is then enabled to see how the remaining subsystem(s) change as a result of the missing members. In this way, valuable diagnostic information as a basis for future intervention can be gathered. This technique has been written and elaborated on by others (Fulweiler, 1967; Minuchin and Montalvo, 1967).

Skynner (1976) has written of his work with one-way mirrors by stating the following:

One of the two co-therapists takes a parent behind the one-way screen to watch the rest of the family interacting. This situation physically enforces observation, reflection and containment of impulses, particularly as the watching parent is able to identify with the reflective comments of the co-therapist sitting beside her. (The parent's self-esteem is also bolstered by seeing that the other co-therapist has similar difficulties to her own in coping with the children!) Parents usually spend several sessions behind the one-way screen, in order to foster a process of reflection and intro-spection which is an almost undeveloped function in such families. The family is helped gradually to make distinctions, to differentiate over-inclusive categories and themes instead of functioning in global, all-or-nothing terms; this is done by interrupting and examining the interaction in the here-and-now, rather than by dis-cussing reports of what has happened elsewhere in the past. The therapist also seeks to identify the prevailing mood and to change it, either by introducing some feeling that is missing or joining in the characteristic family emotion and either exaggerating it so that it becomes obvious, or gradually changing it. [P. 233]

Videotape Equipment

Videotape playback can be used with families in much the same manner as it is commonly employed in the training of therapists. The family members can witness the way in which, for example, they send double-level messages, such as displaying affect nonverbally, that disqualifies the verbal aspect of their message. This technique can also be used to feed back to the members the affect displayed in a situation that may be difficult to capture and explain verbally. A valuable way in which to use this approach is in termination of the therapy, to demonstrate powerfully to the family the gains they have made. Excerpts can be replayed from the first session and compared to the family interaction of the last few sessions. This process reinforces the family for the work they have accomplished and simultaneously encourages them to continue their efforts beyond the formal treat-ment contract. Bodin (1972) has reported elsewhere his findings of a survey among clients in which this technique was employed. The results of this survey substantiate the potential value of utilizing videotape replay in the therapeutic session.

Alger (1976) has presented the following commentary regarding the use of videotape equipment in the direct treatment of families:

Two especially significant values merit emphasis. One is that the possibility of obtaining objective behavioral data, and having it immediately available for integration into an ongoing transaction marks a truly significant advance in the development of the therapeutic art into a combination of art and science. Secondly, the shift of role position which occurs when therapist and family step back from the usual hierarchical positions to that of cooperative researchers in a common task marks another significant move in making therapy a more truly human and mutual adventure. [Pp. 546-547]

Family Photographs

Another technique that we have found valuable is the utilization of photographs provided by the family. When families either volunteer or produce photographs upon request from the therapist, a virtual wealth of information is made available. Milgram (1977) has the following to say regarding the plethora of data provided by photographs:

But even people trying to look their best must work with the materials at their disposal and under conscious control. Close scrutiny of the inadvertant gesture, the unintended clue, or the biologically ineradicable detail adds another level of meaning to the photographs. In this sense, photographs often capture more than the subject, or even the photographer intends.

This is especially true when groups of people are shown in a photograph, for relationships are often expressed through gesture and body orientation. A good first step in interpreting group photographs is to look at the hands. Where are they? Whom do they touch? [Pp. 60-61]

Few families today are unable to provide photographs of themselves, and usually representing various developmental stages of the family. Because of the availability of photographs today, it is valuable to limit the family to a specific number of pictures, as suggested by Anderson and Malloy (1976), based on their use of family photographs in treatment. It is a valuable process when using photographs to ask each family member to select the picture they believe is most important to them, considering their perception of the family. If more than one family member identifies the same photograph, that is fine, considering the primary concern is the individual's interpretation of it. Once each individual's photograph is presented, a valuable process aid has been to ask the entire family to reach a consensus regarding which one they would like to select as "most" representative of them. This process can provide extremely valuable treatment data regarding family interaction patterns, rules, and roles.

In employing this technique with families, the following variables are to be given careful deliberation: any surprise reactions of members to others' selections; who is significantly absent in the photos; what affect is attached to each photo and for what reason; which photo is presented first, most often, and appears most significant to all; closeness and distance of family members reflected in the photos; and which photos have been taken best care of and the reasons for this.

The process seems to activate in the family a sense of connectedness that may have been forgotten. The fact that they as individuals share a common history of hurts, pains, and joys, etc., is a strong bonding element and can be activated through the study of family photographs. Stimulating the awareness or reawareness of their shared history can be a strong therapeutic maneuver that energizes them as a system concerned for themselves within that group and the whole. This approach has provided a valuable assistance in our therapeutic adventures with families and one technique we are unlikely to abandon in the future.

Family Photographs

Each member of the small group (five to eight members) should bring in a significant photograph that he or she believe portrays his or her family. As an individual presents his or her family photograph, the other group members can seek to gather information and further understanding of the presenter's origin and, as a result, their present being. The types of concerns you may want to keep in mind while listening and observing the different presentations are found in the description of the use of family photographs in treatment. Keep in mind that the variables identified for consideration are offered as suggested guidelines and are by no means all-inclusive. As with any other technique, the application is dynamic in accordance with your ability to be creative.

Bibliotherapy

Bibliotherapy consists of assigning readings that could be therapeutically beneficial to the couple or family. This technique, like some of the preceding ones, allows the therapist to make advantageous use of time beyond the usual one hour per week. Many times, families spontaneously offer to the therapist the impact of recently read material upon their relationships. At other times, the therapist can judiciously prescribe readings that might facilitate a family's movement through a particular stage of the life cycle. In order to prescribe appropriate materials, it is important for the therapist to be aware of books with biblio-therapeutic value. Examples of some better known books that have proved of value to us bibliotherapeutically are: *Mirages of Marriage* (Jackson and Lederer, 1968); *I'm OK, You're OK* (Harris, 1969); *Psychocybernetics* (Maltz, 1960); *Your Inner Child of the Past* (Missildine, 1963); *Conjoint Family Therapy* (Satir, 1967); *Peoplemaking* (Satir, 1973); *The Intimate Enemy* (Bach and Wyden, 1968); *Pairing* (Bach and Deutsch, 1973); *Understanding Human Sexual Inadequacy* (Belliveau and Richter, 1970); *Children of Divorce* (Despert, 1962); *The Boys and Girls Book About Divorce* (Gardner, 1970); and *Family Communication* (Wahrtroos, 1974).

TECHNIQUES IDIOSYNCRATIC TO FAMILY THERAPY

The techniques to follow are presented in a section separate from specific related techniques because of their apparent idio-syncratic links to family therapy. Upon examination of these techniques, the reader will see that all are designed to offset the calcified homeostatic nature of disturbed families. These techniques are designed to bring disequilibrium to the family that is homeostatically stuck in their pathogenic patterns. Many of the innovators and leaders in the field have been adept in equipping themselves with techniques such as these to intervene with families therapeutically. Among those individuals identified with the field of family therapy who employ such techniques are Bodin, Bowen, M. Erickson, Haley, Minuchin, Watzlawick, and Whitaker.

Milton Erickson has perhaps most succinctly captured the basic essence of the rationale on which these techniques are based.

> Psychotherapy is sought not primarily for enlightenment about the unchangeable past but because of dissatisfaction with the present and a desire to better the future. In what direction and how much change is needed neither the patient nor the therapist can know. But a change in the current situation is required, and once established, however small, necessitates other minor changes, and a snowballing effect of these minor changes leads to other more significant changes in accord with the patient's potentials. [Erickson's Introduction to Watzlawick, Weakland, and Fisch, 1974, P. 6]

Erickson then characterizes these techniques as he views them: "I have viewed much of what I have done as expediting the currents that need the 'unexpected', the 'illogical', and the 'sudden' move to lead them into tangible fruition" (Watzlawick, Weakland, and Fisch, 1974, P. ix).

The terms *illogical* and *unexpected* are appropriate for the techniques that are described here. On many occasions, these ideas have met with resistance by those in the helping professions. The potential user of these techniques must feel comfortable with them in order to facilitate their effectiveness. Because of this, it is important for each person to assess fully how effectively they are able to integrate these techniques into their theoretical orientations. From our experience and that of others (Haley, 1973; Watzlawick, et al., 1974; Weakland, et al., 1974; Whitaker, 1975), their therapeutic efficacy is convincing. In many cases, these techniques have facilitated changes where the more traditional methods had previously proven ineffective or, in our clinical judgment, would have been.

Encouraging Resistance

This technique is most closely attached to Milton Erickson and can be attributed to his experience in hypnosis. By "encouraging" resistance, the therapist is creating a situation where the client's resistance is defined as cooperative behavior. This has a tendency to defuse or short-circuit the effect the client's behavior normally has on those in his or her environment. An example of this is the couple who resists any attempts to change their frequent fighting. Rather than continuing to confront their resistance, the therapist suggests that they change the duration, time, or place where the fight normally occurs. In this way, the therapist accepts the object of a couple's resistance, i.e. the fighting, but with a slight modification. Once the modification is made, other changes can be added or many times the changes spontaneously occur.

Providing a Worse Alternative

Once the areas for change have been identified, providing a worse alternative tends to facilitate the family's selection of new behavior in a vital area. In one family we saw, it became apparent that the adult subsystem was still relating to the two teenage children as though they were about five to seven years of age. Autonomy for the adolescents was almost nonexistent. In order to change this relationship system, we suggested to the parents that they begin giving their boys three to five "free nights" a week. This suggestion was made with the knowledge it would be rejected by the parents, but would probably help them be more acceptant of some change. At the end of this session, the parents agreed to give the boys one "free night" per week. This change, quite modified from the original suggestion, was a dramatic breakthrough for this family—an action that paved the way for other changes this family gradually but eventually accomplished.

Utilization of Metaphor

Using a metaphor facilitates working with a symptom that the therapist believes may be difficult for the couple to confront for various reasons. Jay Haley (1973) has illustrated this technique effectively in describing how Erickson employed it with a couple that resisted talking explicitly about sexual relations:

> He will choose some aspect of their lives that is analogous to
> sexual relations and change that as a way of changing the sexual

behavior. He might, for example, talk to them about having dinner together and draw them out on their preferences. He will discuss with them how the wife likes appetizers before dinner, while the husband prefers to dive right into the meat and potatoes. Or the wife might prefer a quiet leisurely dinner, while the husband, who is quick and direct, just wants the meal over with. If the couple begin to connect what they are saying with sexual relations, Erickson will "drift rapidly" away to other topics and then he will return to the analogy. He might end such a conversation with a directive that the couple arrange a pleasant dinner on a particular evening that is satisfactory to both of them.

Encouraging a Response by Inhibiting It

Encouraging a response by inhibition is especially appropriate in working with families where one or more members are reluctant to speak and thus potentially handcuff therapeutic intervention. The first step consists of creating a desire or readiness to respond in the silent member but then frustrating their attempt to speak. An example of this is the family with a "silent" father present in the sessions. At one point, the therapist begins to offer conjectures regarding reasons for the discomfort present in the family. In offering these conjectures to the family members other than the father, he deliberately speculates about father's involvement in creating the trouble. During this time that he is speculating, he does not look at father, and when the father is ready to "defend" himself from this "off-base" therapist, the therapist asks the father to wait a minute until he is finished explaining his ideas. Once the therapist is finished, the father is acknowledged, and his time for rebuttal is allowed. The therapist can now join the father by helping him develop his rebuttal, and the probability of father's future involvement is now enhanced.

An example of combining encouraging resistance and encouraging a response by inhibiting it can be given from the authors' experience. A couple had been seen for a number of sessions, and we realized the prominent role that the wife's parents were still playing in her life and resultantly in the marital relationship of concern. We asked the wife to invite her parents in to therapy, and they consented although it involved a round trip of over 350 miles. When the parents arrived for the first time, the wife's father quickly informed us that he was not going to talk because he had already said everything he felt was important. Our response was to say that was fine and he probably knew what was best for him, and we then proceeded to become involved with his wife and daughter. Within a few minutes he wanted to talk, and the response was that he would have to wait, that we were involved with the others right now. In about three minutes, we went to him, and by that time he was literally on the edge of his seat waiting to be heard. From that point on, he was fully engaged in the therapeutic process. Although there is no way of determining with certainty, we believe that if he had been initially engaged regarding his resistance, much valuable time and involvement would have been lost.

Redefining Behavior

Redefining behavior, although simple, can be extremely effective. In dealing with families, it is soon apparent that families are quick to identify certain behaviors as either good or bad and react accordingly. This technique encourages the family to look at behavior from a different vantage point. As it is viewed differently, the behavioral reaction will probably change accordingly. Examples of this are: The mother who is defined by the therapist as apparently "being overconcerned and loving" to her children, who refer to her as the "bitcher"; the husband whose wife defines him to the therapist as "weak-willed and spineless" is defined by the therapist as "overprotective of his wife's feelings and therefore reluctant to act"; and the youngster who is defined by his parents as an "incorrigible delinquent" is defined by the therapist as having similarities to Christ in his sacrificial role of preserving the parents' delusions of a problem-free relationship.

Emphasizing the Positive

Remember that a system can be changed by changing even one element of it, emphasizing positive behaviors can be a potent technique. By selecting a behavior that is satisfying to the whole family and asking them to enlarge on this while working with their "real" concerns, interaction patterns that are responsible for their "real" problems can be effectively changed. An appropriate example is the family that appears fragmented and alienated from each other. The therapist asks the members to identify one thing that seems mildly satisfying to all members. A session could be devoted to the identification of this satisfying behavior, thus giving the therapist a chance to observe the family's communication procedures. During this time, it is often wise to encourage the family to process this item without the therapist's assistance, an action that results in more freedom for observation. Once the behavior is identified, the family is then asked to enlarge it slightly during the ensuing week. Perhaps the family identifies "watching the news" as the most satisfying behavior. During the coming week they may then be asked to watch a particular thirty-minute television show together, without the expectation of verbal interaction.

Hopefully, by building on what is already defined as positive, more motivating goodwill can be generated in the family. This idea was employed with a family that identified watching the news as their most satisfying time. This seemed to be based on the fact that there was no expectation of interaction during this period. Another block of thirty minutes of television watching during the week was assigned; the popular "All In The Family" program. The session following this assignment was the most dynamic of any previously experienced with this family. This was partly the result of the laughter all shared from watching the Bunker family, along with self-insights acquired by comparing their family to the Bunkers'.

Deviation Amplification

By amplifying a deviation, stress is often increased in the system to a point of crisis, resulting in the necessity to reorganize a new set of relational patterns. Minuchin (1974) cites an example, the *blocking of usual communication channels*. In dealing with a family where the oldest child interprets mother's messages to the younger children, resulting in minimal contact between mother and the other children, the oldest child is asked to take a "vacation," and the younger children encouraged to interact and clarify directly with mother. Minuchin similarly identifies emphasizing differences as a means of increasing stress. For instance, the wife who seldom expresses her differences of opinion overtly, but does so regularly passive-aggressively is asked directly to "state her opinion" on an issue just presented by another family member. The side-taking function of Zuk (soon to be presented in this chapter) is another way of increasing stress. Many times, by creating a coalition with a scapegoated family member, unresolved issues can be discussed openly for the first time, resulting in new perceptions and concomitant behavior.

Speaking to One Family Member Through Another

In speaking to one family member through another, the therapist attempts to capitalize on a relationship that is interpreted as positive by the other member with whom he wants to communicate. To exemplify this, imagine a family with a mother and father, and three children. Mother seems to be intensely involved with one youngster, resulting in his acting out in order to avoid being "smothered" by her. The therapist identifies the family member with whom the mother seems to have the most positive relationship. Once this has been accomplished, the therapist engages that person in dialogue, passing on messages he would like the mother to hear. The therapist then makes suggestions to this person regarding what he would do if he were the mother. By communicating to mother in this manner, the therapist attempts to capitalize on the respect and admiration mother has for that person and thus reduce her resistance to the suggestions.

Paradoxical Intentions

Paradoxical intentions has a long history and can be traced back to some early therapeutic pioneers, such as Alfred Adler and Victor Frankl. It has currently been outlined, as defined in this publication, by Carl Whitaker (1975):

It includes a kind of tongue-in-cheek attitude, a kind of put-on by the therapist but is surprisingly useful if it's a natural component of the ongoing relationship. The therapist may so augment or escalate the incongruity of a symptom or bit of the patient's behavior that the absurdity is easily apparent to the patient and he enjoys the implications, as one does after a slip of the tongue. Success with this maneuver demands that it be lovingly done, and this caring is the anesthesia for the amputation of pride that takes place. [P. 6]

This technique, like the others in this section, may appear bizarre and unusual to the uninformed observer. The concern here is not with the aesthetics or acceptability of techniques to a consensus group: changes observed in families as a result of this technique (and the others in this section) are the primary concern.

Paradoxical intentions capitalize on the ability of human beings to disassociate themselves from the situation and observe it for what it is, along with the fact that two antagonistic responses cannot exist simultaneously. This technique facilitates families perceiving a situation differently than what has been customary for them, resulting in a challenge to their previous mental sets. Examples of this technique are given to end this discussion.

(a) give the top of an old coffee percolator to college sophomore schizoid without comment when she leaves the interview; (b) identified patient is accused by parents of having poor ego boundaries—therapist offers blank sheet of paper with large X to "use as ego boundary as needed"; (c) unannounced exit from office and return five minutes later without excuse and with inane reason—"my foot itched"; write a letter during hour to your co-therapist entitled "Why this family won't make it"—offer it to family if anyone questions the behavior. [Whitaker, 1975, P. 6]

Go-Between Process

The go-between process is another effective technique for changing family systems. This technique has been expounded upon primarily by Gerald Zuk (1965, 1968, 1971, and 1972). As Zuk (1971) has stated,

the three terms of go-between-process as conducted by the therapist are: (1) his definition of issues on which the family is in serious conflict and the expression of that conflict, (2) his taking the role of go-between or broker in the conflict, and (3) his siding with or against the family members in conflicts. As the therapist moves from one step to the next and back again, he exerts a critical

leverage on the fixed patterns of relating among family members.
[P. 225]

The go-between process shifts the balance of pathogenic relating in the family so that new patterns of relating can be
practiced in the therapeutic setting. Zuk (1975) states that he
believes there is no more important goal than to change destructive relationship patterns. He says,

> although there may be many goals in family therapy, I believe
> there is only one central goal: the reduction and replacement of
> pathogenic relating. The central aim of the therapist must be,
> in my opinion, to return the family to functioning "within normal
> limits." For each family a judgment of what constitutes "within
> normal limits" must be made by the therapist, in the same way
> that he must decide when readiness for change is not present or
> sufficient so that a course of therapy should not be undertaken.
> [P. 19]

The go-between technique is especially relevant to changing
family rules (Jackson and Lederer, 1969) and myths (Stierlin,
1973). The word *rules* is here defined as the implicit regulations
apparently internalized by the family to maintain their systemic
functioning. *Myths* imply the beliefs that their relationships are
based upon, such as, "We are a *nice* family and therefore never
openly demonstrate *aggression*." Naturally, this is a technique
that places the therapist in a directive position and requires
assertiveness.

In implementing the go-between role, the therapist creates
new rules for relating, such as no interruptions. The therapist
may disclose myths, such as focusing on disagreements and
crystallizing them in families that are fight phobic or characterized as being "pseudo-mutual" in nature (Wynne et al., 1958).
On another occasion, this technique may result in siding with the
family's identified patient to give strength and redefine the IP's
role within the family. Just as therapists may purposefully take
sides to form a coalition, they may be equally adamant about
refusing to take sides in a disagreement between two or more
family members who are attempting to "triangle" them. The
point is that in implementing the go-between process, the therapist directs the treatment situation. This technique puts the

therapist in control of the battle for structure, or who determines what happens in the therapy setting.

The section designed to present techniques in a more traditional therapeutic sense is now closed. In no manner is this overview meant to be exhaustive of the techniques appropriate for use with couples and families. What have been presented are those techniques that have proven to be effective for the authors in numerous situations. An example of a class of techniques that was not given representation are those from the behavioral school. For coverage of many of these fine ideas, refer to the following readings: Wolpe and Lazarus, 1966; Knox, 1971, 1975; Lieberman, 1970; and Stuart, 1975. Techniques more appropriate for specific situations commonly encountered, such as sexual dysfunctions; divorce counseling; marital group and multiple family group therapy; communication problems; and others, are presented in succeeding chapters.

Each person involved with families brings a unique personal and professional history, in addition to a preferred orientation for working with couples and or families that fit that history. This is valuable and should be fostered by those responsible for training family therapists. At the present stage of development for the profession, it appears absurd to state, "This is *the* way to do it." Sager (1976) seems to have captured the value and importance of various approaches:

> All the therapists' skill, artistry, creativity, and training are required to overcome or circumvent resistance to change. To achieve the necessary interactional behavior changes by whatever means are at his disposal—systems methods, psychodynamic and insight approaches, behavioral modification, or any other theoretical approach—is the central task of the therapist. The therapist usually has to work back and forth, utilizing those methods that he believes will be the most effective. A multifaceted approach allows for greater flexibility. [P. 207]

The next section analyzes an adjunct familiar to therapists since around the turn of the century. The aid is that of testing.

TESTING

In the rapidly mushrooming field of marriage and family counseling, testing has been one element of the traditional treatment modality that appears to have been ignored. This lack of attention has come about not as a result of ignoring the value of testing, but rather as a result of the necessary overextension in the area of theoretical and philosophical development for the field.

In this section, the definition of a test provided by Cronbach (1960, P. 21) has been accepted: "A test is a systematic procedure for comparing the behavior of two or more persons." This definition appears to be especially appropriate to the field of marriage and family counseling, in that the major focus is on relationships of at least two or more people. Another advantage of this definition is that a systematized manner of perceiving clients can be especially profitable in determining a treatment strategy and evaluation.

Practical Issues and Concerns

The following concerns are suggested as important for consideration prior to the use of tests in the counseling process.

Am I familiar with the mechanics of this test? One of the best means of becoming knowledgeable about a test is to take it yourself. This experience allows you, at least vicariously, to determine where the potential testtaking experience is on the "threatening-benign" continuum for clients (how threatening or benign the tool is). The next step for familiarization is reference to the manual to gain an understanding of the scoring process, which you can now apply to the answer sheet or protocol. It is recommended that the user of any test have supervision on its use and the administration, scoring, and interpretation of the test.

Is there a need to know? This question revolves around the important issue of whether or not the information derived from the instrument is beneficial to the treatment process of the couple or family. This is suggested to avoid unnecessarily creating client dependency in the treatment process of the couple or family. This situation develops dependency in the clients through the use of assessment instruments, as the clients might look at the therapist and tests as a source of answers to the problems, in contrast to looking at themselves. Answering the question "Is there a need to know?" is a crucial variable in testing.

Can I communicate to the clients the values of this test? If the clients can sense the value of testing at the time the test is given, the probability of cooperation being gained is increased. Not only will the clients be more willing to take the test without attempting to deceive, but they will probably be more likely to receive interpretations without resorting to defenses such as distortion or denial. An explanation of the purpose of testing to the clients can also provide further clinical information. By observing their reaction to a description of what is being assessed, valuable clinical cues may be gathered.

The Interpretation Process

The way that tests have been traditionally used in various settings has led to much suspicion by the general public because of the lack of feedback received by those examined. Because of this fact and also for the therapist to avoid defining himself as an "omnipotent soothsayer" with all of the answers, it seems beneficial to interpret the results to the client, if at all possible.

In interpreting findings of the test to the clients, it is wise to not use jargon. Jargon can not only confuse and frustrate the client but can also provide another bit of unwanted testimony to the therapists' "omnipotence." The therapist, to conveniently determine how communicative he or she is, should frequently stop and ask clients to explain in their own words what they have understood about the interpretations up to that point. It is also worthwhile to frequently solicit feedback from them with regard to how this test information fits in with their own perceptions. A simple but effective approach that facilitates is this: (1) briefly define to the clients what a scale on a test measures; (2) ask them to predict their score on that scale; and (3) then share their test results with them.

Another element of the interpretation process that proves especially difficult for many test users is to remain neutral toward the findings of the test. One way of doing this is to frequently state, "Your performance on this test appears to suggest . . ."

By using this phraseology, the clients are frequently reminded that this is their representation of themselves and not the therapists' definition. This also keeps the responsibility with them and assists the therapist in avoiding the unconscious accusation by the clients that these findings are only their therapists' perceptions.

During the interpretation process, it is extremely important not to get lost in looking at the profile and lose visual contact with the clients. By being especially sensitive to both verbal and nonverbal nuances of behavior, the therapist can determine the impact of the data on the clients and respond appropriately. Are the clients remaining open and receptive to the interpretation? Is one partner using this information to downgrade the other? Is one partner being protective of the other, who is receiving the information? Does the material interpreted appear to threaten the client? Many systemic dynamics can be observed in clients' nonverbal behavior.

The interpretation procedure can consist of interpreting the results to one individual at a time, but a valuable approach that can be employed is the crisscross interpretation procedure. In this process, each spouse completes the instrument with him- or herself as the reference point, followed by completion of the instrument with the spouse as reference point. By following this procedure, the therapist is provided with the following information after scoring:

1. How each spouse perceives him- or herself.
2. How each spouse perceives the other.
3. How each spouse's individual profile compares with the other's perception of that person.

With this wealth of information provided, the results can be used immediately to identify areas of apparent discrepancy and conflict that can be used for negotiations and enhanced understanding. It has also been found that simply having to consider oneself and one's spouse in accordance with a structured format can be therapeutic. As each spouse begins to observe him- or herself and the other, according to the test format, he or she can perhaps be more objective and systematic in considering their differences and similarities. Previous to this time in the couple's relationship, there most likely has been a disproportionate concentration on the differences between them and the liabilities of the other.

Types of Instruments Available for Use and Appropriateness

Cromwell, Olson, and Fournier (1975) have presented a concise paradigm for understanding the instruments appropriate for use in marriage and family counseling. They have provided an excellent organizational scheme and evaluation of instruments available to the individual who works with couples and families. Rather than trying to replicate what they have done, readers are referred to their publication for identification of instruments appropriate for diagnostic and evaluative purposes.

Cromwell, Olson, and Fournier's classification of instruments is based on the premise that in working with relationships there are "insider's" (family member) and "outsider's" (therapist) perceptions. Many times, the perceptions from these two vantage points are in conflict, and there is need for crystallization of these perceptions for the therapeutic process. The two dimensions to be explored are the subjective and objective. By taking these dimensions, they construct a 2 by 2 model with four cells to present graphically the type of data collected and through what means it can be gathered (Fig. 9).

In considering Figure 9, it becomes apparent that there are four basic categories of instruments appropriate for use in mar-

Type of Data

		Subjective	Objective
	Insider	Self-report methods	Behavioral self-reports
Reporter's Frame of Reference	Outsider	Observer subjective reports	Behavioral methods

Figure 9.   Test categorization.

riage and family counseling. (1) The most commonly used are the *self-report methods,* such as questionnaires, structured interview guides, and standardized tests that facilitate self-expression of perceptions. As Figure 9 demonstrates, this provides input to the therapeutic system from the insider's frame of reference. (2) *Observer reports* provide input from the outsider's frame of reference; the report usually occurs after the observer has moved into the family and through the family's encompassing "rubber fence," as identified by Wynne regarding the functioning of the family with which he is working. These tools provide a means of systematizing them. (3) *Behavioral self-reports* are those that rely upon the clients' counting and recording of their own or other's specific behaviors as they occur in regular interaction. These provide relatively objective information that can be used therapeutically either diagnostically or in evaluation. (4) *Behavioral methods* to be employed by that person from the outsider (therapist) frame of reference are also valuable in marriage and family counseling. On the basis of this information, concrete goals can be established for the therapeutic process and can result in facilitating the assessment of success in reaching the same.

Fischer (1976) has provided a valuable paradigm presenting various family and marital dimensions that have been assessed and categorizes them. In the process of ordering the dimensions identified, he provides an excellent overview of research conducted with assessment tools. Bodin (1968) provides another such overview that presents much of the seminal works done in the area of family assessment. The reader is referred to both of these articles for a panorama of the field.

The authors believe it is beyond the scope of this section to present an overview of assessment instruments available. The Cromwell, Olson, and Fournier publication (1975), along with Bruce (1972), provides readers with resources to determine what would be most appropriate for their particular practice.

SUMMARY

This chapter presented specific techniques that can be used to intervene therapeutically with couples or families. In all cases, the techniques are included as a result of the associated success that their use has produced in our work with couples.

This chapter is not meant to be thought of as an exhaustive review of therapeutic techniques and adjuncts, but rather as representative. The techniques employed by therapists working with couples and families are determined by their own creativity, knowledge, and experience, as is true of other forms of therapy. What has been presented in this chapter was tempered by our interpretation of what is more representative of therapeutic intervention with couples and families.

CHAPTER 7

COMMUNICATION TRAINING IN FAMILY THERAPY

COMMUNICATION, VERBAL OR nonverbal, is the vehicle through which family members touch each other and regulate their emotional closeness or distance. Every interaction between two or more family members involves not only the *sharing* of information, but also the *shaping* and determining of the relationship involved. These two dimensions of communication (sharing and shaping) underpin much of this discussion. This chapter maps out frameworks and skills that the therapist can use and share with a family. Communication training is a valuable undertaking in various respects: (1) as a supplement or complement to family therapy; (2) as a therapeutic tool within the therapy process; and (3) as an educational-developmental experience for couples or families. In this chapter, its use as a part of the therapy process is presented.

Therapists and theorists differ in their views of the importance of communication training. Some view communication as simply the expression of one's being and therefore shaped almost totally by one's self-perceptions. Others view communication as shaping a person's being and therefore valuable as an area of therapeutic change. A third view looks upon the relationship between one's being and one's communication as related cybernetically. The latter refers to a mutual influence: being shaping communication, and communication shaping being. Whether communication shapes being or being shapes communication or whether they are cybernetically related (as we believe they are), the process of establishing clear communication patterns is still important. Even if one were to assume that communication patterns are merely a reflection of the status of one's intrapersonal being, the communication patterns between people who have survival value to each other can still become a strategic arena for intervention if only as a way to reach one's being.

BASIC COMMUNICATION PRINCIPLES

Levels of Communication

In Chapter 1, it was stated that in every interaction or communication there are at least two significant levels going on: the report or content level and the relationship or metacommunication level. The *report* or *content level* refers mainly to the verbal messages, especially to the literal, dictionary meaning of the word. In the process of exchanging these messages, the communicators are also engaged in defining the relationship. If the shaping or defining of this relationship were dependent solely on the verbal level of communication, then there would be few problems in relationships because each move to define a relationship one way could be interpreted simply and could be reacted to either by affirmation or rejection. However, there is at least one other level through which the relationship is defined and shaped: This level is referred to as *metacommunication* because it is a communication about the communication (verbal message). The metacommunicative aspect also gives clues about how the verbal aspect is to be interpreted. Human beings are therefore able not simply to say something but also to modify or qualify what they say as it is said. The manner in which the basic message is qualified usually takes place through (1) the context in which the message is shared, (2) the vocal and linguistic patterns, and (3) bodily gestures (Haley, 1959).

Congruence

If the qualification of the basic message is congruent with it, the nature of the relationship is defined quite clearly, and it is more likely that the relationship and its accompanying interactions are without much serious conflict. For example, if a man's words indicate he wants a nonsexual relationship with a woman and his subsequent actions are congruent with that basic message, the woman at least knows her place in that relationship and is more clearly able to either accept or reject the basis on which it stands. However, imagine that the man says he wants a nonsexual relationship with a woman, but these words are uttered only in the presence of his wife, followed by gestures that normally indicate an amorous move. We have a situation where the basic message is qualified incongruently by the context and by the gestures following the words. Incongruency, thus, tends to complicate a relationship because, as the woman in the case experienced, it involves a contradiction in levels.

Congruence, then, is a desirable quality in relationships. Congruence implies that I am willing to take responsibility for my end of the relationship and to be honest about it.

Defining the Relationship

Every interaction explicitly moves to define the relationship. The definition of the relationship involves rules and expectations of what behavior is acceptable to that particular relationship. If a fourteen-year-old son makes a move to hug his father, and says the words, "I love you, Dad," the son is making a move to define the relationship as one in which it is acceptable verbally and nonverbally to express positive emotions. Father is then confronted with two very basic choices: (1) to accept or affirm that definition or (2) to reject it. For example, he may distance himself from his son and say, "I am uncomfortable when you do that to me." In this case, he did not accept the son's definition of the relationship, but he at least did it congruently.

In an early paper (Ruesch and Bateson, 1951), Gregory Bateson stated that it is very difficult for a person to avoid defining his relationship with another. This principle is based on the bilevel nature of communication: that messages not only report or share content but also influence or command it. Haley (1959) acknowledges the difficulty of avoiding or influencing the relationship; he, however, outlines a way in which one can avoid responsibility for defining a relationship. The process basically consists of defining the relationship at one level and then qualifying it at another. Haley writes:

The fact that people communicate on at least two levels makes it possible to indicate one relationship, and simultaneously deny it. For example, a man may say, "I think you should do that, but it's not my place to tell you so." In this way he defines the relationship as one in which he tells the other person what to do, but simultaneously denies that he is and this way. . . . By qualifying his messages with implications that *he* isn't responsible for his behavior, a person can avoid defining his relationship with another. ([P. 157]

Haley breaks down the formal characteristics of any interaction to the following elements: (1) I, (2) am saying something, (3) to you, (4) in this situation. Given these characteristics, a person can then deny or qualify the definition of a relationship by negating any or all qualities or elements. "He can (1) deny that *he* communicated something, (2) deny that something was communicated, (3) deny that it was communicated *to* the other person, or (4) deny the context in which it was communicated" (1959, P. 158).

It is important then to teach families that they are continually defining relationships through processes of interaction or communication. To deny their influence on each other is really to deny reality. The receiver of a message really has three major choices: (1) to accept the sender's definition of the relationship, (2) to reject that definition, or (3) to avoid or disqualify the move on the sender's part. It seems important to teach families to affirm or reject congruently and to assume responsibility for such actions.

Patterns and Rules

Another way to conceptualize the dynamics in interpersonal relationships via communication processes is to think in terms of rules. The concept of *rule* helps one to think about the way the members of a communication process are defining their relationship. Rules tend to be the product of continuing interaction sequences between two or more people. Rules have to do with such issues as who can say what to whom and in what manner and when. One can say then that rules are the dynamic fibers of the construct of *boundary*. Just as every interaction is a push or a definition of the relationship, so every interaction confirms or pushes for a change in rules. *Patterns* are recurring interaction sequences based on rules governing the relationship.

Interaction patterns in couples and families tend to be fairly constant despite the variation in the content of the communication. In the judgment of many therapists and communication theorists, families tend to focus on the content of the communication and lose sensitivity or awareness of the processes they are using to communicate. Haley talks about a case that clearly illustrates the constancy of patterns and the lack of awareness of the couple involved in that particular pattern. In this case, he noted the following pattern: The wife was always criticizing her husband, and he usually defended himself, regardless of the content of their conversation. The therapist then asked the husband to criticize his wife, a move designed to reverse that particular state. After much thought and difficulty, the husband finally threw out a criticism at the wife. In response, the wife said, "That's not a very good criticism." The husband responded, "It was the best one I could think of." If this illustration is representative of the interactions of this couple, a change in that one particular rule or pattern could affect the way they handle a whole range of content issues in their relationship. There is then, potentially, a "multiplier effect" involved when one deals with process patterns.

Given these assumptions, it is valuable to teach families how to become aware of their rules and how to change those rules themselves. The psychological literature, both lay and professional, has given much attention to the importance of personal awareness. Although this is a worthwhile achievement, it seems important to add to that perspective a sense of *interpersonal awareness*: an awareness of the systemic rules and patterns in which the family members are involved.

A Point and a Note of Caution

Teaching couples and families how to metacommunicate, that is to talk about how they communicate, is important for them in order to develop an awareness of their rules and patterns. Another goal of skill development in the area of metacommunication is to increase the congruency between the spoken word and dimensions such as tone of voice and gestures. It is, however, important to introduce a caution at this point. Although the ability to metacommunicate is seen as a valuable characteristic in a family, we also are aware of the danger of using metacommunication as an avoidance mechanism. This happens when family members start attacking the process of the communication as a way to avoid staying with and bringing closure to particular content issues in the family.

There are two general types of communication dysfunctions: (1) to be so lost in the content as to lose awareness of the destructive process patterns being used and (2) to overexamine the process and use it to avoid bringing closure to a specific content issue. If the therapist can avoid these two common pitfalls, he can make communication training in therapy a valuable experience.

INCREASING SELF-AWARENESS

The Awareness Wheel*

The awareness wheel is a valuable tool to facilitate the development of self-awareness. This tool helps one to look within to see what the individual is sensing, and how this is being translated into actions. The immature person is generally reactive; that is, one who blindly responds to the interactive forces in the family setting. The mature person, on the other hand, is able to be more active and is able to determine the way he or she wants to respond to certain forces in the family. To increase a person's ability to act rather than simply react, it is important to increase one's self-awareness.

The awareness wheel (Fig. 10) is the framework we utilize for making sense out of the different dimensions of the self. Look upon the wheel as a representation of your inner self. One important dimension of the wheel is that you are a sensing being; you are constantly in the process of collecting data through your

---

* The following materials draw heavily from the Couples Communication Program (CCP) developed by Miller, Nunnally, and Wackman (1975). (1975).

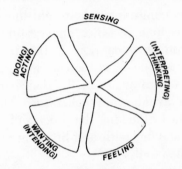

Figure 10. The awareness wheel. (From S. Miller, E. Nunnally, and D. Wackman, *Alive and Aware: Improving Communication in Relationships,* 1975, p. 31. Courtesy of Interpersonal Communication Programs, Minneapolis, Minnesota.)

five senses: You can see, hear, touch, taste, and smell. For example, you *see* some quivering around the mouth of your client (in marital counseling) and you *hear* the softly spoken words "I can't take this anymore."

You might start thinking about what the sense data mean to you. You are now in the process of *interpreting*. You may, for instance, *think* that this person feels despondent and quite hopeless about his marriage. From sensing and thinking, you might then move to your own *feelings*. As you tune in to that dimension, you might discover that you feel uneasy and a little guilty. You may want to look back to the thinking dimension in order to understand those feelings. There you see some possible connection: thinking that you are partially responsible for the couple's inability to snap out of their marital impasse. This thought may have something to do with your feelings of uneasiness and guilt. However, in your cognitive awareness, there is also a belief that this couple is primarily responsible for their relationship. You then become aware of a feeling of relief and a resurgence of confidence. As you turn to your intentions, you find yourself *wanting* to reach out to this person. And so you *do*, with the words: "Do you feel like you're up against a wall, that you're all alone, and that there is no where else to go?" This response is your action, the output that represents the *active summary* of the processes in the other dimensions.

Here are the major elements of the stages of awareness:

Sensing: Seeing the quivering around the mouth of the client; hearing the client's words "I can't take this anymore."

Thinking: The clients feel despondent and hopeless about this marriage.

Feeling: I feel uneasy and somewhat guilty.

Wanting: Wishing to discover cognitive connection to feelings.

Thinking: I am partly responsible for their inability to snap out of their marital impasse; the couple are primarily responsible for their distress.

Feeling: I feel relieved of the burden of responsibility, and I feel confident again.

Wanting: I would like to reach out to this person in distress.

Action: I say, "Do you feel like you're up against a wall, that you're all alone, and that there's no where else to go?"

The above illustrates how you might use the awareness wheel as a tool for sharpening and increasing self-awareness. It is important, in our view, to look upon the awareness wheel primarily as a tool for increasing self-awareness, rather than as a theoretical construct for explaining psychological processes. If, for instance, theoretical explanation is stressed, one will probably want to ask questions like these: Does information always originate with sensing input? Which came first, the feeling or the thought? Was it the intention of the person that then influenced perception selectively and that led to cognitive and feeling processes to suit the original wish?

These questions are theoretically interesting, but need not be answered for you or your client before the awareness wheel can be used as an effective tool. Regardless of what happens within a person, the process of tuning in to awareness can start at any point on the wheel. In the above illustration, the first aspect noticed was the feeling of uneasiness. The therapist could even start with the awareness of what was done and work to the processes involved in the other dimensions. The question of priority is no longer crucial.

It is important to note that awareness of the five dimensions within is *directly* experienced only by the person. This is true even for the doing or action dimension, for awareness of one's action is one thing and another's awareness of the other's action is yet another. This implies that the individual is the best authority of his or her conscious awareness and that he or she is responsible for what is done with that information. Hence, if a person wants someone to know what is going on within him- or herself, then it is important for that person to realize that it is his or her responsibility to share it. This attitude, which is referred to as *self-responsibility*, also implies that person would not allow someone to speak for him or her. This realization, though, has a flip side; the person, in turn, does not speak for his or her partner, but respects the other's right to the ownership and responsibility of his or her own awareness.

Completeness and Congruence

There are two crucial concepts related to the awareness wheel: completeness and congruence. *Completeness* refers to the state whereby a person becomes aware of all the major dimensions of his awareness wheel regarding a specific situation. If that person is not aware of one or more of the dimensions of his wheel around a specific issue, this is identified as *limited awareness*. A person may, for example, be clear about what he thinks regarding a certain incident, but may not be in touch with the depth of the feelings that are being stirred within him. Assume the action was significantly shaped by the person's feeling state. His action then does not make sense in light of what he is thinking about this particular situation. His thinking and doing is not congruent. *Congruence* refers to the coordination of all the dimensions of the awareness wheel. If the therapist thinks that the client is depressed about something that his wife said, and yet the therapist feels guilty about the situation, incongruence of the thinking and feeling dimensions exist. Awareness of this incongruence could lead to a creative process. The therapist may, for instance, discover that in the thinking dimension, the thought "If I had done a good job as therapist, this would not have happened" is prominent. In this light, the feeling reaction begins to take on more sense. It is also a good starting point for change.

The awareness wheel helps a person to organize self-information and to increase self-understanding. In addition, it helps to increase one's choice about what and how to disclose that awareness. The Couple Communication Program has singled out six major communication skills that can be drawn from the awareness wheel framework—five representing the five dimensions and one focusing on the attitude of self-responsibility in the processes of sharing that information. The six skills are: (1) speaking for oneself, (2) making sense statements, (3) making interpretive statements, (4) making feeling statements, (5) making intention statements, and (6) making action statements.

Speaking for oneself means that the person takes responsibility for disclosing important information to the partner but that he or she does not take responsibility for interpreting the partner's awareness. There are two directions to be avoided: over- and underresponsibility. *Making sense statements* refers to the process of expressing to the partner what the other saw or what they heard that led to the subsequent thoughts. *Making interpretative statements* means sharing thoughts clearly. *Making feeling statements* and *making intention statements* imply that the person is able to disclose those aspects clearly and self-responsibly. *Making action statements* could refer to (1) expressing awareness of what was done, (2) expressing awareness of what is presently being done, and (3) expressing awareness of what the person has committed himself to do in the future.

Expression of future-oriented actions and of intentions are sometimes very difficult to distinguish, but the distinction is important and certainly worth the effort. *Expression of intentions* means sharing what the person would like to do or want to do or is considering doing. When the point is reached where the person is not just wanting to do something but has made the decision and commitment to do something at a given place and time, then we can start talking about an *action statement*. This distinction needs to be stressed to highlight the importance of commitment to an action. Awareness of one's intention is valuable information, but it can be carried to the point of continuing to mull over one's intentions as a distraction from having to act. The inability to risk action can be dysfunctional.

Application in Therapy

The application of the awareness wheel in therapy is illustrated in the following dialogue, as the therapist attempts to set up a process aimed at increasing the couple's awareness about an incident that occurred the previous evening. The demonstration proceeds even without formal knowledge of the awareness wheel on the part of the couple. *T* is the therapist; *H*, the husband, Jim; and *W*, the wife, Sue.

T: Yes, I would like to hear about this incident last night. Since you brought the matter up, I would like you to begin, Jim.

H: Well, when I got home, I was still angry about the fact that I was asked to work Saturday. I told Sue, and she exploded at me. She blamed me for not refusing to give in to the request from my boss and accused me of valuing my job over our marriage.

W: You always give in to him.

T: Just a minute, Susan, you'll get your chance in a moment. (*To Jim*) So you got home, with a feeling of anger. I'd like to know a little more about that anger.

H: Well, the boss asked me, at the last minute, to work on Saturday. This is the third week in a row. I really think a lot of it is due to his own lack of planning. I don't like to be caught up in his mess.

T: So, when you got home, you perceived Susan to be angry for your not refusing your boss. What do you think Susan was telling you?

H: Well, she's right here, why don't you ask her?

T: I know that. But I want to know what you think she was thinking. I'd like you to think of what she said and the way she said it and what you saw in the whole process that may have triggered a number of thoughts in your own head. Could you talk about that for a while?

H: Well, I think Susan was disappointed and angry about a couple of things. First, about the fact that we have to give up a Saturday. But I also think that she is disappointed that I wasn't assertive enough.

T: Which of the two reasons do you think is bugging Susan more?

H: There's no doubt in my mind—it's the lack of assertiveness.

T: I like the clearness of your thought on this question, although, of course, Susan may have a different view. Tell me, Jim, what makes you so sure that it's the lack of assertiveness.

H: I just know it.

T: Yes, I'm very clear about your thinking. I would like to know what you saw, heard, or thought about that which may have led to this belief of yours.

H: Well, I've seen her sacrifice several weekends before without complaining. There was also the time last summer when I worked five Saturdays in a row because we wanted extra money for our two-week vacation. Not only were there no complaints, she was most appreciative. So I've seen her tolerate that sort of thing.

T: What about the assertive issue? What was the link between your thought and your observation?

H: Well, on this issue, I've really gotten a kind of mixed message.

T: What do you mean?

H: Well, she really gets angry when I say yes to my mother when I would really rather say no. But when I stand up to her (*pointing to Susan*), she can't stand it.

T: How does she not not stand it?

H: What do you mean?

T: What does she do?

H: Oh, she gets either silent and moody or fights back loudly.

T: So, how would you put the gist of your thinking on this matter of Susan's reaction of your assertiveness or lack of it?

H: I think Susan really wants me to be assertive, but has difficulty when I'm assertive with her.

T: Very good. You've linked the incident last night (and others related to it) with a specific thought about an aspect of your relationship. What were your feelings last night?

H: I was already anxious even before we started talking. In the beginning of the conversation, I felt defensive, almost guilty. I hate that feeling.

T: Any other feelings?

H: Well, when Susan started yelling . . .

W: I did not yell.

T: Susan, I'm not asking you to agree or disagree with him, just to listen at this point. I'm almost ready to shift to you. (*To Jim*) You experienced her as yelling. I believe you were about to relate that to a feeling you had.

H: Yes. I don't like saying this but I was afraid of Susan. Then I became angry and started accusing her of being a nag, a controlling bitch, and of being ungrateful and unappreciative of the work I was doing.

T: Don't let me put words in your mouth, but it sounds like there was hurt there as well.

H: I wasn't very much in touch with being hurt but I'm sure it must be there if you say so.

T: Oh, boy, please don't give me that kind of power.

H: What kind of power?

T: The power of being in charge of what you are aware. You know that better than anybody.

H: But you said I was hurt.

T: Sure. I'd like to feel free to say what I want to say. But it's my own thinking I'm reporting, not yours.

H: Hm.

T: Jim, when you had those thoughts and those feelings, what did you find yourself wanting to do?

H: Let me see. . . . I wanted to pacfiy Susan's feelings.

T: Did you act on that?

H: Yes.

T: How?

H: I tried to convince her that I really wasn't buckling down to my boss and I made a promise that this was going to be the last time.

T: It sounds like your action reflected your defensive feelings.

H: Yes.

T: Any other intentions you were aware of?

H: I wanted the conversation to stop and then I wanted to attack.

T: Were those intentions translated into action too?

H: Only the attack, as I described it earlier. I did not actually attempt to stop the conversation.

T: Thank you, Jim. Susan, I'd like to hear from you now.

The above dialogue could have taken place with only the therapist having formal knowledge of the awareness wheel. In other words, sensitivity to the different dimensions of the wheel could be cultivated by judicious comments and questions in the process of the interaction. The specific communication skills could be cultivated in the same manner. One could, of course, do a formal presentation of the awareness wheel and the communication skills and then begin the process of transferring those skills into the interaction repertoire of the family. Some therapists prefer to have the family experience some of these dimensions and skills before intellectually pointing them out. Others prefer to teach formally and then practice the skills.

INCREASING ACCURACY OF PERCEPTION

Understanding

The awareness wheel is a tool for increasing self-awareness and for expressing the dimensions of awareness. However, no matter how hard an attempt is made to achieve clarity in the expression of thoughts, feelings, and intentions, the receiver of that message could misinterpret what is heard and seen. How then can one be reasonably sure that the message sent is also the message received? The question raised relates to the matter of accuracy of perception. *Understanding* is another term often used to denote this state.

At this point, it is wise to make a clear distinction between understanding (accuracy of perception) and agreement. The reason for making this distinction lies in the common assumption that if one truly understands the other person one is also agreeing with the message that person is sending. If family members think that understanding implies agreement, then they will probably hesitate to make overt efforts to show that the message has been understood, fearing that the other person may interpret such behavior as agreement. Therefore, it is important to underscore to the couple or family that understanding simply means that a person has perceived the other's message quite accurately. *Agreement,* on the other hand, refers to a comparison of one's views about the subject with the other person's position on the same issue.

The importance of achieving understanding may seem elementary at first; that is, it is obviously important to understand what the other person is saying before one can respond to it. However, there is another sense in which achievement of understanding is important in the communication process. Taking the time to understand the other and to make sure that the message received is similar to the message being sent could communicate (through the process) that the receiver cares for the other person and that the sender is respected. Thus, the process of taking the time and the energy to listen and make sure that understanding is achieved may communicate a number of vital relationship messages. In fact, the messages of caring and respect may be much more important in the communication process than the agreement or disagreement around the content issue.

The Shared-meaning Process

The purpose of the shared-meaning process is simply to insure that the message being sent coincides with the message being received. The shared-meaning process, then, is the vehicle used to increase the probability that understanding has been achieved. It is not necessary to resort to the shared-meaning process to achieve understanding, because people engaged in an interaction sequence may in fact be achieving accuracy of perception. What the shared-meaning process adds to the interaction is a greater sense of security in the knowledge that *I know that you know what I know.*

The basic ingredients of the process are quite simple: The sender of the message sends it briefly and clearly, and the receiver rephrases the message in his or her own words and feeds it back to the sender. The sender then either confirms the "translation" or clarifies the message. The shared-meaning process ends when the sender of the message is satisfied that he has been understood by his partner.

Who initiates the shared-meaning process? Either the sender or the receiver may initiate the process. The sender, after sending a message, may request the receiver to feed back what was heard. This is a sender-initiated shared-meaning process. The receiver, on the other hand, may also initiate the process. He does this by beginning the task of rephrasing the relevant messages heard instead of expressing reactions to the sender's message. The question of who initiates shared meaning is important, because it relates to the question of who is responsible for achieving understanding in the interaction process. Both sender and receiver can bear equal responsibility for achieving understanding. If I, as sender, for example, wish to make sure that the message I am sending is understood by my partner, then I will initiate the shared-meaning process. On the other hand, if I am the receiver and sense that the message being sent my way is crucial enough to merit checking out, then I, as receiver, could initiate the shared-meaning process.

The sender of the message has the following tasks to perform: endeavoring to understand the message as clearly as possible; listening carefully to the rephrasing of the message by the partner; and either confirming the accuracy of the message as rephrased or clarifying the message if the feedback by the partner is not substantially accurate. The receiver has the following tasks: listening carefully to the verbal and nonverbal cues; reporting back in his or her own words the relevant messages received; and keeping from expressing reactions to the content and process of the message received.

Application in Therapy

At any point in the interaction between any two or more family members, the therapist can always structure the situation to designate the sender and the receiver of the message. The therapist can, for example, ask the husband to keep on rephrasing a relevant message that he is getting from his wife until a point is reached where the wife says, "Yes, I am understood." At that point, the therapist can ask the husband to share his own awareness wheel around the same issue and ask the wife to rephrase the relevant messages she hears from him. It is probably apparent to the reader that the shared-meaning process can become an excellent prelude to the negotiation process. How a therapist might use the shared-meaning process in an ongoing therapy session is illustrated.

Refer to Susan and Jim, who were in the process of discussing relationship issues raised by an incident that happened the previous night. Assume that Susan is done sharing her own views of the incident and that the couple are now focusing on the issue of Jim's assertiveness in the relationship context.

W: Jim, it's not that I don't want you to be assertive with me. I do. But it doesn't mean that I'll never be angry. But don't back down just because I get pissed or annoyed.

H: What you want is warfare. . . .

T: Hold it a second. I'm not sure you're both talking about the same thing. I'd like you to touch base first before negotiating some changes. Susan, you were trying to get a message across. I will temporarily call you the sender. Now, Jim, you also had a message. But first, I want you to try to understand what Susan is trying to say. I will call you the receiver of the message, at least for a while. Your task as receiver is to listen and to rephrase, in your own words, the relevant messages you hear. Susan, in addition to sending the message as clearly as you can, you also have the task of guiding and acknowledging Jim's attempts to understand you.

W: What do you mean by acknowledging?

T: Simply saying things like, "Yes, you're on the right track," or "No, not quite," or "Partly accurate but not completely." Is that clear?

W: Yes.

T: Go ahead, Susan, please pick up where you left off.

W: I was saying, Jim, that I really want you to stand up for yourself, even with me. But I think that when I stand up for myself in return, you back off. You seem . . .

T: Jim, I'd like you to rephrase what you've heard so far.

H: Well, I understood what was said so far.

T: You may have, but I want to make sure you have. So please rephrase.

H: Well, she said that . . .

T: Jim, please address Susan.

H: (*To Susan*) I heard you telling me that you really want me to be assertive, even with you, and that I shouldn't back off but rather fight you.

W: You got most of it, but there is something there that is not quite right. Let me see. . . It's not that I want you to fight me, necessarily. I want you to stay with the issue, be flexible, but do not back off. When you do, I feel both very powerful and very powerless.

T: Time to rephrase again.

H: What I hear this time is that you want me to stay with the action because when I back off you get somewhat contradicting feelings of being powerful and being very powerless. I don't understand that last part. Could you say more about it.

W: The feeling of power comes from seeing you backing off when I complain. The powerlessness comes from "talking to the wind," when you are no longer really there. Do you follow?

H: You apparently see my backing off as a response to your complaint or to your anger or whatever. That's what gives you a sense of too much power, right?

W: Right.

H: But when I back off, you appear like someone who is talking and talking and talking but getting no response. That's when you feel powerless.

W: Right. Do you see my point?

T: Wait a minute, Susan. Are you asking for agreement or asking to see if he understood you?

W: Both, I guess.

T: I'd like to stick to achieving understanding for the moment. Do you think Jim understands what you have said so far?

W: Yes, it seems that way.

T: You're not sure or reasonably sure?

W: Reasonably sure.

T: Fine. It looks like there's enough understanding to move on. . . . Jim, I'd like you to respond specifically to what Susan shared with you. I want you to share your own thoughts, feelings, wants, and possible commitments in response to what you saw and heard just now.

Increasing Flexibility in Interaction Styles

In Chapter 3, it was seen that flexibility was a characteristic that distinguished the healthy from the disturbed family system; the latter tended to manifest a more rigid or chaotic family interaction structure. The framework to be shared seeks to increase the family's interaction repertoires so that family members are able to express the vast range of their unique individuality. The hoped-for outcome is to create a family system in which a moderate amount of stability is combined with a healthy dose of flexibility.

The Communication Styles Framework

The communication styles framework, as presented in Figure 11, represents a substantial modification of the Hill Interaction Matrix, developed by William F. Hill for analyzing interactions in group therapy. This revision and extension of the framework is the work of Miller, Nunnally, and Wackman (1975).

Figure 11 shows the basic characteristics of each of the styles. Because each style contains various nuances and various verbal and nonverbal characteristics, Miller and associates avoided giving a verbal label to each of the styles. They instead assigned a numerical label to each style and proceeded to define it and to describe associated verbal and nonverbal characteristics. A description of each of the styles follows.

STYLE 1: In Style 1, the person has no intention of changing his own behaviors or attitudes nor those of the partner. The persons major intention is to remain interpersonally safe, relaxed, light, and tensionless. Factual, casual, and businesslike information is exchanged. It is therefore low in self-disclosure, in interpersonal risk, and in its potential to change the relationship. A great percentage of a person's typical day is spent in this style and, we think, rightly so. It is the best style for carrying on routine activities and for expressing sociable, friendly, and playful ways. On the other hand, if all of a family's interaction can be

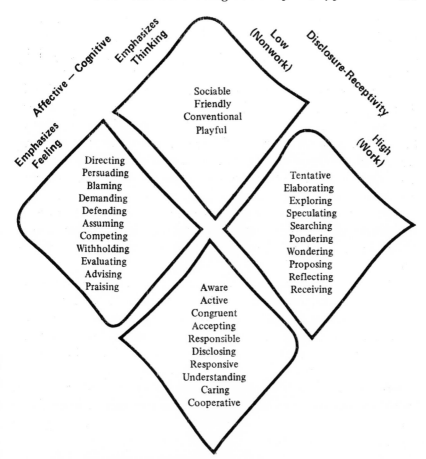

Figure 11.   Intentions associated with each style.   (From S. Miller, E. Nunnally, and D. Wackman, *Alive and Aware: Improving Communication in Relationships*, 1975, p. 208.   Courtesy of Interpersonal Communication Programs, Minneapolis, Minnesota.)

categorized as Style 1, then chances are that the family members are avoiding significant encounters around important issues. Such a family may be characterized as being pseudo-mutual.

STYLE 2:   The person in this style has a commitment to change another person's attitudes or behaviors without an intention to change or to look within him- or herself. The manipulative nature of this style can be manifested either in discounting oneself or the other person. The latter intention is exhibited in labeling, blaming, persuading, and demanding kinds of behavior. Self-depreciating behavior, such as the self-pity portrayed by the martyr complex, can be regarded as a technique for changing another's behavior by eliciting such feelings as pity or guilt. Although this style is high in interpersonal risk, e.g. it may alienate the other or elicit anger, its potential for productive interpersonal work is generally low because of the following characteristics: low self-disclosure, closed-mindedness, and low commitment to the other person. Style 2 interactions may be used creatively to ventilate feelings, to push significantly in a way that perhaps jars the particular relationship, or to respond to occasional emergency situations that call for unilateral action. However, a predominance of Style 2 interaction in a family usually implies a dysfunctional family system.

STYLE 3: In this style, the person intends to explore, examine, and understand his or her own as well as his or her partner's feelings, thoughts, intentions, and actions but proceeds cautiously and safely, speculating more than disclosing directly. The caution comes in testing the safety of the interpersonal water. Its potential for work is great precisely because the person in this style is sending an invitation to the other to work more openly and directly. Self-disclosure in this style tends to be high, but there is more emphasis on the thinking than the feeling dimension. Style 3 is a great style as an opener and as a way of exploring new, risky territory in a relatively safe way. Left to itself, however, it begins gradually to fall flat. The natural progression of Style 3 is a movement toward Style 4.

STYLE 4: In this style, the person intends to communicate completely and congruently. This implies wanting to approach the issue openly and directly and trusting one's own awareness, combined with a sincere desire to understand, to respect, and to respond to the other person's expressed awareness. This style of communication is not characterized by a phony sense of caring, which is often translated into a kind of protectiveness that avoids rather than encounters an issue. There is, however, a genuine intention to value oneself and one's partner, thus setting the foundation for mutual support and caring. The issue of responsibility is clear in Style 4: The person assumes major responsibility for his own life (sensing, thinking, feeling, intending, and acting) without taking responsibility for the other person's life. Style 4 statements, while penetrating and intensely emotive, are always made with an intent to maintain and build both self- and other esteem. This style is thus characterized by high levels of self-disclosure, risk, and commitment to oneself and others.

The Communication Styles Framework

Figure 11 suggested labels for the two diagonal dimensions. One axis is that of *disclosure-receptivity*. This refers to the amount and depth of information shared and received. If one examines the intentions that characterize Styles 1 and 2, it becomes clear that there is very little desire to share much personal and relationship information openly and directly. Style 3 and 4, on the other hand, indicate intentions to search and share personal and relationship messages openly.

The diagonal axis going from right to left (*see* Fig. 11) shows the *affective-cognitive* dimension; that is, the dominance of thinking (cognitive) or the dominance of feelings (affective). Styles 1 and 3 tend to be more cognitive, heavy on descriptions and ideas, but light and tentative on feelings and intentions. Styles 2 and 4, on the other hand, stress feelings quite strongly. Style 4 reveals feelings and intentions directly and with a clear sense of self-responsibility. Style 2 often deals with strong feelings and intentions but usually does so indirectly and overresponsibly.

Because Styles 3 and 4 are high in self-disclosure and receptivity, and because they approach personal and relationship issues directly and openly, they are termed *work styles*. The term *work* implies interaction styles that tend to accomplish satisfactory, growth-enhancing changes in a relationship. Style 3 is more of an exploratory and speculative mode of working around an issue, stepping lightly on commitments and emotions. Because of these characteristics, it has been labeled a *tentative work style*. Style 4, in contrast, is characterized by a desire and ability to lay out one's sensory data, thoughts, feelings, intentions, and actions directly and committedly. It is, thus, called a *committed work style*.

Mixed Messages

Not all interactions are easily categorized as belonging to one or another style. Because people's motives are often mixed, their communication tends to reflect this. "Messages become mixed when any intention or behavior from Style 2 slips into another style" (Miller et al., p. 213). Thus, a statement may have apparent characteristics of Styles 1, 3, or 4, but a phrase, tone, gesture, or context could reveal a Style 2 intention, as in the following examples:

"You're really cute when you're clumsy." (Style 1 with an ambiguous dig, albeit an apparent jest. The tone and context would be the most important clues for determining whether it is a mixed or a straight Style 1 message.)

"I've been somewhat concerned about you lately because I've been wondering about the way you bug people around you." (Apparent Style 3 with a phrase that belies *speaking for all people* about the person's alleged irritating behavior.)

"Every day I pray to God that you'll realize how selfish you are." (Style 4 intention to wish someone good combined with blaming and overresponsible behavior.)

Mixed messages, of course, are forms of the double message and thus reminiscent of the double bind. Without repeating the earlier discussion, we wish simply to reiterate the importance of being able to comment upon the communication (metacommunication). This ability to "communicate about the communication" enables family members to clarify the potentially confusing impacts of mixed messages. There will always be mixed messages. The key, therefore, is the ability to clarify those mixed messages and to go from there with the appropriate style. Mixed messages, incidentally, are classified as Style 2 messages.

Overall Perspective on Communication Styles

The key concept for the family therapist to watch is flexibility of communication styles. This means matching the appropriate style with a person's intentions at any given moment. Although, as Miller et al. (1975, P. 209) point out, Style 4 is the most

effective style for dealing with important personal and relationship issues, it is not an appropriate style for every occasion. The
following paragraphs offer a perspective on the styles:

> If your intention is to socialize and participate in some activities
> together, Style 4 is too heavy. Style 1 would be better here. If
> your intention is to direct and persuade, then Style 4 doesn't fit.
> Try Style 2. If your intention is to explore tentatively and get a
> general overview of an issue, then Style 4 is too focused. Style 3
> is better for that.
>
> In short, each style plays an important role in effective and
> flexible interpersonal communication. Nevertheless, we have two
> major reasons for highlighting Style 4, communication. First, most
> people learn how to use Style 1 and 2 as they grow up. Style 3 is
> often learned as a speculative, "intellectual" style if a person goes
> to college. Style 4 is most often missing in a person's communica-
> tion repertoire. So Style 4 is important to round out your ability
> to communicate effectively. Secondly, we are convinced from our
> research and experience, that Style 4 is the most effective way to
> deal with relationship issues. [Miller, Nunnally, and Wackman,
> 1975, P. 209-211]

Application in Therapy

The communication styles framework could be used to assess
interaction patterns in a particular family system in a manageable
and meaningful way. For example, a family may be described
as one in which Style 1 predominates, with very little overt fighting (a few straight Style 2 messages) some amount of intellectual-
izing about persons and relationships (Style 3), few serious and
open exchanges of feelings and intentions (Style 4), but with
quite a number of indirect, passive-aggressive moves, such as
forgetting, lateness, silence, messiness, and disguised gossiping
(Style 2 mixed messages). Notice how rich this assessment is
in descriptive detail. However, the descriptions are not isolated,
unrelated concepts. They all fit into the scheme of the four
styles. In short, the style's framework gives the therapist a handle
on the family's communication repertoire, showing its strengths
and its gaps. If a family spends too much time on Styles 3
and 4, the therapist is alerted to the advisability of developing
more play- and funtime in Style 1. This way, the family system

is able to refuel and thus resupply itself with the much-needed psychic energy spent in working on relationship issues.

Once an interaction assessment has been made, the therapist can begin intervening with the goal of restructuring the interaction patterns toward greater flexibility. Our experience indicates that Style 4 is the style most often missing among troubled families. The most marked interaction characteristic in troubled families is a predominance of mixed messages. Quiet, fight-phobic families (pseudo-mutual) tend to use apparent Style 1 or Style 3 mixed messages. Then there is the boisterous family characterized by an almost constant state of bickering or fighting in Style 2. Because of these considerations, we recommend having families and couples aim at processing relationship issues in Style 4, with the therapist periodically cutting in to give them process feedback (metacommunication).

CONFLICT NEGOTIATION

Differences, Disagreements, and Conflict

A family that is alive, i.e. one composed of well-differentiated members, tends to deal with interpersonal conflict openly and without fear that members are going to feel devastated by the discovery of differences. Serious conflict is generally a struggle that involves fighting for belongingness and separateness. Being different is threatening because it may be a reminder of one's separateness; in a family system where a sense of belongingness has been impaired, such a reminder is too painful.

We have implied consistently that the way a family deals with differences is probably the best single indicator of its health. If differences can be aired without destroying the sense of belongingness or togetherness, then probably that family is a healthy one. In a disturbed family, differentness is viewed as an attack on the "family ego mass" (Bowen, 1963). Satir (1967, Pp. 11-12) says it well when she writes that among undifferentiated families, differentness "looks bad because it leads to disagreement. Disagreement reminds them both that the other is not an extension of the self but is separate. . . . Differentness which leads to a conflict of interests (disagreement) is seen as an insult and evidence of being unloved."

Conflict is inevitable because differences are inevitable among even the most intimate of human beings. The way in which conflict is dealt with varies greatly: in mixed messages (covert Style 2); in open attacks (straight Style 2), or in open, self-responsible leveling and negotiation. In intimate relations, the question is not *whether* there are conflicts but *how* they are handled.

A Model for Conflict Negotiation

Table I is a model of conflict negotiation that introduces a structure into the negotiation process. The presence of the structure already presupposes that a certain degree of rationality has been introduced in the situation. It may be a superhuman task to expect couples to utilize this system at the moment of intense emotional heat and explosion. To them, we say that is all right. People are not always rational; it seems to us irrational to expect people to be in rational control at all times. Again, it is not a question of whether a family has Style 2 explosions; it is more a question of whether, *at some point,* the members are able to face issues squarely and to negotiate them constructively.

Table I outlines the main elements of this model. The first step is quite fundamental, but not always obvious: identifying the issue and the members' willingness (intent) to deal with it at a given point in time and place. Disagreements on procedural matters could hinder negotiations around important content issues apart from the merits or demerits of those issues (Miller et al., 1975, Pp. 165-168). Steps II and III involve a two-step shared-meaning process, with each taking the sender and receiver role to process various dimensions of the awareness wheel. Step II aims for mutual understanding of thoughts, feelings, and related sensing. We believe that these are the dimensions of awareness least subject to negotiation. Step III pursues the sharing and understanding of intentions (suggested solutions) around that issue. Step IV is the point where real negotiation dialogue takes place, with special emphasis on negotiation of intentions and actions—the two dimensions of awareness that most lend themselves to negotiation.

Table I.

A MODEL FOR CONFLICT NEGOTIATION

Person A		Person B
I. Identify the issue and the members' willingness to discuss it at a particular time and setting.		
II. (a) Assumes role of *sender* and shares thoughts and feelings with proper tie ups with sensing data.	SENDER CONCEN- TRATES ON SENSING, THINKING, FEELING.	Assumes role of *receiver* until sender feels adequately understood (no reactions expressed).
(b) Assumes role of *receiver* until sender feels adequately understood (no reactions expressed).	SENDER CONCEN- TRATES ON SENSING, THINKING, FEELING.	Assumes role of *sender* and shares thoughts and feelings with proper tie ups with sensing data.
III. (a) Assumes role of *sender* and shares a range of solutions (intentions) that he or she is comfortable with.	SENDER CONCEN- TRATES ON INTENTIONS.	Assumes role of *receiver* until sender feels adequately understood (no reactions expressed).
(b) Assumes role of *receiver* until sender feels adequately understood (no reactions expressed).	SENDER CONCEN- TRATES ON INTENTIONS.	Assumes role of *sender* and shares a range of solutions (intentions) that he or she is comfortable with.
IV. Dialogue in Styles 3 and 4 (especially Style 4), sharing reactions to suggestions and moving toward mutually acceptable *commitments* for future *actions*.		

We recommend that, initially at least, therapists structure these processes in the therapy session so they can monitor the interaction. Home exercises in the use of this model (Table I) are encouraged, with close follow-up in the next session. Couples and families should be aware that this structure is a crutch and should be encouraged to try more free-floating conflict negotiation.

SUMMARY

This chapter began with the perspective that it is through communication (verbal and nonverbal) that family members touch each other and regulate their respective closeness or distance. The two levels of communication were discussed and related to the concept of congruence of levels and to the idea that every interaction carries a command aspect that tends to define the relationship in a certain way. These definitions create rules for the relationship. Rules revolve around issues of who can say what to whom and in what manner and when. Patterns are recurring interaction sequences based on rules governing the relationship.

The four major frameworks were presented: (1) the awareness wheel, for increasing self-information and the skills to express it; (2) the shared-meaning framework for increasing accuracy of perception; (3) the communication styles for increasing the flexibility of family interaction; and (4) a model for conflict negotiation based on the first three frameworks. For each of these frameworks, indications were offered for the manner in which they could be applied in a therapeutic setting.

CHAPTER 8

MARITAL GROUP AND MULTIPLE FAMILY THERAPY

E MPLOYING THERAPEUTIC principles with groups is one of the most recent developments in the area of psychotherapy. Treating couples in groups or more than one family simultaneously is one of the more recent innovations in the area of family therapy. Recognition of the effectiveness of working with a group has even moved to the point of working not only with the family group, but also including the entire social network in the treatment setting (Speck and Attneave, 1973). This chapter introduces both the rationale and principles of treating couples and families in a group setting.

Many individuals have discussed reasons for delivering treatment in a group setting as opposed to confining the therapeutic process to just the social system of concern. The following comprise some of the more concise statements that have been proferred regarding advantages or reasons for delivering treatment in a group setting.

Kemp (1970) has offered the following as what the group setting offers to the participants:

(1) A community in which the person may test his evolving attitudes and ideas; (2) the motivation which results from the acceptance of peers and the experiencing of his changing attitudes; (3) the skills of communication with others, which improve his possibilities of developing genuine interpersonal relationships; (4) the encouragement which follows from the participation of others in trying to resolve their conflicts; (5) the acceptance and understanding of peers, with the resulting sense of safety and belonging, which support the process of introspection and expression of feeling in depth. [P. 70]

Leichter (1974, P. 142) presents the following as an advantage of treatment of couples in a group setting: "In essence, a married couples group tends to operate as a 'third family' which in the last analysis means that it gives each individual and couple another chance to come to life and grow, whereas the real family (primary or present) has had a growth-thwarting effect."

The following is a statement regarding the value of multiple family group therapy (MFGT):

> In multi-family therapy groups, each individual has a chance, in the presence of his actual family, to transfer onto other group members as well as to try himself out in ways which his own family is not yet able to tolerate. There is an opportunity for action as well as observation, which often accelerates the process of integration.
>
> Additionally, while in individual family therapy it is mostly the therapist who pays attention to the frequently hidden conflicts of the 'non-problem' children, in MFGT the other families often perceive and challenge the distortions and misconceptions inherent in the polarization and resulting imbalance of the 'good-bad' child axis. As in any good therapy group, the challenge is balanced by support, which in the MFGT is given not only by peers but also by substitute parental figures. [Leichter and Schulman, 1972, P. 176]

Smith and Alexander (1974) have stated the following regarding the process of working with couples in groups:

> In our counseling with couples we find that when a group of couples, all experiencing troubled relationships, meet with competent therapists, there appears a sense of camaraderie and sharing in which there is a desire to aid others, as well as to work on solving the problems of their own relationship. There is a commitment to work together for change, not only for themselves but for the group as a whole. It also appears that the advantage of sharing similar experiences with other couples tends to increase the likelihood of achieving success in improving a couple's relationship. [P. 3]

We have used the group approach to treating couples and families for all of the above reasons and others. The challenge, both personally and professionally, of increasing the emotional field with which one is involved is exciting. Our experience has also been that, through employing the group process, many interventions are facilitated, which results in expediting the therapeutic process. Concomitant with the challenge and excitement of working with groups are many concerns of which the therapist must be aware. The remainder of this chapter discusses these concerns. Marital group work is presented first, followed by the discussion of multiple-family group therapy.

MARITAL GROUP THERAPY

Employing the group approach for treatment of marital problems is of relatively recent vintage. While occasional reference has been made to this treatment modality, Lebedun (1970) indicates that only thirty-nine sources (both books and articles) could be identified. Since 1970, there has been greater interest, as evidenced by the increased number of articles and books dealing with the marital group therapy approach. Considering the apparent increased interest of professionals in this approach, it still must be identified as in the early formative stages of development. In this section we identify what we believe appears to be evident at this point regarding this treatment modality.

Advantages and Disadvantages of Group Involvement

We believe that Kilgo (1970, p. 339) summarized succinctly the advantages and disadvantages of working with married couples in groups. He has organized the pros and cons on a plus and minus basis.

Plus

Influence of peers — Generally a helpful and growth-contributing factor, but could be destructive if too many "badly discordant" marriages in same group.

Reality-reflections — The "many mirrors" aspect of the group; if several persons point out something one is trying to avoid looking at, it is more effective than one counselor's suggestion.

The "not alone" feeling — There is a tendency for couples in marriage counseling to feel that they are

	the only persons having these difficulties, and to be a little ashamed; the realization of the commonality is helpful.
Direct education	Helpful, to see how others have worked out similar problems, or are working them out; it is easier to see other's problems more clearly than one's own.
Satisfaction of helping others	In group counseling, all members in a sense are counselors as well as participants; helpfulness increases self-esteem.
More economical use of counselor time and client money	I could work with several couples at the same time at lower fees.
Minus	
Spouse inhibitions	Either spouse might feel less free to talk in group because of the presence of the others.
Problems too intimate	Couples might be reluctant to discuss some problems as being "too intimate" for group discussion.

The first and second advantages identified by Kilgo are deserving of amplification. Experience suggests that these considerations are probably among the most facilitative in gaining therapeutic leverage with couples. In working with an individual couple, it is a common occurrence to see one spouse deny what is being confronted by the therapist. Many times this denial seems to be amplified by a transference from that spouse to the therapist. When others are available to confront, especially others perceived as peers, the confrontation seems to be more readily accepted. The therapist may even decide not to agree with the confrontation to avoid facilitating the development of denial by the member confronted. The therapist's goal then is solely that of facilitator, as an attempt is made to orchestrate and enable the confrontation to progress. Also contained in this first item is the caution regarding too many "badly discordant" marriages. Couples that are severely disintegrated are not good candidates for a group experience. We have found that these couples are the first to dropout, and justifiably so. What usually happens is that these disintegrated couples either withdraw of their own volition, realizing they are markedly different than the other couples, or are gradually quieted by the others, resulting in dissatisfaction and withdrawal. These couples are in need of more intensive work as a couple prior to movement into a group setting.

THE PRINCIPLE OF UNIVERSALITY: The "not alone" feeling identified in the list is another deserving of greater explanation. Yalom (1970) has referred to this factor as *universality*.

> Many patients enter therapy with the foreboding thought that they are unique in their wretchedness, that they alone have certain frightening or unacceptable problems, thoughts, impulses, and fantasies. There is a core of truth in this, since many patients have had an unusual constellation of life stresses and are commonly flooded by generally unconscious psychic elements. Their sense of uniqueness is often heightened by their social isolation; because of interpersonal difficulties, opportunities for frank and candid consensual validation in an intimate relationship are often not available to patients. In the therapy group, especially in the early stages, the disconfirmation of their feelings of uniqueness is a powerful source of relief. After hearing other members disclose concerns similar to their own, patients report feeling more in touch with the world and describe the process as a "welcome to the human race" experience. [P. 10]

This experience in and of itself can be curative in providing group participants with a new sense of motivation for changing. This new-found motivation results from the new hope that is gained from realizing they are not bizarre or atypical. Any therapist who has sat in therapy sessions with a number of couples is soon struck by the similarity of problems experienced and is able to put marital difficulty in perspective. Naturally, most couples who engage in marital therapy do not have this observational opportunity, other than what they discover in the group setting.

SPOUSE INHIBITION: The first disadvantage identified by Kilgo (*see* list, p. 203) is also present in working with the couple individually. Occasionally, in seeing couples, one of the spouses attempts to initiate a session with the therapist alone.

Many times, this effort on the part of the spouse is an attempt to win the battle for structure and therefore attempt to defuse his or her need for this individual session. The effort to defuse is generally accomplished by explaining to the spouse requesting the session that we would be dishonest with the other spouse by allowing this rendezvous; unfair to the spouse requesting the session in that they would then wonder if we are doing the same for the other; and unfair to the relationship and therapy in that if this "secret" is that important it should be integrated into the relationship and therapy. Along with the above, the ability of the therapist to communicate competence in dealing with stressful situations greatly aids a couple in feeling comfortable to be open in the therapeutic setting.

The Persistent Spouse

Establish a scenario where there is a "married couple" and therapist or co-therapists, with one of the spouses requesting an indiviudal session. Try to experience as fully as possible how you would handle the situation in such a way that the battles for structure and initiative (*see* Chap. 3) would not be controlled by the client. Switch roles and process the experience with the goal being to discover alternative styles in handling this type of situation in a facilitative manner.

INTIMACY OF THE "PROBLEM": The last disadvantage to be referred to is that of the couple who perceives an element or concern in their relationship as too sensitive for exposure in the group. This is a legitimate issue and one that theoretically can be dealt with in the pregroup screening interview. During this interview, the therapist should attempt to determine whether the couple is capable of both benefitting and contributing to the group experience. The key to both benefitting and being of benefit to others seems to be most highly correlated to the couple's openness and can be determined by both the couple's own self-perceptions and the therapists' clinical impressions gathered in the interview.

Considerations for the Marital Group Therapist

Most individuals who have written about group therapy or group counseling have identified concerns such as those about to be identified. These concerns are common to the author's experience and what seems vital to facilitating successful married couple groups.

THE PREGROUP INTERVIEW: As mentioned above, the pregroup interview allows the marital therapist an opportunity to determine the readiness of the couple for a group experience. Another important task of this interview is for the therapist to begin to win the battle for initiative by explaining to the couple their responsibilities in the group and what they might do to increase their probability of benefitting from the experience. Time is also well spent in dealing with common concerns group participants voice and answering questions the potential participants may volunteer at this time. There is also a need to help the couple begin to identify what they want to accomplish through the group experience. This moves the therapist and couple into the development of a therapeutic contract that should be then disclosed to all participants in the first session.

The Pregroup Interview

Identify two people to serve as co-therapists and two to role play a couple having a marital group therapy experience explained to them. The "married couple" can ask questions they think they may have moving into this type of experience followed by the therapist helping them to begin to formulate goals to be worked on in the group setting.

SIZE: Groups of four to six couples seem to provide the most vital and productive groups. In groups consisting of greater than six couples, it becomes difficult to keep certain members from lurking in the shadows of anonymity of their own volition or otherwise. Larger groups also create problems for the leader in attempts to attend to all members sufficiently, resulting in the group taking on a classroom aura. Fewer than four couples eliminates the potential for differences that generate energy for the group being manifested. Fewer than four couples also eliminates the potential "island of refuge" or relief for some members that occasionally is needed in the life of the group.

Naturally, if the task of the group is more educational in nature, such as some parent-education groups, an increase in group size appears to be justified. The recommendation of four to six couples for the group size is offered for the group that is going to be heavily reliant upon interpersonal interaction to accomplish its goals.

GROUP COMPOSITION: Differences in age for married couple groups seems to be of less importance than is true for other types of groups. This seems to be the case as a result of the universality of the marriage experience. Considering this, a blend of couples of different ages and in various developmental stages of marriage is more facilitative than it is detrimental. One exception to this is the group composed of married couples who are relatively well integrated, except for one couple, who is struggling for development. In this case, the less developed couple may be intimidated and not take advantage and benefit from the group experience.

The advantage of various ages and developmental stages being represented has become obvious to us. The younger members can remind the older ones of "how it was" and also relate more closely to parent-child problems that may be presented by the older members. The older members can likewise provide insights based on their experience to the younger members.

LENGTH OF THE SESSIONS: In groups of four to six couples, experience has demonstrated three hours to be a productive time limit for each group session. Three hours is a time frame that enables all to be attentive and is sufficient to allow this number of people adequate interaction time.

The importance of adhering to the three-hour limit seems important for two reasons: (1) This is a vital element of the battle for structure (*see* Chap. 4). (2) By not adhering to it, dawdling on the part of the couples is reinforced, and this may well be a problem in their relationship already.

FREQUENCY OF MEETING: Ten weekly sessions have proven to be the most productive. This seems to be in line with what others suggest as a productive number of therapeutic sessions (Mann, 1973; Weakland et al., 1974). By initially identifying the number of sessions the group will exist, a note of reality is immediately introduced to the group. This also communicates at the metalevel that time is limited and if the couples want to benefit they should become actively involved as quickly as possible. This quite naturally leads to the battle for initiative (*see* Chap. 4) and encourages the couples to be self-responsible and capitalize on the group experience.

SETTING: The setting does not seem to be as important as the ability of the facilitator to establish a therapeutic environment. The environmental consideration that is important is allowing for enough physical space to facilitate conducting nonverbal exercises that involve movement, as can be found in *Helping Families To Change* (Satir, Stachowiak, and Taschman, 1975) and other sources. Comfort is also a consideration when considering the setting; either comfortable furniture, a carpeted floor, or both seems essential.

OPEN OR CLOSED GROUP: If the group is going to rely on rather intense interpersonal interaction to reach its goals, it should be closed to new members after it commences. If the group is not reliant upon interpersonal interaction, i.e. parent-education groups, an open group can be managed successfully.

HOMEWORK ASSIGNMENTS: We strongly advocate using homework assignments in therapy, and a group setting is no exception. In this regard, we agree with the rationale offered by Smith and Alexander (1974, P. 15) for use of assignments in marital group work: "Assignments are usually given at the close of each session for two reasons: (1) It is felt that an assignment helps the couple concentrate on the overall purpose of the group on a more continuous basis, and (2) the exercises are designed to improve the clarity of communication and perceptions between the couple."

If the group has identified a topic such as communication (*see* Chap. 7) as its primary concern, the assignments are then designed to accomplish the goals in this area. If the group has more of an individual problem-solving orientation, each couple may have an idiosyncratic homework assignment. We have taken the initiative to make assignments for couples; had the group arrive at homework assignments for each couple; and encouraged each couple to design its own homework assignment—all with equal success. We always follow up on the homework assignments at the beginning of the next session to facilitate the group reinforcing success or providing feedback to the couple who experienced difficulty in successfully completing the assignment.

DRESS: The pregroup interview is the time to advise the

participants to wear comfortable clothing, as advocated by William Schutz in *Elements of Encounter* (1973). Having the women wear slacks and other nonrestrictive clothing, as is advised for the men, facilitates movement and allows them to assume comfortable positions without inhibitions.

ENDING THE GROUP EXPERIENCE: The termination phase of the group seems to be the most predictable element of the group's life. The characteristics of this phase have been captured and identified succinctly by Schutz (1973):

> Groups or relations that are about to terminate or markedly reduce their interaction exhibit fairly characteristic behaviors: absences and lateness increase; there is more daydreaming; members forget to bring materials to the group; discussion of death and illness is frequent; the importance and goodness of the group is minimal; general involvement decreases; often there is a recall of earlier experiences. As a member of a terminating group, you usually want to discuss with the group the events that were not completely worked through at the time they occurred; in this way, you hope that your relations will be resolved successfully. Often when you feel that your actions in an earlier meeting were misunderstood, you will recall the instance and explain what you really meant to say, so that no one will be angry with you. Sometimes you want to express to other members that comments they made earlier were important to you and made you feel better. On it goes, with all unresolved incidents, they are more capable of accepting separation. [Pp. 56-57]

Although elements of the process Schutz has identified definitely appear in married couple groups, they do not seem to be as evident in groups of couples as they are in groups of unrelated individuals. This seems true of marital groups as a result of the fact that each member will probably be leaving with his or her spouse and in that sense the group does not terminate completely, as do most groups. Acknowledging this, the bare fact of termination is still present, even if in moderation. A common pattern for dealing with separation is discussion of a potential get-together for the group members at some future date. Schutz (1973) refers to this as the "fantasized reunion," and appropriately so. Rarely does this reunion materialize, but it seems to ease the impact of the separation.

It seems wise to attempt to end the group with a feedback exercise. Examples of what have been employed at this time are (1) psychological gift giving—each member gives each other member a gift of verbal feedback regarding what has been appreciated about the other; and (2) mailbox—the members remove their shoes and use them as their own mailbox. Each member then writes a note to each other member and deposits it in the appropriate mailbox. Closing the group sessions with this kind of exercise seems to facilitate optimism in the members that can be carried out of the group and encourages them to continue working. These exercises also use the skill of feedback, which is usually developed during the life of the group and reinforces the power of its use for the departing couples.

Synthesis of Marital Group Therapy

We are intentionally not devoting attention to appropriate or beneficial topics for marital groups. This seems to be best defined by what the facilitator is comfortable with in discussion. The one underlying element of married life that seems to continually arise in these groups, if it is not identified initially as the task of the group, is the improvement of communication between the couples. As Smith and Alexander (1974, P. 9) state, "In nearly every case the underlying problem is found to be poor or non-existent communication between the parties. When there is improvement in this area, an improvement in the total relationship generally ensues."

Chapter 7 has identified both cognitive maps and processes for developing communication skills that are appropriate for implementation in groups of the nature under consideration here. Our experience, like that of Smith and Alexander, definitely suggests that communication is the "lifeblood" or "heartbeat" of marital relationships. By using this as a focus, regardless of presented content, we have been exposed to considerable success and satisfaction in our marital group experiences.

MULTIPLE FAMILY GROUP THERAPY (MFGT)

Most of the advantages previously identified in working with groups of couples are also appropriate for working with groups of families. The following comprise some of the chief values of the MFGT approach, as identified by some of the innovators of this therapeutic modality. Virginia Satir seems to have delineated the chief value in working within the MFGT framework as she discusses her experience with groups of families:

> While I do make a lot of use of structure, it is always within the framework of trying to see whether it is true that, for example, you are the only one who thought your mother did not like you. There are millions of people who have that kind of experience, but before you find that out from others you think you are all alone. People discover they are not alone in thinking, "I'd like to wring my father's neck!" They find that everybody has these kinds of thoughts and feelings, and not because they had parents but because people are people. They can then stop beating themselves and start building and growing. [Satir, Stachowiak, and Taschman, 1975, P. 213]

As Satir is referring to the dynamic of universality within groups, Leichter and Schulman (1972) refer to what they identify as a value offered via the MFGT approach:

> We have found that one of the great values of MFGT is that it makes possible interaction between group members across family lines. Youngsters can "have it out" first with adults who are not their parents before they get ready to deal with their own. For the acting-out youngster with his difficulty in tolerating genuine feelings and interchanges, for the husband or wife who is afraid of his marital partner's reaction, the presence of substitute figures in the group offers a particularly good opportunity for the breaking through of some family taboos, such as expression of anger or other feelings. Reactions to group members other than one's own are often less guarded and may reveal hidden feelings and attitudes in a person which the real family is unaware of. [P. 170]

Laqueur (1972), one of the first to write about MFGT, identifies the reason he believes the implementation of this approach has reduced the frequency and length of hospitalizing schizophrenic patients and enhanced the potential for preventing future crisis:

> The difficulties inherent in the treatment of individual families which include a schizophrenic member have long been recognized. MFGT provides a unique setting for the resolution of the core conflict which, in our opinion, plays a major etiological role in

schizophrenia. More specifically, we see the schizophrenic patient's main problem as a conflict between his struggle to achieve differentiation, on the one hand, and his need to maintain his symbiotic attachment to primary family objects, on the other. The presence of other families and other hospitalized patients in the treatment setting seems to stimulate the patients to engage actively in the struggle toward increasing self-differentiation and independence. In MFGT sessions patients and parents tend to recreate the primitive, long-standing family situations which gave rise to, and have served to perpetuate this conflict; thus, a patient or a relative may identify with a member of another family on a given occasion and learn by analogy with much anxiety than is less usually associated with such learning. [P. 403]

Our orientation to MFGT is more traditionally treatment oriented in that concerns being manifested and brought into treatment by the family are dealt with now. We assume that by following this procedure the family can be induced to change their current relationships, which are reinforcing, and set an operant chain effect into motion. The work they have completed to initiate the change is rewarded by the change, which also is a cue to continue working to effect further productive change. Although some prefer this orientation to MFGT, others see groups of families and work in a modified fashion. Bowen (1976) sees families in groups, but perceives his role as being more of an educator. He sees the family members in a group setting of other families to teach them about triangles and emotional systems. In the process, Bowen's role is more characteristic of the teacher, and then coach, as he encourages them to put their new learnings into effect in their nuclear and extended family network. Bowen (1976) identifies his process as somewhat different from the traditional therapeutic approach and has mentioned his distaste for the term *psychotherapy* as descriptive of his work with groups of families.

Before moving into the technique of MFGT, readers are referred to the ten considerations identified earlier for the marital group therapists (*see* pp. 205-209). These considerations are as appropriate for internalization prior to beginning work with a group of families as they are for a group of couples. With that understood, attention is directed to the technique of MFGT.

The Technique of MFGT

We have found many of our constructs and techniques to be similar to those identified by Laqueur and his associates. Considering this, it may be valuable for the reader to refer to three excellent articles for further resources (Laqueur, 1972, 1976; Laqueur, LaFurt, and Morong, 1971).

Other than the availability of a multifamily therapy group, the following variables are valuable when used as criteria for inclusion of a family: (1) If the family is isolated and seems to lack sufficient skills to reach outside their own system, the MFGT experience can be valuable for developing these skills; (2) if the family system is extremely calcified and resistant to change in individual family therapy, the MFGT experience may provide them with new models; (3) there is potential for change as a result of confrontation from peers, if it is a single-parent family, which is becoming more and more common (the other families can provide parental substitutes); and (4) *all* family members are interested in trying the MFGT approach.

Those factors that seem to serve as criteria for excluding a family from MFGT and adhering to individual family therapy are lack of motivation by family members to engage in this type of experience and the family whose "ego" appears too brittle and could result in promoting a defense such as withdrawal from therapy.

We found groups ranged from fourteen to nineteen members, depending on the size of the families involved. The size is also affected by the "vertical representation" of the family. By *vertical* the implication is a representation of greater than two generations (parent-child) for each family. Whenever possible, it is advisable to include grandparents to provide a three-generational perspective of the family. Grandparents are included not only for reasons expounded on in Chapter 2 of this book, but children of some families without living grandparents are given an opportunity to gain exposure and insights to grandparent figures and the role they play in family functioning. The presence of at least one set of grandparents in a MFGT situation is extremely valuable, and therapists are advised to attempt to engage at least one couple that represents the third generation in every family group.

Our groups generally last for three to eight hours, depending upon the situation. Typically, the group lasts three hours, but occasionally sessions are scheduled for longer periods of time if the group seems to have identified material deemed therapeutically crucial that will need more time for elaboration. This occurred in one group composed of four families. Three of the four families identified simultaneously how an experience with the death of a family member seemed to be unresolved and affecting present family functioning. The co-therapists used an eight-hour session on that occasion in order to facilitate, as fully as possible, the completion of the mourning and the integration of insights, so that the families could move beyond their current homeostatic set.

Once involved with the families in the MFGT session, the therapist should be aware of the following levels of observation identified by Laqueur and his associates (1971, P. 90):

1. Phenomenological description referring to the concrete statements and actions which occurred in the event [observed by the therapist].
2. Communication description which focuses on the mode of communication, be it direct, or unconscious, via gesture, movement, intonation, or otherwise.
3. Psychodynamic description reflecting intrapsychic process, i.e., affective and experiential factors evidenced in the present behavior of each individual.

Once the observations are noted, what is done with them therapeutically is determined by the clinical judgment of the therapists, i.e. confronting the family openly, confronting the family metaphorically, or asking other families what their impressions were of what just transpired among those who just finished interacting. The above observational cues facilitate the therapist breaking the code the family uses for communication, but to use it therapeutically is an idiosyncratic issue depending on therapist style and orientation.

Mechanisms of Change in MFGT

Laqueur (1973, Pp. 404-405) has identified what he refers to as mechanisms of change in MFGT: "This includes (a) the use of families as co-therapists, (b) competition, (c) delineation of the field of interaction, (d) learning by analogy, (e) learning through identification, (f) learning through the identification constellation, (g) "tuning-in," (h) learning through trial and error, (i) the use of models, (j) focus of excitation, and (k) the amplification and modulation of signals.

Each of the above dynamics of change found in the MFGT experience are discussed at this point. We have combined Laqueur's points *d* and *i* into a single issue. A variable that seems important for consideration is that these mechanisms of change be perceived in the MFGT setting through general systems theory, as expounded on by Bertalanffy (1966, 1968). The GST approach, as identified and applied to families (*see* Chap. 1) in this book, is especially appropriate when working with a group such as is found in the MFGT experience.

THE USE OF FAMILIES AS CO-THERAPISTS: The presence of other families becomes valuable in implementing the accepted therapeutic techniques, such as confrontation, support, interpretation, and reflection, etc. On many occasions these interventions, emanating from what is perceived as a peer, can have far more therapeutic impact than if they were to originate in the therapist. Using other families as co-therapists may develop quite spontaneously, while at other times the therapist may need to orchestrate the therapeutic advantage offered in the presence of the other families. An example of orchestration is that of asking one family that has a problem similar to one being presented currently to present their observations to the family in focus at that time. In this case, the family the therapist utilized as co-therapist is asked to offer not only their experience of a similar nature, but also observations regarding the process they perceive in operation in the identified family.

COMPETITION: The competition inherent in the MFGT experience seems to expedite change. This seems to be related to what

Schutz (1973) refers to as "sibling rivalry" that is manifested especially in the beginning stages of the group. As the group participants attempt to please the leader, change evolves. In this same sense, the families seem to compete in their efforts to improve. Laqueur (1972) reports that it is his experience that this initial competition seems to shift into cooperation, and our experience validates his report.

DELINEATION OF THE FIELD OF INTERACTIONS: This concept refers to the effort on the part of the therapist to facilitate understanding by the families of the systemic nature of their relationships. The effort is directed at realizing how each member affects each other and how forces and stress from the suprasystem (the social environment) affect them as a subsystem (family). This process results in all participants being better able to express fears, joys, frustrations, and other feelings that up to this point have been prevented from being expressed. An example of this construct was a family that was concerned about the father's tendency to withdraw from interaction with them. As the situation was explored in the MFGT setting, it became evident that the father was experiencing stress in the form of pursuit for more production on his part on the job, was unable to deal with this on the job, and became preoccupied with attempting to resolve the situation through introspection. He would go home and continue to engage in introspection—his family responded to his "withdrawal" with pursuit for his involvement, which resulted in compounding his stress. As the family discussed this, with the aid of the other families present, they became aware of the fact that the father was acting in this "withdrawing" fashion in order to protect them from having to "worry," as he was.

This served as an excellent example of the cyclical nature of subsystem affecting subsystem, resulting in a compounding of the "problem." The authors believe this is also a good example of what Watzlawick and others (1974) suggest as being central in "problems" of human relationships. Their contention is that the identified problem is not the real problem, but rather the solution to the perceived problem. The solution, as utilized in the family mentioned above, was destructive until the family fully understood how the solution was creating stress. Once uncovered, a new process that facilitated a flow of support from one member to another, that encouraged creative problem solving and a community feeling that replaced the alienation that existed before, was employed.

LEARNING BY ANALOGY AND MODELING: Families are able to learn more constructive means of problem resolution through observing other families resolve dilemmas of a similar nature. As mentioned earlier, just the realization that there are others that have survived similar stresses is many times therapeutic and provides the motivation needed to induce change.

LEARNING THROUGH IDENTIFICATION: The MFGT setting offers family members of all ages the opportunity to identify with members of other families in a similar situation. The idea of the facilitator orchestrating the MFGT process becomes vital at this juncture. By appropriately reinforcing adaptive behavior manifested by members, the facilitator can increase the chances of that behavior being identified with, in opposition to maladaptive behaviors.

LEARNING THROUGH THE IDENTIFICATION CONSTELLATION: Laqueur (1972, P. 408) states the following regarding this phenomenon: "This is a more complex mechanism than simple identification, and one that probably is unique to MFGT. Identical family configurations give rise to something that might be called an identification constellation." This similarity of family configuration seems to greatly expedite the identification process. An example is two families with the oldest child being adopted and the second child being a natural child. These two families would probably identify more readily with each other than they would with other families in the group.

"TUNING-IN": This construct refers to identification of one situation with another. As a particular situation is discussed by family *A*, it may be a cue to a member of family *B* for an insight into a situation in his or her family. Although it may not be identical, it stimulates the process of generalization and application to a situation that is real in family *B*.

LEARNING THROUGH TRIAL AND ERROR: In the MFGT setting, members have the opportunity to adopt new behaviors, implement, evaluate through feedback, and accept for integration or reject. There are numerous sources of feedback on which the family can draw. In individual family therapy, the therapist is the primary unit providing feedback, whereas in MFGT the family has readily available its fellow group members.

FOCUS OF EXCITATION: Laqueur (1972, P. 410) states, "A new, more realistic type of behavior manifested by one individual or family, as distinguished from their usual behavior, can act as a focus of excitation for the whole group, if it is used skillfully by the therapist."

To illustrate this point, a MFGT session the authors were engaged in once will be used. The situation comprised twenty-one members representing four families in the third session of the group's history. This group was manifesting defensiveness to a degree that had resulted in a low-keyed and apparently nonproductive experience to that point. About twenty-five minutes into the session, a sixteen-year-old girl, a member of one of the most closed families, identified with much animation how upset she was with her parents for quieting them (the family) from fully disclosing their feelings regarding a situation that had occurred during the week. This girl had been identified by her family and the other participant families as the "well child," which resulted in her apparent "disloyalty" having considerable impact on all present. This act had a therapeutic effect upon not only her family, but served as the catalyst to the other families involved as they began to explore and expose themselves to one another. This particular group evolved into what we agree is the most vital and energetic we have engaged in a MFGT meeting.

THE AMPLIFICATION AND MODULATION OF SIGNALS: As therapists become aware of various situations and dynamics, they can ask a member they believe is particularly sensitive to comment on the process. In this sense, the member identified can amplify the observation and resultant insight for the identified family, who in turn can respond and amplify it for the other participant families. Without this amplification process, the insights may have never been acknowledged.

In this same sense, signals can be modified. As families

become aware of how other families have lived through similar situations and perhaps even benefitted, they place their dilemma in a more realistic perspective. By perceiving their "problem" in a new perspective, they are now able to perceive more realistic alternatives.

Synthesis of MFGT

This exposition has perhaps helped the reader identify the constructs and techniques of MFGT. The MFGT method is a powerful and facilitative approach for all participants. Perhaps the best way of summarizing this approach and what is attempting to be accomplished is to again quote Laqueur (1972b, P. 633): "Multiple family therapy is a tool to teach individual families a great deal about their behavior by setting up mirrors (in reality and subsequently on film and on videotape) in which they can compare the things they are doing to each other."

SUMMARY

In this chapter, the basic principles of working with couples in a group situation and families in the group setting were presented. Although these are the two most prominent modalities in which the group approach is used in marriage and family therapy, a more recent innovation implementing group principles is gaining in prominence. This approach is referred to as *network therapy,* as developed and refined by Ross Speck and Carolyn Attneave (1972, 1973). Their description of network therapy is as follows:

> In network therapy we assemble together all members of the kinship system, all friends and neighbors of the family, and, in fact, everyone who is of significance to the nuclear family that offers the presenting problem. In our experience, the typical middleclass urban family has the potential to assemble about forty persons for network meetings. These meetings are held in the home. Gathering the network together in one place at one time releases potent therapeutic potentials. [1972, P. 637]

As this, along with marital group therapy and MFGT, is a relatively recent innovation in the field, new innovations implementing group principles and practices may yet be on the horizon. Perhaps one of the readers of this volume will be the innovator of the new approach and join the other creators mentioned in this chapter in applying group principles in a new and more effective delivery system.

CHAPTER 9

COUNSELING AT TWO CRITICAL STAGES OF FAMILY DEVELOPMENT: FORMATION AND TERMINATION OF MARRIAGE

PREMARITAL COUNSELING

T HE PHRASE *premarital counseling* is used to describe the work that a professional counselor does in helping a couple to prepare for marriage, whether the work is focused on specific problems (remedial) or whether it is for enhancement (developmental) purposes. Acknowledging the inadequate education for marriage and family life that the general population receives, premarital counseling could represent the first and last opportunity for planned exposure to the development of interpersonal competence. Divorce and marital satisfaction studies do not speak well for people's abilities to experience relationships competently. Add to this the problems between the parent and child, and the picture becomes even bleaker. Premarital counseling* allows the therapist to build in skills and a sense of interpersonal awareness that could help couples avoid some pitfalls or at least solve problems more quickly and skillfully. Therapists quite frequently talk about the ease and the joys involved in working with couples who have not built up a vast reservoir of hurt, sadness, and anger. Couples seeking premarital counseling often fall into this category.

---

* David Mace (1972) prefers to use the term *marriage preparation* as the more general term to encompass the whole gamut of premarital work. He limits the term *premarital counseling* to therapeutic work that focuses on specific problems. Although Mace is technically more accurate, we generalize "premarital counseling" to include both remedial and developmental aspects. This is partly an attempt to broaden our concept of counseling to include developmental, enhancement-oriented work that addresses general and specific issues. It is also partly a capitulation to convention.

Purpose and General Approaches

The major purpose of premarital counseling is to facilitate a couple's preparation for successful marriage. Marriage, in western culture, is meant to be the most important and most intimate relationship people can have. To help two people achieve success in such a relationship is no small matter. With that major purpose in mind, more specific goals of premarital counseling can be discussed. Three come to mind: (1) to assess the qualities of the relationship and evaluate the readiness of the couple for marriage; (2) to develop the personal and relationship strengths of the couple; and (3) to do some specific problem solving and negotiation. The last two are complementary, because good developmental work generally involves application to some of the specific conflicts in a relationship. Likewise, good therapy, in our view, usually leads to some form of enhancement focus.

Mace, in his preface to the book *Getting Ready for Marriage* (1972), offers a general typology of the ways or approaches that have been developed by professionals in premarital work. The first he calls the *facts-of-life approach*—basically a didactic approach designed to impart knowledge about marriage and family life. The assumption that ignorance is the prime cause of marital trouble is presumably the basis for this approach. The second approach focuses specifically on the couple, helping them to evaluate themselves, each other, and their relationship. The third approach focuses on counseling the couple on specific difficulties about which they have asked for help.

We agree with Mace that the second approach is the most effective one, while certainly not limiting one's options to one approach. Mace (1972, P. 10) writes, "The core of marriage preparation, therefore, lies in the second approach, with some of the first included incidentally, and the possibility that the third will develop as a result of the new awareness that the couple will be almost sure to achieve."

The rest of this section is an elaboration of the above statement with due emphasis on the second and third objectives. The second approach involves more than just an evaluation of the couple as persons and as a relationship. It also involves a range of growth-oriented experiences (in and out of the counseling office) to enhance the relationship in the present and as preparation for the future.

Interpersonal Space and Courtship: Blessing or Blindfold?

Much has been written about romanticism during courtship, both in the professional literature as well as in fiction. The general sense is that the fire, the thrill, and the ecstasy during courtship soon fade after marriage. It seems that one of the key factors influencing this phenomenon is captured in the concept of "space" (*see* Chap. 1). During courtship, couples usually have built-in space—structured times apart. This is in part the result of separate residences and in part of cultural expectations.

The interactional characteristic of most courtships is often the key to understanding a multitude of personal and relationship struggles in the premarital stage. It is of utmost importance to understand the patterns of togetherness, separateness, pursuit, and withdrawal. Moments of togetherness are usually experienced with a sense of deep joy and satisfaction precisely because they were preceded by moments of separateness and take place with the assurance of being followed by another episode of apartness. The majority of couples at this stage view the moments apart with great disdain or at least as something to be tolerated, not anticipated. The ecstatic moments together are seen as indubitable proof that their match is indeed matchless, mature, and uncommonly open and honest.

Conflicts are often buried or not allowed to reach the level of hard-nosed negotiation. When the conflict becomes too intense, one or the other can always elect to go home, be apart, and breathe more easily for a while. After a night or two of this separateness, the forces of togetherness are usually so strong that conflictual issues are easily set aside and forgotten. The image that best fits this coming together is the scene portrayed in many movies where two young, beautiful lovers run toward each other in slow motion. The need for sexual and emotional affirmation is so strong that the unpleasant aspects of conflict negotiation are simply unable to emerge.

Many premarital couples are simply entranced by this experience. They are led to believe that their relationship is not in need of any additional attention and that they in fact possess all the skills and knowledge needed to fashion a successful marriage. In light of this, it seems that one of the most crucial tasks for the therapist is that of equipping the couple with the skills to negotiate togetherness and separateness *explicitly*.

Furthermore, exploring, a person's family of origin can also reveal the basic themes and experiences around the issues of belongingness and separateness—themes that are evoked in the patterns of interpersonal space. This element is detailed later in this chapter.

In addition to assessing the couple's interactional patterns, it is important for the therapist to help the couple experience aspects of relationship dynamics not yet significantly expressed in their own relationship. For instance, the party who tends to initiate more of the times together might be told to initiate times apart. The other, then, can be instructed (for a few days at least) to pursue the partner intensely and demandingly. The latter, as pursuer, might then experience some of the loneliness, rejection, sadness, and anger that often accompany such a move. These feelings can be amplified by instructing the pursued party to increase efforts to avoid the pursuer. The avoidance must be done in indirect ways if the experiment is to have realistic impact. This tends to develop in the pursuer the ability to empathize with the partner at a time in the future when they may be pursued. The pursuit could then be seen as a thirst for closeness and affirmation rather than a desire to control or suffocate.

The built-in space that most couples experience during courtship can be a real advantage because it gives them a feel for the functional and satisfying rhythm of closeness and distance. There is at least a subconscious realization of this experience. However, this built-in space can also act as a blindfold to the conscious awareness of the couple, as just described. The blindfold could cover many opportunities for growth and skill development. The therapist-educator can be helpful in the process of capitalizing on the opportunities for personal growth and interpersonal competence.

Suggested Aspects for Premarital Exploration

The discussion on interpersonal space was meant as an overall comment on a quality of the courtship structure as known in the United States. We would now like to focus on a number of more concrete issues for exploration. Although the following exposition is not exhaustive or comprehensive, it represents what appear to be the more crucial aspects to be examined in premarital counseling. In many cases, the reader is referred to chapters in the text where a specific topic is dealt with more thoroughly.

CHOICE AND A COMMITMENT TO GROWTH: Because marriage in the North American culture is primarily seen as a voluntary arrangement, it is important to help couples clarify the choice element involved in their decision. This explicit attention may seem redundant to the reader and often seems ridiculous to the couple. But experience indicates (as does the literature, e.g. Lederer and Jackson, 1968) that many couples enter marriage with motives dictated by external forces. Lip service is paid to love as the basis of their choice. A decision as monumental as marriage is rarely made with one overriding motive. It is the result of a complex of important and powerful forces, including social expectations, parental pressure, loneliness, economic security, self-growth, and love.

The object of the clarification process in therapy is not to eliminate all forces other than love, but to become aware of their impact on each person and to help each party own aspects of the impacts and disown others. The key factor is choice. A couple may choose to follow a parental request and in so doing own that decision as theirs, thus assuming full responsibility for it. They could also choose not to follow it. The processes of owning or disowning the decision may be as important as the content of the decision itself.

Making the choice of the partner explicit is a way of celebrating the sense of commitment that couples have toward each other. This kind of self-chosen, self-directed, and fully owned commitment is the best foundation upon which to build a marriage. The nature of the commitment is a steadfast promise to help each other grow as persons in the relationship.

COMMUNICATION AND CONFLICT NEGOTIATION: David and Vera Mace (1977) believe that the three essential ingredients of a happy marriage are (1) commitment to growth, (2) an effective communication system, and (3) the creative use of conflict. We have just addressed the first. Now the importance of training in communication and conflict negotiation is stressed. We believe that these areas ought to occupy a significant portion of premarital counseling. The reader is referred to Chapter 7 for specific ideas on communication and conflict negotiation. It seems that through devoting an entire chapter in this book to communication skills, we have emphasized the importance we place on that element of the marital relationship.

FAMILY-OF-ORIGIN EXPLORATION: Perhaps one of the most neglected areas in premarital counseling is the role that the families of origin can play in the therapy process. In the literature, there is great awareness about the parent's attitude toward the proposed marriage. However, the dialogue usually stops with the question of whether or not the parents approve of the marriage. We propose a much more detailed exploration of the impact that the families of origin play in the formation of the self, the mate-selection process, the loyalty shifts necessary in marriage, their interaction patterns, and their marital-family goals. We also suggest involving the families of origin in the actual counseling sessions.

Using the ideas and techniques discussed in Chapter 2, we suggest that at least an hour be devoted to exploring each persons genogram, with the partner present. This is not just a journey into the past, but a journey into the present effects of past experiences with one's family. These two hours of work tend to be eye-openers for the couple and are an excellent foundation for the live sessions with the families of origin.

The following is a format that has proven itself to be valuable: One session is devoted to one's family, with the other person present, or not present, depending on the therapist's inclinations.

If the other is not present, we recommend that he or she listen to the tape of the session. Another live session is devoted to the other partner's family, with similar arrangements for the one whose family is not present. A third live session then involves both partners and their families, whenever possible. We realize, of course, that geographic considerations sometimes make these live sessions difficult, especially with families who cannot afford the expense involved in such trips. However, we strongly suggest that the therapist propose such sessions, regardless of the circumstances. It is difficult to predict what measures a given family is willing to take to accommodate a family member's request. The therapist may be selling the couple short by assuming that such live sessions are impossible to conduct.

We believe that the family-of-origin sessions are among the most helpful and powerful aspects of premarital counseling. Sessions with one's family of origin are helpful at any time before, during, or after marriage. However, they take on a special meaning at the premarital stage because one of the major tasks to be accomplished in the transition from courtship to marriage is the shift in primary loyalties. In our culture, it should shift from one's family of origin to one's newly formed intimate group—the marriage and family of one's own making. These family-of-origin sessions could set the tone for the kind of belongingness and differentiation acceptable in these family groups. The development of "couple identity" is facilitated without the fear of losing their rightful place in the family network. We know of no better way to prepare a couple for marriage.

NEGOTIATION OF MORE SPECIFIC CONTENT AREAS: Specific issues are the areas that premarital counseling and education have traditionally emphasized. We view the task of facilitating the communication and negotiation of these areas as helpful in marriage preparation. We suggest that these are the content areas to be focused on while doing the training in communication and conflict negotiation. This way the therapist can teach process skills while facilitating the exploration of key content areas.

The important aspects of the key content areas are not detailed; the areas that seem significant are listed. A perusal of the premarital literature shows a fairly consistent choice of areas identified as important. The following are examples:*

1. The meaning of marriage and related expectations
2. Communication and interaction patterns
3. Sex and the expression of affection
4. Money
5. Children and parenting
6. Extended family and in-laws
7. Friends
8. Recreation-leisure
9. Education-occupation
10. Division of tasks in the home
11. Spirituality-philosophy of life

It is neither possible nor advisable for the therapist to bring closure to each of these issues. The goal is simply to get the couple started, to break down the fear of exploring these issues, and to get a taste for success in the negotiation process. After all, the major initiative resides in the couple.

DIVORCE COUNSELING

Premarital counseling deals primarily with what could be in a relationship. Divorce counseling is primarily directed toward what will be, but also involves equally an examination of what has been and what is, as well.

Divorce means the end of the marital relationship, but not the end of the family. In fact, it may mean a more complex family system: a one-parent family with arrangements for some contact between the children and the nonresident parent who, in turn, may marry someone with or without children from a previous marriage. In a way, then, divorce could lead to the extension of family ties.

A Tough Dilemma: Easy Divorce or No Divorce?

The minute there is talk about divorce counseling, there is the immediate implication that divorce is a real and legitimate

---

* For the sake of completeness, we have included those areas already discussed earlier; hence, the redundancy.

option for couples. The very existence of divorce counseling is a reflection of a slowly growing societal trend toward viewing divorce as a viable but difficult solution to a difficult problem. It is not a question of idealizing divorce as a wonderful or beautiful experience, because however the experience is perceived, it is still painful. It is rather a question of making divorce a real option, as opposed to a path so laden with personal, social, economic, and spiritual costs that to call it a matter of choice stretches that human capacity beyond the range of the mortal.

There are some very tough questions that need to be answered by the couple, counselors, and legislators; among others, the question of the acceptability of divorce, the ease with which it can be legally obtained, and the seriousness of effort that couples bring to a marriage prior to terminating it. At the core of these issues is a very delicate dilemma seldom confronted head-on in the divorce literature. One aspect of the dilemma is based on a belief that growth in a relationship often comes at the point of conflict and from the process of dealing with the conflict. Hence, those couples who give up at the first sign of failure to deal with the conflict may never achieve significant growth. Since people tend to choose mates around complementary dimensions, the path toward symmetry may never be started. Wallerstein and Kelly (1977, P. 6) state, "Thus, the divorce period produces a three-cornered potential—a crisis engendered capacity for (potentionally helpful) change; the external demand for major decisions regarding future parent-child relationships; and a (sometimes) heightened motivation for improvement."

The other aspect of the dilemma appears when society does not make divorce a real choice, either legally or through rigid social expectations. If divorce is not a real choice, then staying married is not either. In such a society, the closest thing to having an honest choice is whether or not to marry (even then, pressures toward marriage are usually so strong as to question this). But once married, without an open path to divorce (or annulment), there is no choice but to stay married. Any insight into the basic laws of relationship dynamics, e.g. those governing togetherness and separateness, shows that this situation tends to "push" people away from emotional commitment to the marriage, as a way to preserve their own individuality by creating a sense of pseudo-distance.

This is not the place to raise all the related issues in divorce; that requires another volume. The following are attitudes that seem important for couples and therapists to keep in mind: (1) One's current mate, in most cases, represents that person who is most able to elicit those relationship situations and dynamics from which one can grow the most, and vice versa. (2) If one chooses not to work out a relationship struggle with the current mate, one will most likely encounter similar relationship struggles with a future mate, but in any case, it is important to grant the individual the right to decide whether, as well as when and with whom, he or she will work out such issues. (3) We encourage laws and social expectations that realistically portray the validity-legitimacy of divorce, as well as its difficulties and related consequences, and that provide structures that could educate and support people's efforts in these matters.

What we are saying is this: "There are probable payoffs to working through issues in your present relationship; however, you do not have to do it now or ever. If you choose not to at this point, please realize that you will probably have to face them in your next intimate relationship. Running away from the present struggle does not usually mean running away from the struggles toward intimacy. If you choose never to struggle, you are most likely choosing never to achieve an ongoing, committed intimacy. Keep in mind also that in the process of divorcing, you can achieve much growth and, thus, prepare yourself for your next relationship, if you choose the route of intimacy once again."

Defining Divorce

In ordinary conversation, the term *divorce* generally refers to the legal process of terminating the formal marriage contract between two people. In this discussion, the legal aspect is viewed as a substage of a much larger and more inclusive process. Divorce, in our minds, starts from the first serious thoughts and discussion couples have about it, continues on to the moment of what seems to be a final decision, and includes all the emotional, social, economic, and legal aspects related to the termination of a marital relationship.* It is important, then, to think of divorce as more of a dynamic process, rather than as an event that legally culminates and ends in a courtroom at a specific point in time.

The Phases of the Divorce Process

Emily Brown, one of the authorities in the field of divorce counseling, suggests a helpful typology for the divorce process (1976, P. 411). She divides the divorce process into two major phases: (1) the decision-making phase—from the first consideration of divorce to the time when the decision to split is made; and (2) the restructuring phase—this involves the implementation of the decision made. Building upon the work of Bohanan (1970), Brown conceptualizes the restructuring phase as embodying five overlapping subprocesses: emotional, parent-child, legal, economic, and social. It is important for the family to deal successfully with the process surrounding these five issues if the ex-spouses and the children are to develop stable, creative, and autonomous life-styles.

Defining Divorce Counseling

To the lay person, the term *marriage and family counselor* refers to one who works only with those couples who are trying to stay together or who, faced with a couple seeking divorce, does all in his or her power to convince them to keep their marriage going. Fisher (1973) suggests that professionals who include divorce counseling in their service call themselves *marriage and divorce counselors*. However this misconception* is

---

* Although our discussion uses the vocabulary of *marriage, marital,* and *divorce,* all of which imply a legal aspect to the relationship in question, we are aware that the processes we are talking about apply to nonlegal relationship investments as well. The absence of the legal bond could, but does not necessarily, make the process less complicated. Legal procedures, if wisely undertaken, could facilitate the transition from being married to being single.

* This was not really a misconception a decade ago because marriage and family counselors often operated under the assumption that their function was to "save" marriages. Consequently, their training emphasized improving relationships and underplayed handling the divorce process.

cleared up, we believe that every marriage and family counselor should be equipped not simply to aid in the process of improving relationships but also in handling its dissolution. If divorce is difficult for a counselor, it is important to be straight and clear about one thing: the importance of giving the couple a suitable and facilitative arena for decision making around the issue of divorce or no divorce. This is not simply sound ethics but also sound therapy.

In our view, then, divorce counseling is a specialty area in the field of marriage and family therapy. More specifically, divorce counseling is a process whereby the therapist (1) helps those in the decision-making phase of divorce to assess their needs, strengths, and shortcomings, and thus facilitates their arriving at a satisfactory decision (to stay married or to divorce); and (2) helps couples and families facing divorce in the process of restructuring their individual lives and relationships. Divorce counseling, despite its crisis-laden aspects, is more than just supportive counseling. It is a process for working through the inevitable feelings of hurt, loss, and anger—feelings that if not faced head-on, could be the motivating force for creating triangles, usually with a child as the third point.

Wallerstein and Kelly (1977) have documented from their extensive experience with families experiencing divorce the similarities of the divorce process to grief work with families who have experienced death. It is also a process for understanding the patterns that emerged in the family system in general and in the marital relationship in particular. The emotional decourting and the interactional understanding that could result from the counseling process tends to be preventive and promotive in effect. The children's chances of growing up with a healthy sense of self-esteem and autonomy become much greater; the ex-spouses' chances of developing a healthier relationship in the future tend to be increased.

The Decision-making Phase

Research indicates that the decision-making process (from serious discussion to final decision to divorce) among couples who finally decide to divorce takes the majority of couples roughly one to two years to complete (Goode, 1956). Many of these couples approach the family therapist with a decision already made. In this section, those couples who come without an agreed-upon, stated decision to get a divorce are discussed.

In some cases, both spouses come to counseling having seriously discussed divorce as an alternative. We find these couples generally more open and ready for an exploratory look at their relationship. In cases where one spouse wants in and the other wants out, the motivation for seeking counseling is a crucial factor in the process. In some cases, it is the spouse wanting out who makes a move toward counseling. That spouse may already have decided on the divorce, but is tacitly asking the counselor to help the other accept the decision or even expecting the counselor to recommend or decide on divorce as the best solution. On the other hand, Whitaker (1970) has discussed his belief that some spouses come in for divorce counseling with the hope that the counselor will become a replacement for the spouse they are hoping to leave. In this sense, the divorce counseling becomes a way for the spouse desiring divorce to appease his or her guilt by finding a "surrogate spouse" for the partner they are leaving. When the counselor is sought by the spouse who wants to save the marriage, he or she may be "asking" the counselor to convince the other spouse to stay.

Covert motivations do not always exist, but because it is so important for a therapist not to take on the role of decision maker (the battle for initiative), it is well to be alert to these factors. It is important to be mindful that the element of free choice by the spouses about whether or not to stay married may be the most therapeutic element in the counseling experience. Therefore, it is important to set a therapeutic structure that enables couples to assess their situation somewhat objectively, thus avoiding a premature decision, but one does not discourage them from making some decisive moves. Divorce talk is usually a sign that one or both spouses have not made a solid, internalized commitment to the relationship. Hence, the process of facilitating the decision making around this issue is of the essence.

A time-limited therapeutic contract is especially facilitative in the decision-making phase. We usually recommend a six-session exploratory phase before terminating the counseling relationship or renegotiating the contract for a new phase in counseling, divorce, or otherwise. The initial contract includes the intent on the part of both spouses to (1) be as honest as possible about their thoughts, feelings, and intentions; and (2) to put their heart into giving the relationship a fair second chance. The last point is included as an attempt to minimize the situation where one spouse has really decided on divorce, but is going to go through the motions of counseling so he or she can say to him- or herself and to others, "I have tried; but, as you can see, it is hopeless." Remember that we are dealing with two people who are, in essence, saying: "We are here to find out whether we want to make it together or not."

During the time-limited contract, we recommend taking a strong stand against allowing the use of divorce as a threat—unless one member is ready to make a final decision to divorce. Such threats are considered below-the-belt weapons. This injunction has nothing to do with sharing feelings of closeness or distance. It is one thing to say, "I am angry and feel distant from you right now." It is quite another thing to say, "You do that again and I am leaving you for good." This element of the contract does not prevent a spouse from creating emotional space—even though leaving for a limited time. Leaving for a day or two is not to be equated with leaving the relationship. In our experience, troubled couples tend to equate these two. We may, in fact, encourage brief episodes of physical separation, as long as these episodes do not come under the rubric of "threat." If this contract is acceptable, we would proceed almost as if we were doing marital and family therapy, with, however, greater sensitivity to the exploratory nature of the counseling.

Structured Trial Separation

Some couples come to the therapist already in a state of trial separation, and others ask the therapist about the advisability of such a move. If after exploring the different alternative structures open to a couple during the decision-making phase, one or both of the spouses express a strong preference or insistence on trial separation, we generally recommend acceptance of that preference and suggest a structure for it. The purpose of the trial separation is identical to the purpose of divorce counseling at the decision-making phase. Toomin (1975, P. 354) states, "The purpose of this counseling procedure is to help separating individuals understand their relationship, resolve their conflicts, decide whether their future relationship will be together or apart, and grow through the separation process." Creation of a structure through which couples might more genuinely take an autonomous move toward or away from the present relationship is the objective. By structuring time apart and thus creating emotional space, couples could hopefully assess their individual and relationship needs more realistically.

The contract we make with a couple contains several major elements. We generally prefer to have the structured separation time coincide with the length of six weekly sessions. If we take missed appointments into account, this period generally lasts approximately two months. During this time, husband and wife live separately. As with nonseparated couples, the recommendation is that they not use divorce as a threat. We also suggest that they not take any steps toward contacting lawyers or making any arrangements for property, custody, or related matters. Couples are encouraged to meet, excluding sexual contact unless mutually agreed upon. Either partner may initiate a move toward togetherness with an explicit agreement that there is no assumption or expectation that the other partner must say yes.

Children maintain their natural environment with the parent best able to care for them. At another point in the book, data is presented that clearly indicates that children are able to handle openness much better than covertness. Hence, we feel comfortable about including the children on the drawing up of these agreements. We are not denying difficult moments for the children, for they will naturally experience feelings of confusion and ambivalence. However, it is our judgment that these feelings of confusion and ambivalence are inevitable in a marital conflict, whether that conflict is played out in a situation of togetherness, separation, or divorce. However, one thing seems clear; trying to hide conflicts from children not only is seldom successful, but is quite often injurious to their psychological growth.

We also recomend an agreement not to seek sexual involvements outside the marital relationship. A sexual involvement could easily develop into a triangle that keeps the couples from experiencing reactions resulting from the time they are spending apart. Exceptions to this rule are couples whose normal life-style involves outside sexual involvements or who explicitly seek counseling as a means to incorporate such a life-style into their currently monogamous pattern. In general, we view extramarital involvement at moments of conflict with great suspicion. We realize, of course, that in saying this, we may be reflecting biases of our own kind and personal subculture. Nevertheless, it is our honest judgment that this is a valid therapeutic route.

Because structured separation stresses the element of choice more than a situation where couples are living together, it tends to be a tremendous aid in the development of self-differentiation. The move to be together must be consciously and explicitly initiated, and the acceptance of that move is more difficult to take for granted. Thus, the choice to stay married, if made, becomes more genuine since there is room to move in, as a result of the apartness created by the structure. The choice to leave the marriage and proceed on to divorce is likewise based on a more realistic assessment of the situation, not on the fantasy of relief.

Marjorie Toomin (1975) studied eighteen couples who completed the structured separation with counseling. She observed that the first and immediate experience of the separation was a shock reaction. She noted that the shock was accompanied by somatic disorders such as headaches, gastrointestinal disturbances, and upper respiratory infections. The shock reaction was generally followed by an eight- to twelve-week affective cycle. In one group of separated couples, the first four to six weeks were characterized by depression and withdrawal. In the other group of couples, the first four to six weeks were characterized by a time of euphoria and activity. During the next four to six weeks, the depressed or withdrawn group start to feel more open and more active, while the euphoric group begin to experience tendencies to withdraw and become more depressed. Thus, a period of intermediate affective inactivity level develops. Toomin (1975,

P. 357) writes, "It is on this base that the person can best either grow as a single individual or begin to establish a new dependency relationship." This cycle, incidentally, is the rationale for a three-month separation period.

The Restructuring Phase

The restructuring phase begins once the decision to divorce has been made. This is the time to implement the various aspects that the decision to divorce entails.

Wallerstein and Kelly (1977) stated:

> Many decisions made during the divorce in regard to the subsequent structuring of relationships including custody and visitation, have long-term consequences for the future of the child and the parent-child relationship. Yet often the impetus and direction for these changes derive entirely from the stress-laden interaction of the family disruption. It would seem of considerable importance to provide the opportunity at this time for thoughtful consideration of consequences and alternatives. [P. 6]

We believe Wallerstein and Kelly's admonition in the last sentence is advice well taken and what we hope to facilitate in working with divorcing couples. This section looks at the counseling goals for the restructuring phase, outlines some considerations for the counseling structure, and focuses on certain aspects of the counseling process in this phase of divorce considerations. Throughout the discussion, it is important to keep in mind that it takes two people to make a marriage but it takes only one to break it. Who initiated the divorce process is important information and a perspective to keep in mind throughout the counseling procedure. The initiator in the divorce has usually been through a much rougher experience during the decision-making phase. He or she may experience a tremendous relief soon after the immediate separation. However, once emotional space has been created, our experience tells us that many spouses at this point may experience a desire to get back into the relationship. Obviously, this kind of feeling or orientation is difficult for these people to understand. The noninitiator, on the other hand, may feel depressed and angry and eventually may be inclined to play the distant uncaring member role. If the therapist keeps in mind the dynamics involved in the systemic tug-of-war around relationship space, it is much easier to understand and cope with the counseling situation.

Divorce Counseling Goals

Below is an outline of the general goals to which divorce counseling, at the restructuring phase, must address itself.

CLARIFICATION OF THE SITUATION: This simply means bringing reality to a scene so filled with fantasy and distortion, a scene so filled with denial and all sorts of defensive maneuvers. The major task at this point is to make sure that the couples understand what the decision is; that at least one person in that relationship has made a decision to end the marriage. The noninitiator of the decision may often find it difficult to hear the reality of that decision; the therapist can help by creating a structure to ensure that messages are clearly heard and a response is made. It is similarly important to make the initiator especially aware of owning that decision and taking full responsibility for it. When the decision is accepted by both the initiator and noninitiator, a much more productive context is usually created. When the noninitiator refuses to accept the other person's right to end the relationship, many kinds of games tend to emerge, often at the expense of the children.

DECOURTING AND MOURNING: *Courting* is the process of becoming progressively more committed to a relationship where two people seek much of their togetherness and identity. *Decourting* is the process of letting go, the process of loosening the expectations of togetherness, support, companionship, and power, to the point, ideally, of being able to genuinely wish the best for the other. Since anger and love tend to be different faces of deep emotional investment, they tend to play a major role in the decourting process; hence, these feelings have to be dealt with in some significant way in decourting. Generally, the most therapeutic method is to identify these feelings, own them, and express them, preferably in front of the divorcing partner.

Esther O. Fisher (1973, P. 55) graphically defines divorce: "Divorce is the death of marriage: the husband and wife together with their children are the mourners, the lawyers are the undertakers, the court is the cemetery where the coffin is sealed and the dead marriage buried." The loss of a relationship, like the death of a loved one, needs to be mourned. The hurt that lies behind the anger must be felt, accepted, and given expression in some appropriate way. Otherwise, the anger and the hurt will likely be expressed indirectly, often through the formation of triangles with the children.

UNDERSTANDING THE PAST AND PRESENT: At some point in the divorce counseling, it is important for the family (spouses and children) to understand the relationship patterns that led to the divorce and how the other members of the family were involved or influenced by them. Although the major focus is on the marital relationship, it is important for the therapist not to forget that there are other subsystems in the family, the members of which have been vitally influenced by the marital subsystem. It is important for each family member, especially the husband and wife, to understand his or her contribution to the relationship patterns. In processing these matters, it is important to avoid implying that anyone is to blame, but it is appropriate to elicit ownership of responsibility. Time and effort to understand the past has several payoffs: gaining interpersonal insights, a chance for family members to mourn and to forgive each other, and, most importantly, such efforts contribute to understanding of the present. Accomplishing these tasks increases one's chances of avoiding the duplication of such dynamics in one's current and future relationships.

PROCESSING LEGAL, ECONOMIC, AND SOCIAL QUESTIONS: The family therapist can be of great service to the family by providing them with an open structure for discussing legal, economic, and social issues, many of which affect the children as well as the spouses. If these decisions are left solely in the domain of the legal system, the adversary nature of law may seriously contaminate what has been accomplished in counseling.

PERSONAL GROWTH OF FAMILY MEMBERS: In the final analysis, divorce counseling aims to enhance the personal growth of the ex-spouses and of the children. The crisis of divorce is an excellent time to develop self-differentiation among members through individual, conjoint, and intergenerational counseling.

Divorce Counseling Structure: Some Notes

We prefer to see couples together when clarification, decourting, mourning, and understanding and the processing of economic and legal matters are taking place. Although the situation can be explosive, a skilled therapist can conduct honest, open, and flexible sessions. We also recommend including children, especially in the beginning of the counseling process. This is especially important until the children get a clear sense that their parents are indeed getting a divorce and that they can face their problems clearly without falling apart. This is also true whenever matters relating to the children, such as custody, are being discussed. Our goal is to demystify for the children whatever fantasies they may have regarding their parents' divorce. We consider this essential, and the validity of this belief is documented in research conducted with children of divorcing families in the following statement from the researchers: "The widespread regressions, symptomatic behaviors, and fearfulness which we observed in the youngest children can, at least in part, be attributed to the absence of explanations and assurance of support from their parents" (Wallerstein and Kelly, 1977, P. 13).

Wallerstein and Kelly (1977) have also identified an assessment process for evaluating children of divorce to determine the impact upon them and sources of therapeutic intervention. The dimensions of this divorce-specific assessment process are: (1) an abbreviated assessment of the overall developmental achievements of the children with the information coming from school personnel, the parents, and direct observation of the children by the clinician; (2) an assessment of each child's unique response to and experience with the parents' divorce—this includes the child's knowledge of the divorce, the child's affective responses, effectiveness of the child's defenses, pervasiveness of the child's responses (school, home, peers, etc.), and finally an inquiry into the development of new symptoms since the divorce process began; and (3) an evaluation of support systems surrounding, and available to, each child, including parent-child relationships, siblings, extended family, school, and peers.

We strongly recommend several sessions with a spouse and

his or her family of origin. At this point, we prefer not to have the ex-spouse of the divorcing spouse present in the session. We think that involvement of the family of origin is the most facilitative route to personal growth. The family of origin (parents, brothers, and sisters) can also serve in a much-needed supportive role. It seems to us that this supportive role is more appropriately played by the family of origin than by the therapist. The supportive role is crucial for at least two reasons: (1) it is a strongly felt need, and (2) it can prevent the divorcing spouse from prematurely becoming involved in another intimate relationship. Another concern that suggests that the family of origin be involved is if the spouse is going to return to live in the family of origin household. Dell and Applebaum (1977) have written effectively about the danger of *trigenerational enmeshment* or the process whereby roles and rules that result in autonomy become blurred and nonfunctional. Our goal in this situation becomes that of attempting to clarify boundaries and insuring as much differentiation as possible for all concerned.

Premature involvement or early marriage is the most powerful stumbling block to a successful divorce. Such involvement could be entered into in response to the painful loss of a relationship and can thus prevent adequate decourting and mourning. The new partner usually becomes a fantasy of what the old partner could have been. This situation prevents personal growth, which is another way of saying that it blocks movement toward self-differentiation and individuation. This is the reason that premature involvement often results in the creation of relationship dynamics similar to those that prevail in the previous one. On this question, Brown (1976) writes, "No matter how good the relationship appears to be, and how 'different' the new partner, the individual needs to experience singlehood for a sufficient period of time to gain or regain autonomy. This does not mean that the individual should be an island unto himself, but that he or she needs to know through experience that he/she is capable of caring for his/her own needs."

For these reasons, we recommend a six- to 12-month moratorium on significant reinvolvement with another person. We suggest building this into the therapeutic contract. This moratorium on significant reinvolvement, despite its apparent harshness, does not in any way imply noninvolvement in outside activity, social or otherwise. Dating, for example, and meeting other members of the field of eligibles are generally positive signs of adjustment. We encourage such activities, as soon as the divorcing spouses are comfortable. It is the exclusive attachment to one person that is at question here.

SUMMARY

This chapter presented material on the practice of both premarital and divorce counseling. In both areas, the purpose was discussed, along with practical considerations and approaches.

In the section on premarital counseling various elements that seem crucial for consideration were identified and discussed. Among the elements for consideration presented were: the role of interpersonal space in courtship and marriage; choice and commitment to growth; communication and conflict negotiation; the role of the individual's family of origin in the past, present, and future; and negotiation of specific content areas such as money, recreation, division of tasks, parenting, and friends.

The section on divorce counseling discussed the dilemma of divorce in our society. Part of this dilemma is the important role the availability of divorce has in reaffirming that each individual stays in the marriage by choice, and, contrarily, how quickly many people opt for divorce before really working to effect changes in their marriage. Attention was then turned to the phases of divorce counseling—decision making and restructuring. Elements of effective divorce counseling as it occurs in each of these phases and how approaches such as a structured trial separation can be effectively incorporated into the process were discussed. The considerations suggested for application were offered within the context of the following goals of divorce counseling: understanding the influence of the past and present on the relationship; now and potential future impact; processing legal, economic and social questions; and promoting the personal growth of the family members involved in the divorce.

CHAPTER 10

CHILDREN AND THEIR PARENTS

Tʜɪꜱ ᴄʜᴀᴘᴛᴇʀ ꜰᴏᴄᴜꜱᴇꜱ on the child's place in family therapy
and on the role that parent education could play in the therapeutic process. It is important for the beginning family therapist
to be aware of the major frameworks in parent education for
several reasons: (1) acquisition of additional frameworks and
tools for handling problematic behavior in children; (2) the
ability to equip the parents with methods to shape children's
responses; and (3) equipping the therapist with the language
for dealing with parents whose mental maps are oriented in this
educational direction.

The major frameworks discussed in this chapter are presented
in the language and orientation of their developers and pro-
ponents. The reader is therefore advised to integrate these ideas
into his preferred theory of human functioning and therapeutic
intervention.

CHILDREN'S ROLE IN AND OUT OF THERAPY

Throughout this book, emphasis has been focused on the
family as an interactive, interdependent system. Considering
this, it is important to acknowledge the impact each family
member has on the total family functioning. "Therapeutic tradition" seems to have it that children are not valuable resources
in therapy. This belief most likely evolved as a result of the
interface between the verbal nature of most therapeutic orientations and the child's natural developmental deficiency in verbal
skills. Regardless of what the reasons may be for the lack of
importance placed upon the role of children in the therapeutic
setting, these must be dispelled for the sake of therapeutic efficacy
and for the benefit of the family involved.

Rationale for Including Children in the Therapy Sessions

Acknowledging the ecological nature of human problems as identified by Auerswald (1972) and Bateson (1972), among others, the need for involving as many members of the system as possible in therapy is obvious. Zuk (1968, P. 43) has defined family therapy as "the technique that explores and attempts to shift the balance of pathogenic relating among family members so that new forms of relating become possible." Naturally, the most effective means of observing pathogenic relating—triangulation, mystification, binding, disqualifying, etc.—is through having all elements of the family system together and interacting.

The presence of the children in the therapeutic setting provides the family therapist the opportunity to: (1) observe first-hand the interactional patterns between the children and parents; (2) observe the interlocking roles, i.e. the "crucifier" and the "martyr," in the entire family; (3) hear the children's perceptions of the family directly from them; (4) use the children as therapeutic allies by monitoring family change outside the session and by reporting their observations in the therapeutic setting; and (5) actively including the children in assignments given to the family to be completed between sessions.

By having the children present in therapy, the family benefits in the following way: (1) A growing appreciation and respect for one another is usually fostered, (2) All members more fully understand the how and why of their change, thus facilitating the activation of change in the future as stress is encountered by the family, (3) The preventive element of family therapy for the offspring of the children of this family is implemented. This last statement implies that the children can learn how families change from the therapeutic process.

The above advantages for both family and therapist are true, regardless of the ages of the children. Even the newborn infant's presence can contribute to the therapeutic endeavor, as stated by Taschman: "The family interaction patterns in the presence of even an infant (who will not directly benefit from therapy himself) will often give the therapist valuable clues to the family relationships" (Satir, Stachowiak, and Taschman, 1975, P. 28).

An example of this situation is the couple, who, when seen alone, seemed to interact quite openly, but when their infant son was present had significant difficulty in relating. In the presence of the infant, the mother was frequently involved in checking diapers, preparing the bottle, and other activities that the husband responded to with much consternation and quiet withdrawal. Without having the infant present in at least one session, the therapists would not have been able to observe this pattern, which was extremely significant in their treatment. This observation also became the basis for evaluating the effectiveness of change in this couple's relationship. As the therapeutic process progressed, the father became more actively involved with the infant, resulting in both the mother and father learning how to share not only the responsibilities of parenthood, but the joys with one another.

Utilizing Children in the Family Therapy Process

Considering the above, it seems imperative to include the children at some point in the therapeutic setting, regardless of their ages. If the choice is not to include the children all or most of the time, they should be included at least once.

Through actively involving oneself with the children, one can not only learn a considerable amount of information about the family, but also begin to change the family process. Haley (1976) has indicated that the children's answer to why the family is in therapy reveals information to the therapist about secrecy in the family and what sort of splits there may be among the family members. The youngsters' responses can disclose where the alliances and/or coalitions are, who is the scapegoat, who is being parentified, who the youngsters look to for permission to speak, what are silencing mechanisms utilized by the family to keep the children "quiet," and other clues that are equally important to the therapist in developing a design for therapeutic intervention.

Younger children and those without the ability to speak yet provide valuable insights for the therapist. How responsibility for young children is distributed and assumed within the family is determined through observation. Haley (1976) comments:

> For small children, it is always best to have toys and puppets
> in the room so that the child is given the opportunity to communi-
> cate in a 'play' form. The estimate of the child's ability to play
> may be important, as well as the parent's ability to play with the
> child when they are asked to by the therapist. Toys and play
> activities allow action in the room rather than merely conversation
> so the therapist can observe the family members dealing with one
> another. [P. 29]

Zilbach, Bergel, and Gass (1972) have presented an excellent
discussion regarding the importance of including young children
in family therapy and how the medium of play can facilitate
their expression. Through the inclusion of normal play materials,
such as drawing paper, crayons, blackboard, chalk, watercolors,
finger paints, blocks, dollhouse, and dolls, the child is provided
symbols to facilitate communication in the sessions. This also
gives children the opportunity to defend themselves by escaping
into play from the material generated in the session which is too
stringent for their developing egos. Through the results of the
child's play (drawings, paintings, furnishing a dollhouse, etc),
the underlying feeling of the family is many times disclosed.

In the same sense that the child's lack of verbal ability is a
disadvantage to the therapeutic process, a powerful advantage
is also gained. The young child relies extensively on a basic
intuitive instinct, which is more sensitive to affect than adults'
cognitive powers. Once the child has a medium for expression
such as play, the wealth of information gathered by his or her
instincts becomes available in potentially powerful ways. Zilbach,
Bergel, and Gass give the example of the boy who painted a
picture of a bleeding heart with the inside colored black. He
was doing this while his parents were critically presenting their
difficulties with him to the therapists. The therapists in this case
interpreted the boy's production as representing his wish to get
close to his parents and his depression about being unable to
do so.

Intervention can many times be initiated by the therapist
through interaction with the children. Through the therapist's
addressing the children with concern and respect regarding their

perception of the family's situation, all present observe what, in many cases, is an alien way to relate to "kids." This implicitly communicates to all present that this (the therapeutic setting) is an environment where everyone is regarded as important and worthwhile. This move results in powerful modeling for the parents and is effective in joining the children and acquiring their involvement in the therapeutic process. As Ackerman (1970) has suggested, not only should the therapist indicate it is safe for the child to talk, but that there is in the therapeutic setting enough confidence and power to counteract the threat of punishment. Just as there is need to provide safety for the child, there may be times when it is necessary and wise to assist the parents. This is what Bloch (1976, P. 175) states while discussing the role of children in family therapy: "Throughout, the emphasis seems to be on rebalancing. If one is dealing with a scapegoated terrorized child, the therapist must side with the child. . . . If at the other extreme the child turns into a destructive monster and terrifies the patient, the therapist must again equalize the relationship."

The process of assisting parents in relating to their youngsters may come in the form of encouragement and support of their actions or actual intervention by the therapist to model for the parents. In implementing this type of intervention, we believe it is wise to acknowledge Bloch's (1976) admonition about the danger of being motivated to this action out of a sense of competitiveness with the parents. If the therapist determines that competitiveness with the parents appears to be the motivator for intervening with the children, it is probably time to discuss the case with a colleague and/or have a co-therapist sit in a session for consultation.

Inclusion of the children in family therapy not only demonstrates acknowledgment of the family theory orientation and capitalizes upon its advantages, but also makes the therapeutic process more alive and challenging for the therapist. Their presence contributes valuable data to the therapist that cannot be gathered with the same degree of quality in any other means. Just as the presence of all family members implies they were, and are, involved in the development of their situation, it also allows all the opportunity to be actively involved in reaping the benefits of bringing about change.

A trend of recent years is that of education of parents regarding more effective parenting. This is an effort that we applaud, recognizing that as parents change themselves there will be other resultant systematic changes that occur. Oscar Christensen, of the University of Arizona, concluded that many parents have difficulty with their children primarily because they lack information or are functioning with misinformation regarding how to rear children (1971). One apparent shortcoming of most orientations to parent education is that the educators work solely with the parents and do not capitalize on the opportunity for direct observation of the parent-child relation. The opportunity to observe directly increases the impact of the education that is to be carried out.

The remainder of this chapter is devoted to an overview of three primary orientations to parent education: (1) parent training (via Thomas Gordon and Carl Rogers), (2) the Adlerian approach, and (3) behavior modification. The following material presents information that can be imparted educationally with the aim of effecting changes in a family system. As each of these three approaches to parent education are presented, the reader is advised to consider how these newly acquired parenting skills would affect the total family.

PARENT TRAINING

Many of the ideas presented in this section are from the works of Carl Rogers, who introduced the client-centered approach to therapy in the early 1940s, and Thomas Gordon's Parent Effectiveness Training Program (1970). Both approaches attempt to help people (families) become more congruent in their relationships. Congruence is used here to mean the communication of true feelings, negative as well as positive. Rogers (1961, P. 315) has stated the idea in defining the meaning of congruence, "It is as though the map of expression of feelings has come to match more closely the territory of the actual emotional experience."

Carl Rogers's Thoughts on Family Functioning

Carl Rogers believes that family relationships are much richer, as are all human relationships, when they are based on honesty. When relationships are built on pretenses, one of the participants is generally defensive for fear the other might discover what he is truly like and reject him. When assuming this defensive posture, it is hard to imagine two or more people making and maintaining functional human contact. This contact can be facilitated in families by communicating the impact that a person's action has on one's feelings rather than attempting to coerce the person into changing because he is wrong. When a person attempts to coerce another to change, the message generally comes out as a put-down.

Another consideration of Rogers for family living is real two-way communication. This is understanding another person's thoughts and feelings thoroughly, with the meanings they have for him, and to be thoroughly understood by this other person in return. This experience is one of the most rewarding a person can have, but it occurs all too rarely in families, as well as in other human relationships. Gordon has identified various techniques for implementing this.

From Rogers's point of view, once these previous concepts are accepted and integrated into the personality, the next step is that of being able to allow another person to be separate. Many of us are probably not fully cognizant of how we pressure those around us to have the same views and feelings that we experience. This ability to allow another person to be independent comes about only after the person has learned to accept himself. Once this is accomplished, the family circle tends to move in the direction of becoming a number of separate and unique individuals bound together by deep understanding of at least a portion of each other's private worlds.

Thomas Gordon and Parent Effectiveness Training (PET)

Gordon, who was associated with Rogers, has taken many of Rogers's concepts, elaborated upon them, and applied them to a parent training program. This program was first implemented by Gordon in California in 1962. Since that time, the PET Program's impact has increased rapidly and is now in operation in most cities around the nation. Gordon's ideas are grounded in the belief that children do not rebel against parents, but rather against the destructive methods of child rearing almost universally accepted by parents. This approach hopes to assist parents in influencing children to behave out of a genuine consideration for the needs of parents rather than out of fear of punishment or withdrawal of privileges. The PET model is based on the establishment of an effective total relationship with a child, in any and all circumstances.

Gordon recognizes three types of parents as currently being in existence. The first type are the "winners" who dominate and force their will on the child. The second type are the "losers," who give children complete license for fear of frustrating needs. The third kind are the "oscillators," who are not sure what to do and thus vacillate between the two extremes. Gordon presents the *no-lose* method of child rearing, which depends on the parents' learning the skills of nonevaluative listening and effective communication of their own feelings. This means the parents recognize their humanness and that they should not feel guilty if they do not love their children in the same manner or to the same degree from day to day. However, an essential consideration is that parents effectively recognize what it is that they are feeling. As a result of this philosophy, Parent Effectiveness Training (PET) recognizes that parents are inconsistent, as their feelings change from day to day and situation to situation. If parents were to attempt to be consistent, it is impossible to be authentic in dealing with their children. This is accompanied by the idea that parents believe they must always present a united front to their children. This leads to unfair treatment of children in that it amounts to parents' "ganging up" on their children and in many cases leads to "unrealness" on the part of one of the parents. When one of the parents feel accepting toward a child, but their behavior communicates unacceptance, the child really becomes confused. The child now receives contradictory cues and is placed in a bind. Parents often operate under the illusion that they can deceive children from detecting their true feelings. Gordon (1970, P. 25), however, states, "In a relationship as close and enduring as the parent-child relationship, the parent's true feelings seldom can be hidden from the child."

PRINCIPLES OF COMMUNICATION IN THE PARENT EFFECTIVENESS TRAINING MODEL: According to Gordon, when parents say something to a child, they often say something about him. The most important thing to say to the child is, "I accept you," and there are many ways to do it. One way of communicating this is by letting the child be. Rather than unnecessarily interfering with the child, parents should allow the youngster the freedom to be separate. Parents should attempt to allow children to be involved in activities on their own and make, and learn from, their "mistakes." Another method is "passive listening" or silence. Therapists have long been aware of the value of silence in therapy to allow clients to think for themselves. Parents should also be aware of the value of silence and how it can communicate acceptance. With this technique, the person is given the freedom to explore in the presence of a person who is listening intently.

Another technique is that of active listening, involving the roles of "sender" and "receiver." This approach differs from passive listening in that the "receiver" here is more active. This approach is aimed at reducing misunderstanding of the sender's message. This technique is based on the concept of feedback. The receiver gives feedback to the sender as to how he interprets what has been sent. In this way, the sender has an opportunity to determine if he is truly being understood. The receiver puts into his own words what he feels the sender's message meant—not evaluation, opinion, logic, analysis, or question.

Active listening accomplishes many tasks important for good parent-child relationships. It helps children discover exactly what they are feeling, rather than suppressing or repressing them. The child is also helped to accept his feelings, even the negative feelings he may experience. This method also increases the amount of warmth in the relationship. Whenever one feels understood and accepted by a person, feelings of warmth seem to grow toward that person. Problem solving by the child is facilitated through active listening.

Before active listening can be used effectively, the potential user must possess certain attitudes. The parent must want to hear what it is the child has to say and have the time to be effective. Genuineness in the desire to help must also be present. Parents should also be willing to accept whatever the feelings are that the child wishes to express. This implies, in many instances, allowing the child to be different and separate from you as a parent. Along with this concept, parents should attempt to realize that feelings are transitory and that hate can turn to love or pessimism to optimism quite rapidly.

PROBLEM-RESOLUTION SKILLS: According to Gordon, there are two *win-lose* approaches to conflict resolution: (1) the parents win, even if power has to be resorted to or (2) the child wins at the expense of the parent. In both approaches, one of the parties is defeated and generally feels quite resentful.

Another approach to problem resolution is the one Gordon advocates. This is referred to as the *no-lose* method of resolving conflicts, referred to as *Method III*. This method is used frequently by equals in possession of power. When there is an equal amount of power possessed by two individuals, there are obvious reasons why neither desires to resort to power as a means of problem resolution. In Method III, the equality is assumed and both win because the solution must be acceptable to both. Method III facilitates the development of better relationships in several ways. First, children are motivated to carry out the solution because they were part of the decision-making process. They have been invested in the problem solving and thus feel a commitment. This method also develops the child's thinking skills. Use of Method III also facilitates the development of more love and respect in the relationship and lessens hostility. Another advantage of Method III is that it requires less reinforcement by parents and thus eliminates the need for power. This approach thus enhances a child's self-concept through the communication of respect and equality.

The no-lose method explained is greatly facilitated by the use of active and passive listening. During this process, feelings are explored and acceptance is communicated. Along with this, Gordon has identified six steps in the implementation of Method III:

1. Identifying and defining the conflict
2. Generating possible alternative solutions
3. Evaluating the alternative solutions
4. Deciding on the best acceptable solution
5. Working out ways of implementing the solution
6. Following up to evaluate how it worked

CHANGING THE ENVIRONMENT TO AFFECT CHILDREN'S BEHAVIOR: One of the most well-known means of changing behavior through environmental manipulation is enriching the environment. This is simply a procedure of providing children with a great many interesting objects and activities to do. These objects and activities might consist of toys, paints, crayons, puzzles, and friends, etc.

There are also times that impoverishing the environment is important; examples are bed- and mealtime. If the child is overstimulated just before these times, it is unfair for the parents to expect him to change his feelings immediately.

Childproofing the environment is another approach parents can use in this category. This is done by using unbreakable glasses and cups; putting matches out of the child's reach; removing expensive, breakable objects; making upstairs screens secure; removing slippery throw rugs; and avoiding the purchase of furniture with sharp edges.

Substituting one activity for another is an example of another effective technique. Simply taking something away from a child without offering a substitute usually results in the child feeling angry and somewhat rejected. Replacing the object removed with something else is more acceptable to the child and results in less conflict for the adult.

The Adlerian Approach to Parent Education

Alfred Adler began developing his concepts while he was still a student of Freud's and continued to do so after the two parted ways. Adler theorized that since personal problems ultimately emanate from social interaction, such problems could be resolved more efficiently with group methods than by treating the offspring in isolation and returning them to the family in which the conflict exists. The premise underlying this technique is that the counselor helps the parents to develop new attitudes toward their offspring. An issue of primary concern for the counselor is that of helping the parents to understand the goals of their children's behavior. Various phases of the Adlerian counseling process have been identified and are now discussed.

The *relationship phase* is based on mutual trust and respect. Without the proper relationship being established, the counselor should not attempt to go any further. In addition, throughout the process, careful attention should be given the relationship, and if a disturbance occurs, it should be given immediate attention. The reason such importance is attached to this phase is that it is more than a means of counseling; it is also a prerequisite for the cooperation necessary in counseling. This appears to be especially true in working with parents of exceptional children, who may look for the slightest innuendo made by the counselor to terminate the counseling relationship that they perceive as becoming more threatening.

The *exploration phase* involves the exploration of the child's life-style, the basic premises on which he or she operates, his or her basic mistakes about himself and life, and the goals he or she has set for him- or herself. In working with parents, this is a vital stage as the counselor attempts to understand what the goals are that the parents have set for their child and themselves as parents.

Revealing goals, or *interpretation,* is one of the most important steps in promoting the last phase of reorientation. The goal is to try to make the parents aware of what it is they are doing to perpetuate their present situation. Adlerians believe that recognition of self-determined goals and purposes promote motivation to change more rapidly than other methods. Bringing the parents' real intentions of their behavior to their attention is the concern in this phase. As Adler pointed out, an effective therapeutic technique is "spitting in the patient's soup." He can continue what he is doing, but it does not taste so good.

The last phase is *reorientation.* It is a mistake, according to the Adlerians, to suggest that the client should change his behavior. As long as the parents maintain their outlook, they cannot act differently. At times, simply thinking the problem through together leads the parents to an awareness of the mistakes in their concepts and ideas and result in change. In this stage, encouragement is the most effective tool for assisting parents in changing behavior. As most people do not realize their own contribution to the present situation, so they fail to recognize their own power and ability to produce a change.

As in all counseling, the art of listening is paramount on the part of the counselor. Only through listening is it possible for the counselor to detect what the parents' beliefs and attitudes are. Through listening, the counselor can formulate a tentative hypothesis and then gather further information to validate or dispute it. It can also be emphasized here that good parent-child relationships depend on understanding children's goals. In addition, the useful dictum that a child needs encouragement as a plant needs water for growth can be emphasized. The counselor can communicate here how parents often discourage their children, through good intentions, by assuming too much responsibility for them.

GOALS OF CHILDREN'S MISBEHAVIOR: In assisting parents in the understanding of their children's goals, the Adlerians refer to the following model. Adlerians believe that if parents can learn to understand the reasons behind a child's behavior, they are in a better position to correct it. Children's behavior, from this point of view, is seen as the result of a child's mistaken assumption about the way to find a place in the family and gain status. By not being aware of the meaning of the child's misbehavior, the parents respond by falling for the child's scheme and reinforce the mistaken goal. Adlerians recognize four such goals: (1) attention getting, (2) a struggle for power, (3) revenge, and (4) using disability as an excuse.

Attention-getting behavior is manifested when the child wants attention and service. Parents can generally determine whether this is their child's goal by observing their own reaction. If the parent's reaction to the child's behavior is one of feeling annoyed and a need to remind and coax the child, it can be assumed that attention getting is the child's goal.

The child with *power* as his goal is striving to be the boss.

When this is the child's goal, the parents usually respond by feeling provoked and enter into a power contest with him. What most parents do not know is that the child's goal is to get the parent involved in the struggle, not necessarily to win it. From the child's point of view, though, once the parent has joined the battle, the child has already won it.

Revenge is another goal. The child manifesting this type of behavior believes everybody is against him, and the only way to get recognition is to retaliate against adults for the way he feels he has been treated. This child is attempting to hurt those in his environment. Parents can determine if this is the goal of their child's behavior by examining their feelings in response to the behavior. If they feel deeply hurt and a sense of wanting to "get even," this is a good indicator that revenge is the child's goal.

Behavior designed to achieve the goal of *display of inadequacy* can be most frustrating. The child whose behavior is motivated by this goal wants to be left alone, with no demands made upon him. If the parents' first impulse is to react by feeling despair and not knowing what to do, this is probably the goal of the child's behavior. It is through this method that the child tries to avoid further humiliation by not attempting anything and risking failure or ridicule.

The four types of behavior mentioned above occur only when the child is discouraged and is not able to find his place in the family or peer group in a constructive manner. The Adlerians do not recognize children as being "bad," but rather as being unhappy, misguided, and discouraged. When the children feel this way, they resort to the behavior patterns identified above in order to gain what they perceive as significant. If the child is discouraged in his efforts as he utilizes one of the goals, such as attention getting, he descends to the next goal until he is so ultimately discouraged that he manifests "assumed disability," which is the final stage of discouragement.

ADLERIAN TECHNIQUES FOR EFFECTING CHANGE: The Adlerians have developed several techniques, or concepts, that are discussed as ways of implementing the aforementioned knowledge. The Adlerian counselor frowns on punishment as it has been used throughout history. Punishment from this frame of reference is used to express the power of personal authority and retaliation. Rather than use punishment, the use of natural and logical consequences are encouraged. Both of these techniques allow the child to experience the actual result of his own behavior.

Natural consequences are the direct result of the child's behavior. For example, a child is careless in his behavior, falls down, hurts his knee. The next time, he will be more careful. The parents must be careful not to destroy any of these valuable opportunities by a miscalculated zeal to keep their child from discomfort but rather allow him the chance to learn from experience. The only time at which parents must interfere is if the child is endangering himself or others.

Logical consequences are established by the parents and are a direct and logical consequence of the transgression that is not arbitrarily imposed. An example of this is the child who comes to dinner late and finds that his plate has been removed. It is important though that the parents not assume a defensive posture and begin to lecture, but rather maintain a friendly attitude. The parents can assume that the child was not hungry enough to come for dinner.

In both instances, the parent allows the child to experience the consequence of his actions. With these techniques, the child experiences the social order in which he lives and thus is motivated toward proper behavior. Natural consequences are always effective, and logical consequences can only be applied if there is no power contest involved. If logical consequences are enforced with power, they simply degenerate into punitive retaliation. The power of logical consequences is that it distinguishes between the deed and the doer so that the idea of worthlessness is not being communicated to the child but rather his act. In addition, the child is relieved of the feeling that he is subject to the whim of an authority over which he has no control. The use of natural and logical consequences gives the child the choice of deciding for himself whether or not he wants to repeat a given act.

Encouragement is another basic concept of the Adlerians. *Encouragement,* as used here, means faith in, and respect for, the child as he is. A child becomes discouraged when parents have standards that are too high or overambitious for him. When the child becomes discouraged it is then that he misbehaves because he believes that he cannot succeed by useful means. Adlerians feel strongly that a child needs encouragement like a plant needs water for growth. Because of this, parents should try to refrain from telling the child he can do better, for what is being communicated then is that he is not good enough as he is.

In times of parent-child relationship stress, it is believed best to act rather than talk. Talking should be restricted to friendly conversations. In cases where the child demands undue attention or tries to involve the parent in a power struggle, *withdrawal* is the best approach. If nobody pays a child any attention, his tantrums or annoying behavior gain no satisfaction for him. "The less attention a child gets when he disturbs, the more he needs when he is cooperative," is the tenet to remember in this respect.

Adlerians have postulated that a "dependent" child is a demanding child. As a result of this, parents should allow the child to be independent and never do for him what he can do for himself. Children only become irresponsible and dependent when they are not given responsibility and independence. Although parents may believe they are giving when they act for a child, actually they are taking away the child's right to learn and develop. When parents act for their children, they are probably communicating to the child that he is weak and helpless. The child who has always had things done for him is inevitably helpless when left to his own resources. A child who always "forgets" usually has a mother who always remembers. In cases similar to this, if the parent feels sorry for the child, he will shortly feel justified in feeling sorry for himself and soon believe that life owes him something.

The last concept to be mentioned in this section is the *family council*. This is a regularly scheduled gathering of the family in which all members are invited to express both positive and negative thoughts pertaining to the family structure and process. In this approach, each member has an equal vote and should be training for living in a democracy. During these meetings the parents should refrain from lecturing or imposing their will on the children. If a negative situation is brought up by any member the emphasis should be on what "we" can do about it, and not simply dwelling on the situation itself. The chairmanship should be rotated every week, and decisions that may be thought of as being poor should stand until the following week. It is during these times that logical consequences can be discussed and established.

For pamphlets and books on the Adlerian approach to parenting, the reader is referred to the Alfred Adler Institute, 110 South Dearborn, Chicago, Illinois. The Institute has available many fine publications with much bibliotherapeutic value for parents.

The Behavioral Approach to Parent Counseling

The behavioral approach is based on the premise of teaching parents how to manage or change their child's behavior through the management of consequences of behavior. In this section, consequences are understood as connoting any event that follows a response that can strengthen or weaken that response. Consequences can be understood as being synonymous with rewards or punishments. It is important at this point to clarify the difference between punishment and negative reinforcement. Punishment has been defined as an environmental event that decreases the rate of the response it follows. From the definition, the reader should be able to ascertain that punishment is incurred after a child demonstrates a type of behavior that is generally unpleasant from the adult's point of view.

The concept of negative reinforcement suggests that unpleasant or undesirable behavior is prevented before it actually occurs. Negative reinforcement consists of removing something that could be punishing, so the child avoids the punishing event by doing what is required of him. The most common form of negative reinforcement resorted to by adults is that of threats. The child is advised that if he does not do something desired of him, unpleasant consequences will be the result. It is reasoned then that the behavior desired of him is reinforced by avoiding unpleasant consequences.

The behavioral approach assumes that behavior is not random

but rather operates on the basis of general principles or laws of behavior. It is also assumed that when a parent knows about these principles of behavior, he or she knows what to do to change present behavior patterns of the child. As a result, the counselor is cast in the role of a teacher. The steps vital to this process consist of determining what the undesired behavior is; getting an accurate measurement of how frequently it occurs and under what circumstances; establishing a specific behavioral goal for behavior change; implementing behavior modification techniques to change the behavior; and finally, evaluation to determine how effective the behavior modification techniques were in changing behavior.

ESTABLISHING THE BASE LINE: The first step in the behavioral approach to assisting parents is that of establishing a reference point from which to measure change. In order to determine whether what the parents do is effective, an accurate measure of the rate of the undesired behavior must be procured. This measure is referred to as the *base rate* or *base line* and is used to establish goals and to determine if there is changed behavior as a result of changed consequences or variables. To establish the base rate, the parents should be requested to count the number of times the specified undesirable behavior is demonstrated by the child. The parents can assess and record the behavior every time it occurs or record it only during randomly selected periods of time. If the behavior occurs infrequently it is wise to have the parents record it every time it is presented. If, on the other hand, the behavior is demonstrated frequently, it might be wise to have them randomly select a few minute periods each hour during which they chart or record the behavior. To check on reliability of the recorded base line, it might be suggested that the parents keep separate base lines for comparison purposes.

With good base line measurements established, the parents can be much more efficient and precise in changing the specified behavior. This procedure also gives the parents constant feedback to indicate that some alterations are needed in the program as presently designed.

GOAL SETTING: After the behavior has been charted, the next

step is that of establishing an adequate behavioral goal. The goal must be defined precisely so it is possible to determine the steps needed to achieve the desired end goal, or terminal behavior. The steps should be precisely defined, with each one being an important link in the learning process. As a result, the steps in changing behavior should be a logical, sequential series of intermediate goals.

At this stage, the counselor should help the parents determine what is reinforcing for the child, so that a payoff for desired behaviors can be determined. The parents can decide what is rewarding for a child by paying particular attention to what happens immediately before and after a specified behavior to determine what constitutes reward. Another simple but effective means of establishing what is rewarding for a child is to ask him what he likes. Once the parents know what they will use as a reward with the child, have the child's behavior charted, and have a specific terminal behavior identified, they are ready to begin shaping the child's behavior.

CHANGING CHILDREN'S BEHAVIOR: This stage implements behavior modification techniques. Probably the one technique that is used most frequently is that of shaping a child's behavior through the use of positive reinforcement. As already mentioned, most behavior is affected by its consequences. The probability of behavior recurring is related to the effect it has on securing positive or negative outcomes from the environment. With this knowledge in mind, the parents are advised to issue whatever is reinforcing for the child immediately upon completion of the desired behavior. Timing is important, as has been documented in a considerable amount of research, which demonstrated that the sooner the reward appeared after the desired behavior, the more effect it had. Another important consideration is the idea of consistency of reward administration. If the reward is administered too infrequently, the child may not associate the reward with the desired behavior. This idea is referred to as *schedule of reinforcement*.

The idea of rewarding the child after every instance of the desired behavior is referred to as a *continuous schedule of reinforcement*. Another form of a reinforcement schedule is the *intermittent schedule.* This may take the form of a *ratio schedule,* where the desired behavior must occur a specified number of times before the reward is administered, or an *interval schedule,* where a certain amount of time, during which the child was demonstrating desirable behavior, must elapse for the child to be rewarded.

Research has demonstrated that the *variable ratio schedule* maintains the highest rates of responding and is the least resistant to extinction. In the variable ratio schedule of reinforcement, the child is reinforced or rewarded after he has demonstrated the desired behavior a number of times. The number of times the behavior must be present before he is rewarded is not static, but everchanging. For instance, he may be rewarded the first time after he has demonstrated the desired behavior twice, then after demonstrating it four times, then three times, then twice, and so on. The main consideration is not to let the child go too long before he is reinforced, for the desired behavior might not occur any longer if a reward is not collected. This is an individual matter and a consideration that must be individualized to each unique child, depending on his or her age and emotional maturity.

Another consideration in using positive reinforcement to shape behavior is that of rewarding successive approximations. As discussed in the section dealing with deciding upon the behavioral goal, or terminal behavior, the goal consists of a logical sequence of behaviors leading to the terminal behavior. The parents should not believe they can get the desired terminal behavior with one administration of a reward or that it will ever occur immediately. Because of this, the parents should be encouraged to reinforce approximations of the desired terminal behavior and in this way shape the child's behavior toward the end result. If this concept is not thoroughly understood by the parents, it could lead to much frustration and the eventual destruction of their program for behavior change.

Before leaving the concept of reinforcement as an agent of a behavioral change, the various categories or reinforcers are discussed: (1) edibles, (2) social stimuli, (3) tokens, and (4) the Premack principle.

The *edible* category of reinforcers is quite self-explanatory. The child is administered something he can eat or drink after each demonstration of desired behavior. The main concern here, as with all reinforcers, is that the edible is something the child likes.

Social stimuli or reinforcers are probably the most frequently used form of reinforcement. These are verbal or physical displays of approval and commendation on the part of the person administering the rewards. Rewards such as commenting "Good," or a pat on the shoulder or head are administered.

Token reinforcers are those rewards that are symbols, with some value, that the child can collect and later redeem for something he wants. Tokens are administered to the child in direct proportion to the types of behavior he or she is manifesting. The more desired the behavior manifested is, the more the value of the tokens received.

The last category of reinforcers is that of the *"Premack principle."* This means employing a behavior that occurs at a high frequency as a reward for behavior that occurs at a low frequency. Although the name is rather esoteric sounding, this is probably an idea parents have been utilizing for thousands of years. An example is the parent who allows the daughter to watch her favorite television show for helping with the evening dishes.

Along with shaping the desired behavior through positive reinforcement, the parents may want to attempt to eliminate opposing, undesirable behavior. The three most prevalent behavior modification techniques for eliminating undesirable behavior are punishment, negative reinforcement, and the process of extinction. In an earlier discussion, it was indicated that punishment is an unpleasant stimulus imposed on the child after he demonstrates undesirable behavior; negative reinforcement occurs when the child realizes that if he does not demonstrate the desired behavior, a negative or unpleasant stimulus will be administered to him. Extinction simply consists of not reinforcing a behavioral act in any way.

At the beginning of this discussion, it was pointed out that behavior occurs in relation to the reinforcement it elicits. If behavior produces no reinforcement it will disappear, the premise on which *extinction* is based. Although the concept of extinction is simplistic sounding, it can be extremely difficult to implement. For instance, in the case of undesired behavior, the child usually gets some reward out of seeing his parents becoming agitated and giving him attention, even if it is of a negative nature. When the parents decide to utilize extinction they must be certain all sources of reinforcement are eliminated completely and not just reduced. The key lies in avoiding any controlled reward when an unacceptable behavior occurs. The extinction procedure seems to be most effective when used simultaneously with a positive reinforcement program. In essence, then, what the parents are doing is systematically redistributing the rewards for new behaviors. The older, undesired behaviors no longer receive rewards, and the opposing, more desirable behaviors are heavily reinforced.

Another example of a behavior modification technique that is used to shape behavior is *modeling*. This is the process whereby children are exposed to role models participating in what is deemed desirable behavior and being reinforced for it. In the procedure, neighborhood children or siblings of the problem child, might be used as role models for the child to imitate. To shape the child's behavior, he is exposed to modeled behavior that is relatively close to his current behavior, with the difference in the direction of the desired terminal behavior. By viewing behavior that is slightly different from his own and observing the model rewarded for this behavior, the child tends to adopt that behavior pattern. The child is then exposed to more demonstrated behavior patterns that are in the direction of the identified terminal behavior. As a result, the child's behavior is changed through observation of modeled behaviors. Although modeling appears to be most effective when using live models, it has been demonstrated that effective changes can be implemented by having a child observe models on film or videotape. The most important consideration in implementing this concept is that the child must observe the models receiving what he perceives as being desirable reinforcement for demonstrating desired behaviors.

The last behavior modification principle to be discussed is that one known as *negative practice*. Negative practice is based on the premise that continued repetition of an undesirable response satiates the need for its occurrence and thus extinguishes it. This technique is most appropriate for an annoying verbalization that a child resorts to continually or a motor behavior that has become irritating to those in his environment. In this approach, the child, under the direction of an adult, repeats the unacceptable behavior over and over until he is bored, fatigued, and no longer derives satisfaction from the act. After this extensive repetition, the act takes on negative properties and is extinguished from his repertoire of behavior responses. This concept is one that has not received nearly the amount of research that previously mentioned behavior modification techniques have and thus must be used with discretion.

EVALUATION OF THE CHANGE PROCESS: The last step to be discussed in the process of changing behavior, from this approach, is that of assessing the effectiveness or degree to which the terminal behavior was achieved. As previously mentioned, assessment of effectiveness of the behavior modification program occurs continually to determine if the sequential steps are operational and if the rewards being used are truly reinforcing. The final assessment is whether or not the child has achieved the desired terminal behavior. Occasionally, time that elapses before the terminal behavior occurs is included in the behavioral objective, but this should be given careful consideration before being included as part of the stated objective. In one way, it might serve as motivation for the parents, but it can also serve as a source of frustration to the parents who do not achieve their goal by the end of the designated time period. As a result, it is wise for the counselor to consider the needs of the parents before including time as a part of the behavioral goal.

This has been a review of basic concepts with which the counselor working with parents from a behavioral approach should be familiar. For a more detailed discussion of these principles, the reader is referred to publications such as the following: Becker, 1971; Krumboltz and Krumboltz, 1972; Madsen and Madsen, 1972; Patterson, 1971; and Patterson and

Gullion, 1968. Although it has been amply demonstrated that laymen can implement behavior modification techniques effectively, it is recognized that professionals familiar with behavioral principles should develop the behavioral objectives. One of the most important steps in changing behavior is that of developing sequential steps to the terminal behavior. If the steps are constructed in such a manner that too much distance exists between them, the objective collapses. Another consideration in constructing the steps is that they are logical and follow one another in sequence.

One last consideration for the counselor is that of reinforcing the parents' efforts. Times may occur when the parents are frustrated with the lack of evident progress being made, and it is at these times the counselor should offer encouragement and point out what successes have been achieved as a result of the behavior change program. Only through consistent application of reinforcement and other behavior modification techniques can they be effectively implemented; this should be emphasized in working with parents.

SUMMARY

Regardless of which of the above modalities or combinations the therapist decides to employ, there are certain guiding principles that seem appropriate for consideration. Attempt to make certain that the parents fully understand what they are deciding to do. Facilitate both parents discussing what they want and how they are going to get it. This diffuses the possibility of the two of them becoming irritated with one another or the change process and discontinuing their efforts. Once they have arrived at an agreed-upon plan, role playing can be valuable to their efforts. Establish a scenario in the session that allows them to practice what it is they have agreed to do. It is also valuable for the parents to discuss ways in which they can monitor and support one another in their efforts to bring about change in relationships with their children.

Working with parents on parenting skills can be a valuable

way to change families. It can effectively change parent-child relationships and in the process change the quality of the parent-parent relationship as well. This process, then, sets into motion a very positive circular process of parents feeling better about their relationships with the children; the children feeling the same way; and the parents feeling more comfortable and supportive in relation to each other.

CHAPTER 11

SEX, ALCOHOL, AND DEATH IN THE FAMILY

Tʜɪꜱ ᴄʜᴀᴘᴛᴇʀ ʟᴏᴏᴋꜱ at the influence of three apparently different variables that have commonalities in regard to the family unit. Sex, alcohol, and death have been identified and accepted as having a significant impact on family life. Along with this acknowledged impact, each of these three has until recently been regarded as taboo material for open discussion. Considering that sex and death influence every family, and alcoholism is affecting at least nine million Americans, these are variables that the person who plans on working with couples and families must comprehend. In arranging this chapter, consideration was given to the developmental stages of families, as in Chapter 3. This thinking resulted in presenting sex first, as this is an issue that generally confronts couples quite soon in the development of their relationship. Alcohol seems to be presented as a concern by families in the middle, or child-rearing years. Death, other than accidental, generally affects the family toward the latter child-rearing years, as grandparents die, followed then by parents. This is the reason for its placement in this chapter.

SEX IN THE PERSPECTIVE OF THE MARITAL RELATIONSHIP

As knowledge of human sexuality has made rapid advances in the past two decades, so has the treatment of sexual dysfunctions. Professionals have moved from the era of regarding sexual dysfunction as psychopathological. Most treatment modalities for sexual dysfunction today are based on short-term treatment directed at the elimination of the specific problem.

As Kaplan (1974) and others have stated, it seems that most

sexual dysfunctions occur in people who are quite functional in other areas of living. Many therapists who specialize in treating sexual dysfunctions have documented how often the roots of sexual dysfunction rest in variables such as fear of being rejected and humiliated by the partner, anticipated failure to function, and real and/or imagined demands to perform in accord with unrealistic criteria. It seems that therapists have now developed enough of a sense of security and maturity that they can attend to these simpler and more immediate problems. Historically, to have dealt with such immediate and "surface" problems would have been heresy, due to its lack of concern with "in-depth" study.

Sexual therapy, as a separate field, has as its primary goal amelioration of the sexual dysfunction. Those who are primarily identified with sexual therapy, and especially of the brief intervention format, report positive results. Among this group are Masters and Johnson in St. Louis and Kaplan at Cornell University, who report success in greater than 70 percent of the cases treated for secondary impotence. Along with a specific set of therapeutic intervention skills it seems another variable accounts for the success reported by those who work from a brief intervention posture.

Relationship difficulties are often reported simultaneously with sexual difficulties. Which came first is often a mute question, for it seems the process is predictable. The difficulty is followed by hurt, irritation, frustration, and other emotions that confound the difficulties in the sexual arena, which result in a more intense sense of hurt or irritation, etc., or even worse, one of apathetic indifference. If the process disintegrates to one of apathetic indifference, it is unlikely a therapist will have contact with the couple and it is more reasonable to suspect the divorce attorney will be visited. Considering the pattern identified above, a crucial consideration becomes that of intervening to break the counterproductive nature of the behavior. One means of doing this is to focus specifically on the sexual dysfunction in an intense and direct fashion. As change is effected in the area of their sexual functioning, feelings of a more positive nature begin to pervade the relationship and result in even more favorable sexual functioning, which then intensifies the positive feelings and so on.

The reader may see that the destructive process brought into the therapeutic setting has been disrupted and changed to a more positive and relationship-enhancing process.

Although much attention has been given to sex therapy in recent years, it seems realistic to believe that the prominence of sexual problems as a primary concern of clinicial couples has not changed significantly from DeBurger's (1975) study. He indicates that his study revealed nearly one-fourth of the couples perceived their marital trouble as being a result of some form of maladjustment in sexual relations. Albert Ellis (1969), took a somewhat different approach to identifying the pervasiveness of sexual problems in discordant relationships. He identified one hundred consecutive couples who came to him for therapy. As part of his routine questioning, he asked them about the presence of sexual problems in their relationship, and if present, the type of sexual difficulty experienced. He determined that in only six of the one hundred couples seen were there no reported sexual difficulties. This rate of reported sexual difficulty, among a clinical population, is consonant with our experience as well as with other clinicians with whom we have discussed this matter.

Acknowledging the prominent role of sexual difficulties in discordant relationships, the concern with etiology and treatment still stands. We believe to become overly involved with the question of what came first, the destructive and negative affect that characterizes the relationship or the sexual dysfunction, is in most cases time consuming and not much more than mental exercise. What seems to be of primary importance is to intervene and change the process in the relationship that is resulting in dissatisfaction for one or both partners. Considering this, there are various options available for intervention purposes.

Among the options available, one is to treat the specific sexual dysfunction. A primary advantage of this option is that the dysfunction itself is generally easier to identify and define than most other relationship issues. The famous educational philosopher, John Dewey, has stated that a problem well defined is half-solved, and this seems to be appropriate for treating relationships. The specificity with which the problem is identified allows the therapist to select problem-specific techniques, and both the therapist and couple can then more readily assess their effectiveness. A major disadvantage of attacking the sexual dysfunction unilaterally is that if the problem is more pervasive to the relationship, it may not be responsive to the sexually oriented interventions. The failure of the therapeutic interventions then results in a greater sense of frustration and hopelessness for the couple, which may then compound the relationship difficulties.

Another option available to the therapist is that of treating the couple's sexual problem as symptomatic of a pernicious relationship problem. The basic idea in this approach is that as the couple improves, for example, in the area of communication, their general affect held toward one another will change, which then stimulates sexual activity of a more satisfying nature. In this example of concentrating on improving their communication skills, along with the more positive effect engendered, they may also be able to discuss openly their sexual likes and dislikes for the first time and negotiate a more satisfying sexual relationship. Again, the reader is alerted to the "ripple effect" that is so prominent in working with a social system. Intervention is directed toward one element of the system, and as change is effected in the target area, the results ripple out to other dimensions. A major disadvantage of this approach rests in an answer to a "what if" question. What if the couple's identified sexual dysfunction is just that and not symptomatic of other more "major" difficulties? The chances for further compounding their situation then becomes a possibility. They begin to experience increased frustration with their spouse and relationship secondary to the lack of change, and the amplified affect results in less of a commitment to the relationship and hope for change.

The last option to be identified is a combination of both of the above. It seems safe to assume that sexual dysfunctions can exist as the only area of concern for a couple or as a symptom of more pervasive relationship issues. As already mentioned, we acknowledge that the greatest majority of couples seen are going to be indicating dissatisfaction with the sexual element of their relationship. With this in mind, it seems judicious to pay particular attention to the couple in the first few interviews to determine what weight will be placed on the sexual issue for treatment.

If the couple places great prominence on sexual dissatisfaction, this is a cue to focus attention on it in intervention. When the couple gives secondary or only passing acknowledgment to the sexual concern, we may also decide to give it the same regard in treatment considerations. If the latter option is chosen and it is determined that we are not progressing at a rate satisfactory to either the couple or ourselves, we may return to the sexual issue originally identified. The reason for returning to the sexual concern is that it may have a more prominent role in the relationship than either spouse was able to identify for various reasons. Many times we have found that returning to the sexual dysfunction when at an impasse stimulates the therapeutic process. Change can be quickly engendered in the sexual facet of the relationship, which leads to renewed hope and positive affect for both partners and serves as a catalyst to change throughout the relationship.

Common Sexual Dysfunctions

An overview of the more common sexual dysfunctions are presented in this section. Readers who are interested in a more thorough discussion of this area will find books by the following authors worthwhile: Belliveau and Richter, 1970; Kaplan, 1974; and Masters and Johnson, 1966 and 1970.

Before presenting a description of the various sexual dysfunctions, a quote from Masters and Johnson (1970, P. 2) seems appropriate: "There is no such thing as an uninvolved partner in any marriage in which there is some form of sexual inadequacy."

Masters and Johnson clearly captured a basic tenet that we hope the reader has comprehended throughout this book. In a social system as complex as marriages and families, if "one individual has a problem," then everyone else in that system is involved. In the area of treating sexual dysfunction, it is especially tempting to perceive the problem as "belonging" to an individual. If the husband is experiencing erectile failure, it is "easy" to say that this is "his problem" and treat him individually. With the woman experiencing vaginismus, it is likewise tempting to say "she has a problem" and treat her individually. "After all isn't it their body?" Naturally, the answer to this question is yes. To the "yes" though, must be added a "but." Yes, *but* the problem is occurring within the context of *their* relationship. Because of the consideration given to the context in which the problem is manifested we, along with those such as Masters and Johnson, Hartman and Fithian (1974), and Kaplan (1974), want both partners involved to enhance both understanding and treatment effectiveness with the situation.

Premature ejaculation is one of the more common sexual dysfunctions presented in a clinical setting. There are basically two ways to define this condition. One is to look upon the man's inability to delay ejaculation long enough for the woman to have orgasm 50 percent of the time. If the woman is unable to experience orgasm for reasons other than her partner's rapid ejaculation, this definition does not apply. Masters and Johnson (1970) use this definition because it considers satisfaction of both partners as the primary criterion. Others define premature ejaculation as an inability to delay ejaculating for thirty seconds to a minute after the penis is in the vagina. Regardless of which definition is utilized, premature ejaculation is the most common sexual dysfunction of men and also the most easily relieved. *Primary prematurity* refers to that condition where the male has never been able to control orgasm. *Secondary prematurity* describes that condition where the male developed a problem after a history of good control.

Ejaculatory incompetence is the opposite of premature ejaculation. In this condition, the male is unable to ejaculate while his penis is contained in his partner's vagina. Most of these men can ejaculate through masturbation or even fellatio, but have a mental block against allowing their seminal fluid to enter the vagina. In its milder forms, the male may only experience this difficulty in specific anxiety-provoking situations, such as when with a new partner or when he experiences guilt about the sexual encounter. Seldom is a physical-organic condition related to this dysfunction. Common explanations for this condition are a strict religious upbringing, suppressed anger, fear of abandonment, and/or ambivalence toward his partner. As with the

premature ejaculator, the male with this dysfunction often antici-
pates failure and frustration, which compounds and often leads
to his inability to maintain an erection.

Male impotence is that dysfunction defined as the male being
unable to develop and maintain an erection to allow penetration
of the vagina or because of being unable to maintain his erection
long enough after vaginal penetrating to ejaculate. *Primary
impotence* is characterized by that situation where the male has
never been potent with a female, although he may be able to
maintain a good erection in other situations. The male who has
functioned well prior to onset of the impotence is characterized
as experiencing *secondary impotence*. Fatigue, excessive drinking,
undiagnosed diabetes, hepatitis, low androgen levels, depression,
and guilt have all been linked to impotence in the male.

The reader will notice that as attention is turned to the more
common female sexual dysfunctions, many of the same etiological
sources are identified as were true of males. Belliveau and
Richter (1970) seem to have caught the essence of the rationale
for this situation.

> But what if a person has not had the opportunity or the informa-
> tion with which to construct a positive value system about sex?
> Worse yet, what if everything a child or young person growing up
> has heard or been taught about sex is negative? Of course, in these
> instances, the signals from the psychosocial system will exert a
> negative influence on sexual functioning. Both sexes need positive
> signals from both systems to be sexually capable. To this extent,
> the sexual problems of men and women have similar sources.
> [P. 158]

Female orgasmic dysfunction is that situation where the
woman is having difficulty experiencing an orgasm. This is
probably the most common situation presented by females in
the clinical setting. *Primary orgasmic dysfunction* pertains to
the woman who has never experienced an orgasm by any means.
Women with *secondary orgasmic dysfunction* responded orgasm-
ically at one time but no longer are able to respond. Reasons
offered for the presence of this condition are: excessive and
punitive religious beliefs; ambivalence or blatant dissatisfaction
with her partner; marriage to a sexually inadequate male; and

lack of sufficient emotional maturity to develop female identification and development of a functional sexual value system.

Vaginismus is that condition where the female experiences an involuntary tightening or spasm in the outer third of the vagina, resulting in either a complete inability to be penetrated, or the woman experiences penetration, but only with considerable pain. Reasons for this dysfunction consist of fear of pain resultant from vaginal penetration; family background that associates sex with sin; a husband's impotence; psychological effects of rape, and more pervasive relationship problems. Physical problems that may result in vaginismus are a rigid hymen, inflammatory pelvic diseases and tumors, hemorrhoids, and childbirth pathologies. Naturally these are conditions that should be ruled out by the physician in a physical examination prior to sexual therapy with the couple where the female partner indicates vaginismus is a problem.

Dyspareunia (painful intercourse) and lack of erotic response to sexual stimulation is the last female sexual dysfunction to be mentioned. This condition is very commonly encountered in the clinical setting. In most cases, a physical examination does not determine the cause. It seems that a combination of psychological and physiological events related to the attitude she holds toward the partner are the primary instigators. The pain is usually caused by the lack of vaginal lubrication.

Vaginal lubrication is the female response to sexual stimulation that parallels the presence of an erection by the male. In the absence of vaginal lubrication, the woman is probably neither physiologically nor psychologically ready for intercourse. Women plagued with this condition quite naturally derive little, if any, erotic pleasure from sexual stimulation. This dysfunction is most commonly associated, as one might guess, with the woman who has no affection, respect, or understanding for her partner and usually perceives none of these emanating from him. Fears such as pregnancy, pain, or inadequacy in the male may also precipitate this situation. Infection and physical conditions such as childbirth scars may also result in painful intercourse and the resultant resistance to sexual activities. Thinning of the vaginal walls, which is common in the fifty-to-seventy-year age-group may also result in painful intercourse. The presence or absence of these conditions is determined by physical examination.

Before leaving the overview of common sexual dysfunctions, it seems important to emphasize a point. At no time in the previous discussion was lack of proper information or the presence of sexual misinformation specified as an etiological factor in sexual dysfunctions. In no way should this be interpreted to mean lack of information or misinformation is not a factor in sexual dysfunctions. In fact, the opposite is true.

There is probably no more pervasive reason for the presence of sexual dysfunctions than lack of information or being misinformed. We agree wholeheartedly with Masters and Johnson's (1970) resolute assertion that ignorance, more than anything else, results in sexual dysfunction. It is for this reason that information about sexual functioning should assume a prominent role in sex therapy. We remember the couple we saw together in which the wife indicated she had been experiencing primary orgasmic dysfunction. In questioning the couple regarding their sexual behavior, we learned that at no time in their nine years of marriage had the husband's penis ever been contained in her vagina for longer than two minutes. Both partners were under the impression that two minutes of penile-vaginal penetration was at least of a "normal" length of time, if not exceptionally long. This was a "well-educated" couple with a prosperous business in the area.

Treatment of Sexual Dysfunctions

In treating the sexually dysfunctional relationship, it is valuable to conduct a brief history-taking process. The format we follow is similar to that presented in the Group for Advancement of Psychiatry's book *Assessment of Sexual Dysfunction* (1974). The areas this format attends to are childhood sexuality, adolescence, orgastic experiences, feelings about self as masculine or feminine, sexual fantasies and dreams, dating history, direct sexual experience with partners and others (both pre- and postmarital), and other information that seems appropriate to the couple. Examples of other information worth pursuing, depending upon the couple, are the exploration of effects and treatment of a rape or pursuing thoughts and feelings surrounding a homosexual encounter one partner experienced some years ago. The determination of what to explore outside of this history format is determined by reactions of the therapists to the couple as they present their histories in the clinical setting.

In the area of childhood sexuality, the following have proven to be valuable to determine: family attitudes about sex; how sex was learned about and from whom; childhood sex activity (sight of nude body, self-stimulation, and sexual exploration with another); childhood sexual myths; and any contact with the primal scene.

In exploring the period of adolescence, it is important to ascertain the following: preparation for adolescent physiological changes (who informed, nature of information, age at which received, and feelings regarding how the information was relayed); masturbatory activity; heterosexual contact; and homosexual encounters.

Orgastic experiences may be touched upon while explaining other areas already mentioned. Information clinically valuable to explore at this juncture, if not already covered in a previous section, includes: frequency of orgasm during sleep and accompanying dreams; age and frequency of masturbation, along with feelings about and methods used to achieve orgasm; age when necking and petting were begun and with whom and how often; age at first intercourse and with whom and resultant feelings; and other coital experiences since the first encounter.

Regarding the individual's self-perceptions as masculine or feminine, it has been proven valuable to determine feelings about body size; appearance (handsome, etc.); voice; hair distribution; genitalia; and ability to respond sexually (both giving and receiving). We have found Hartman and Fithian's (1972) idea of having individuals evaluate their physical being and the components from head to toe a valuable asset. Each spouse is asked to score him- or herself on an imaginary continuum from 0 to 100, with 100 being maxmium. Hartman and Fithian have found that those who like themselves give themselves a rating of 85 to 100 and people with a poor self-concept a rating below 50.

Through completion of this sexual history, the therapist can identify sources of gross misinformation in the forms of myths, such as the importance of penis size; perceived "pathological" nature of group masturbation while in junior high; coitus is the only "right" way to achieve sexual satisfaction; the male is always the aggressor; and oral sex is "dirty"; etc. We have repeatedly been exposed to situations where couples have needlessly deprived themselves due to sexual misinformation and attempting to live in accord with absurd myths. In regard to the role of myths on the sexual performance of couples, Lederer and Jackson (1968, P. 123) have said, "If the various manifestations of sex were accepted as natural, and if people could abandon the view that there is a single absolute standard to be reached by all who are normal, the unhappiness of many couples would decrease and their performance would automatically improve."

The last area of concern in exploring the couple's sexual relationship revolves about their ability to communicate directly and honestly about their sexual likes and dislikes. It is not uncommon for the sexually dysfunctional couple to manifest marked inability to discuss their difficulty without hostility or other emotions that confuse and compound their dilemma. When the difficulty in communicating seems to be a contaminating factor, the techniques outlined in Chapter 7 are valuable to implement in conjunction with conveying corrective sexual information.

The Sexual History Process

Select a male and female to depict a couple who are concerned about their sexual relationship. Identify two people to serve as co-therapists. Allow the "couple" to identify the sexual dysfunction they want to present to the therapists. Begin the session with the couple briefly presenting their concern and then move into the sexual history-taking process. The therapists may select to have some notes outlining the format for conducting the history-taking. The couple should be encouraged to improvise in order to introduce as realistic a flavor as is possible.

Upon completion of the history taking, process the experience from the perspective of both the couple and therapists. Follow this step with the opportunity for the observers to share their perceptions.

Rather than attempting to give an overview of treatment techniques, it seems more appropriate to refer the reader to books such as Kaplan's *New Sex Therapy: Active Treatment of Sexual Dysfunction* (1974); Masters and Johnson's *Human Sexual Inadequacy* (1970); and Hartman and Fithian's *Treatment of Sexual Dysfunction: A Bio-Psycho-Social Approach* (1974). In these books and others like them, specific sexual techniques are presented in detail and accompanied in many cases with illustrations. The reader who refers to these resources will probably be struck by how relatively simplistic the techniques appear to be. Considering this, it must be remembered that, with the aid of these techniques, sex therapists are reporting success of up to 100 percent in treating some of the sexual dysfunctions explained earlier.

It seems appropriate to close this section by recommending to potential practitioners the importance of them assessing their own perceptions of their sexuality and sex in general. Without the practitioner being comfortable with sex and sexuality, there is always the risk that clients will be either consciously or otherwise discouraged from disclosing problems of a sexual nature. This is not only a disservice to the clients, but certainly not facilitative to the practitioner's reputation. Readings, workshops, and films, such as those available from the Center for Marital and Sexual Studies of Long Beach, California, and therapy of different persuasions can all contribute to practitioners' developing greater comfort with the important aspects of their own sexuality.

Sexual Self Analysis

Organize a small group of four to five others and discuss what may be difficult for you in conducting sexual therapy. Examples of areas that may be problematic for you are: discussing certain types of sexual behaviors; knowledge of sexual vocabulary and what is appropriate usage; discussing sexual behavior with certain types of individuals; and potential problems of interface between your sexual value system and the clients'. After identifying what might be problematic for you, attempt to specify what action you might pursue to resolve the situation.

ALCOHOLISM FROM A FAMILY THEORY PERSPECTIVE

Recent projections place the number of alcoholic North Americans at nine million, with many authorities placing the figure even higher. With the assumption accepted that an individual is a member of a social system comprised of many relationships, of which at least some are of an intimate nature, the fact becomes clear that millions more are affected by alcohol than the above projection implies.

The frequently heard statement that alcoholics are on skid row has now been clearly identified as a myth. A prominent psychiatrist, Dr. Ruth Fox, has indicated that only 3 percent of the total alcoholic population is on skid row (*The Alcoholic American*, 1973). Most alcoholics are found in homes, offices, places of business, and in every walk of life.

Another myth revolving about alcohol is that regarding females. A frequently heard statement, "Women hardly ever become alcoholics," is now clearly identified as being untrue. In large cities women alcoholics appear to match men one for one, while in the rest of the country one in every five alcoholics is a female (*The Alcoholic American*, 1973). Women are probably less noticeable as alcoholics than men because they are less exposed to the public view, and they often do their drinking at home.

Alcoholism as a Symptom of Family Dysfunction

Considering the above brief facts, it seems apparent that alcoholism has the potential to rear its ugly head regardless of sex, socioeconomic class, and other factors. We believe that what is referred to as "the disease of alcoholism" is all too frequently related to the dynamics of family dysfunction and that the alcoholism is a symptom of these dynamics in operation. Murray Bowen (1974) has indicated this same belief and identifies family therapy as the preferred treatment modality for alcoholism. He explains the etiology of alcoholism intergenerationally, by stating that alcoholics handle the emotional attachment to their parents, especially the mother, by denial of the attachment and by a superindependent, overcompensating posture.

The concept of alcoholism being a symptom of family dysfunction also seems to be validated by Dr. Marvin Kamback (1976, P. 5) of the University of Maryland's Hospital Alcoholism Division when he states, "We have had cases where the alcoholism simply disappears without specific treatment of the alcoholic member when the family begins to function better."

Gallant, Rich, and Bey (1970) have reported a success rate of 45 to 56 percent when treating acoholics by concentrating on their family relationships. At first glance, this success rate may appear mediocre, but one must remember that for years the alcoholic has been identified as probably having the poorest prognosis of all the cases that may enter a therapist's office.

In another study reported by Corder, Corder, and Laidlaw (1972), utilizing an intervention strategy directed at the family, success was again reported. The control group in this study was twenty alcoholics treated in the traditional residential four-week treatment program. The experimental group was composed of twenty alcoholics exposed to a treatment program with an emphasis placed on intervention with the marital relationship of the subjects. Post-treatment follow-up after six months revealed that eight of the nineteen experimental subjects were drinking compared with seventeen of the twenty control subjects. McDowell (1972) has identified the efficacy of family treatment with the alcoholic. In this article, he discusses the program utilized by the National Council on Alcoholism at Kansas City and its adaptability. He believes the family approach provides an answer to much of the frustration and confusion in the treatment of alcoholism.

Dr. William Bosma (1974, P. 4), Director of the Division of Alcoholism and Drug Abuse, University of Maryland Hospital, has pointed to the need for a vast increase in the availability of family therapists to treat families where alcoholism is a problem. He reports that a four- to six-month follow-up of sixty Maryland families who received family therapy for problems related to parental drinking showed that the majority improved greatly, with sobriety achieved in over 60 percent of the alcoholic parents.

The studies are reported as documentation and support of

what Smoyak (1973) has stated as her contention: The family system, rather than the drinking individual, is the problematic unit. In this sense, the alcoholic individual is viewed as the signal of system distress. As a result of this belief, solutions are sought at the family system level, rather than at the more traditional subsystem-person level.

Considerations for Family Therapists in Treating the Alcoholic Family

The systems approach to conceptualizing the etiology and treatment of alcoholism is the one with which we resolutely concur. Whether it is explained on the basis of the intergenerational systemic point of view, as with Bowen (1974), or in the horizontal, one-generational perspective, it seems to be the soundest theoretical and pragmatic explanation of alcoholism. Our own preference is to understand the "alcoholic system" both vertically (intergenerationally) and horizontally. In this process, attention is given to the families of origin of both spouses and the impact those experiences are having on their relationship (*see* Chap. 2), along with the systemic nature of their current family. An example of this is the wife who has come from her family of origin perceiving herself as a debtor and the husband who leaves his mother and father with a self-perception as a creditor. Remembering from Chapter 2 that the creditor feels he has payments coming to him as a result of leaving the family of origin shortchanged and the debtor feels a need to pay off the debt she feels she has incurred in her "oversolicitous" family, there is a complementary couple. Both sense the potential in one another to balance their ledger of interpersonal accountability.

As the husband begins to drink, his wife is able to take care of him, provide excuses, and take on more than her fair share of responsibility for family functioning, etc., in order to remove herself from the status of debtor. He can function in an irresponsible fashion with her as a result of his self-perceived creditor status, and the gears of destruction are set in motion. Soon, this pattern gets out of hand, and the system begins to appear like the "run away equation" of which Lacqueur speaks (1972). Father becomes more disinterested and unable to function in an intimate relationship, leaving mother experiencing an emotional vacuum. She thus turns to her oldest child and "parentifies" (Boszormenyi-Nagy and Spark, 1973) her to fill this void. The daughter is now expected to fulfill her mother's emotional needs, which are usually met in the adult subsystem. This results in the daughter developing migraine headaches and a drastic reduction in her school achievement as an adaptation to the stress. Neither of the parents are emotionally available to their children to provide needed love, nurturance, and support. The mother points this out to the husband, who feels guilty about the developments and drinks more, which escalates and compounds the system dynamics.

To try to analyze and place blame for the vicious cycle being implemented and maintained is a fruitless effort. A cursory examination reveals one would have to search back intergenerationally and probably never arrive at a justifiable conclusion. As a result, blame as an issue is disregarded, and intervention and change are of primary importance. The concern is one of restructuring the current destructive relationship, or system patterns, and replacing them with more constructively adaptive ones. Considering this, the treatment takes on an overt appearance of being remedial in nature. Upon further evaluation, though, it becomes evident that the effort has a strong preventive flavor to it. This appears as a result of the realization that the children of this marital relationship will be able to leave and construct their own families without the scars that otherwise would be present.

The Impact of Alcoholism on Children

The influence of the alcoholic family on children has been heavily documented. Bosma (1974, P. 4) reports that a review of an inner-city Baltimore pediatric behavioral clinic revealed that 60 percent of the children seen there had an alcoholic parent. Chafez, Blane, and Hill (1971); Haberman (1966); Kelly (1973); Kammeier (1971); Shade and Hendrickson

(1971); Fine (1975, P. 4); McGilvray (1975, P. 3); and Ludi (1975), among others, all report findings that concur with Bosma's equally dramatically.

Perhaps insight into the impact of alcoholism on children can be best captured by quoting from the findings of Dr. Lee Yudin, Jan Holmes, and Shirley Heinemann (1975) of the West Philadelphia Clinic. These findings evolved out of a study of children with an alcoholic parent.

> Compared with normal children, those in a family with parental alcoholism are less able to maintain attention, less responsive to environmental stimulation, and more prone to emotional upset. They tend to be anxious, fearful individuals who have great difficulty in containing or regulating their excitement or mood. They are subject to aggressive behavior and show evidence of deficient learning of certain moral codes of conduct. There is also evidence that they are socially isolated, and preoccupied with inner thoughts rather than a concern for what is going on around them. [P. 4]

The preventive nature of intervening from the family therapy orientation with the alcoholic family can be appreciated for another point as well. Along with others, Barron (1970); O'Neal, Robins, and King (1962); and Shade and Hendrickson (1971) have documented the disproportionately high number of children from alcoholic families who later become alcoholic adults themselves. By working with the alcoholic family, this vicious cycle can be broken for the benefit of generations as yet unknown.

The Acknowledged Developmental Stages of Alcoholism in the Family

The family approach is also advocated in order to prevent what has been reported by Cohen (1966) from happening. He indicates that, in many cases, once the alcoholic husband stops drinking, the marriage becomes worse. He explains this on the basis of the shift in the marital balance of responsibilities and role performance that occurs with the husband's sobriety. Without total family involvement in the treatment process new roles, rules and communication patterns are not accepted and understood by all members. This could (1) either temporarily or permanently disorient and place stress upon the family or (2) result in the family attempting to restore equilibrium in its system by overtly, or more likely covertly, encouraging the alcoholic to begin drinking again. A publication of the National Council on Alcoholism, *Alcoholism and the Family*, reports the following principles that determine family equilibrium and therefore must be considered in the treatment process:

1. All members are assigned (and assume) roles and are related to each other in characteristic ways.

2. There is a set of regulations that governs the roles members are to assume and the ways they are to relate to each other; these roles and patterns of relationship constitute the family equilibrium.

3. Any attempt to shift the family equilibrium from within, i.e. a change in a member, which is the case with the alcoholic member, may evoke resistance from the family system, which seeks to maintain its equilibrium.

4. No matter how sick it may appear to the outsider, the established equilibrium represents the family's attempt to minimize the threats of pain and disruption (Rooney, 1975).

In the same publication (Rooney, 1975), three stages of deterioration in alcoholism (Jellinek, 1960) have been intertwined with seven stages (Jackson, 1954) the family goes through in the course of dealing with the alcoholism. These stages appear to be of considerable value in understanding the dynamics of the alcoholic family when intervening.

STAGE I. The Family Tries to Deny the Problem

The alcoholic in the early and middle phases of Dr. Jellinek's study (1960) is denying the problem by rationalizations and by unwillingness to discuss his drinking.

The nonalcoholic reacts to the loss of control and to specific episodes and is ashamed but accepts the alcoholic's rationalizations. The spouse feels rejected, unloved, and unwanted as the alcoholic becomes more preoccupied with drinking. The nonalcoholic also feels inadequate as a person when continued efforts are made to please and to be accepted by the alcoholic.

At this point, the family is unlikely to seek help for alcoholism. The family uses the process of denial to preserve its stability.

STAGE II.   The Family Tries to Get Rid of the Problem

Without treatment, the alcoholic moves to the middle and crucial stage in the three-stage process described by Dr. Jellinek. Symptoms in this phase include dropping or losing friends, change of family habits, devaluation of personal relationships, decrease in sexual drive, flashes of aggression, and dominating behavior. These symptoms make it increasingly difficult for the family to cope.

In Stage II, the family becomes aware that the drinking is not normal but, because of the stigma on alcoholism, they refuse to recognize it as alcoholism. Fear of discovery by friends, employer, and others mounts, and the family tries to cover up. The family members feel they should solve their own problems and so resist seeking outside help and advice. The increasing isolation magnifies the importance of family interaction and events. A sort of group collusion takes place in which the alcoholic maintains considerable power over the family.

The alcoholic's chief aim is to continue drinking; the spouse aims to prevent him from drinking. The struggle over drinking culminates in quarrels, recriminations, and psychological withdrawal on the part of one or both partners.

The on-again relationship begins to affect the children, and they may begin to show signs of emotional disturbance. The spouse begins to feel self-pity and to lose self-confidence as the nonalcoholic's behavior fails to stabilize the alcoholic's drinking. The family's behavior may also become deviant and out of control.

STAGE III.   Chaos Threatens the Family

In this stage, the family tends to lose hope and to drift into irresolution. The family continues habits of Stage II—nagging, berating, or chilling with silence. Arguments now begin to be touched with violence, and the children become tools in a husband-wife struggle. The disturbance of the children becomes more marked as this occurs. The nonalcoholic worries about insanity and the inability to make decisions or act to change the situation.

The spouse begins to avoid sexual contact when the other is drinking, which in turn reflects emotional withdrawal in other areas of family life. Accusations are made of impotence or frigidity, which adds to the nonalcoholic's concern about sexual functioning.

Fear is one of the major characteristics of this chaotic phase as few problems are met constructively. The spouse becomes ambivalent. The family may seek help at a time of crisis then withdrawal, feeling the situation beyond hope or help.

STAGE IV. The Family Tries to Reorganize (In Spite of the Problem)

The spouse begins to manage the family alone. The children lose respect for their alcoholic parent and talk back or treat the alcoholic as an inferior. The alcoholic may make desperate efforts to regain their respect and affection by excessive fondling or by giving them stiff lectures about children's obligations to their parents. The alcoholic may be resentful of the children and attack them physically or verbally. The children, however, on the whole, become more settled in their behavior as the nonalcoholic assumes greater responsibility within a new family equilibrium.

At this point, the alcoholic may accept the need for help and treatment. If recovery begins, the family moves into Stage VII. If not, the family moves into Stage V.

STAGE V. Efforts to Escape the Problem

In an effort to escape the problem, the partners may separate, which may lead to the termination of the marriage. This happens when the alcoholic enters the chronic phase of alcoholism, as viewed by Dr. Jellinek. The emotional difficulty in making this decision is enormous. The children may vacillate between thinking their parent "spineless" for staying with the alcoholic and considering the spouse unfair for leaving. Surprised by the spouse's determination, however, the alcoholic may seek help, may begin to recover, and the family then moves into Stage VII.

STAGE VI. Reorganization of Part of the Family

In this stage, the family regroups without the alcoholic

partner. Unless the alcoholic, who now may die or undergo some irreversible physical and mental damage, seeks help, the family will not progress into Stage VII.

STAGE VII. Recovery of the Entire Family

The seventh stage is possible if the alcoholic achieves sobriety. The readjustments needed are numerous. The family itself must recover as well as help the alcoholic rehabilitate himself and must overcome fears born of frequent past disappointments and discuss problems not related to drinking. The family must develop trust and realize that since they are part of the problem, they must also be necessary as different behavior is experienced and integrated (Rooney, 1975, Pp. 2-5).

Summary

This section facilitates the development of a systematic understanding and appreciation of alcoholism by the reader. The literature on alcoholism is rapidly becoming replete with reports regarding the family therapy treatment modality as its value is recognized. We are resolutely convinced of the value of this approach on the basis of our experience.

DEATH AND THE FAMILY

Death, as a loss event, plays a vital role in personal development because it focuses and amplifies the human search for belongingness and separateness, ingredients identified earlier as basic motivating forces in life (*see* Chaps. 1, 2, and 3). The death of a significant person provides the opportunity for facing squarely and starkly the interactional issues of closeness and distance. Because belongingness and separateness are viewed as constituting the dynamic faces of identity, death, in stirring up these issues, also stirs up the meaning dimension in our lives. Identity is intimately tied up with the quest for meaning—who am I, what am I about, in relation to whom and to what?

This section deals with the therapeutic aspects of the death experience in treating couples and families. Although the primary focus is on therapy applications, the necessary theoretical base is supplied, when appropriate. The student who wishes to delve more deeply into the subject of death is encouraged to pursue the following sources: Becker (1975); Bowen (1976); Kavanaugh (1972); Kübler-Ross (1969); Maddison and Raphael (1976); Paul (1967); and Schoenberg et al. (1975).

Death as a Crisis

The death of a family member is generally accompanied by effects that enable it to be called a crisis. At the system level, a crisis disrupts the homeostasis to such an extent that a family's usual coping mechanisms become ineffective. The potential for systemic change is high, especially for change that is initiated from outside the family (therapy or social service, etc.). The concept of *crisis* implies a time-limited state because, by definition, anything that is ongoing would then imply a normal state. This, however, is not to say that a crisis has only time-limited effects. On the contrary, a crisis usually has long-lasting effects because social systems rarely return to the precrisis equilibrium. The postcrisis adaptation could move the marital or family system to a more open or closed style of relating. (*See* Chap. 1 for connotations implied in the concepts of "open" and "closed" systems.)

At the indivdiual, intrapsychic level, a crisis also stresses and disrupts a person's usual coping devices. In the case of death, bereaved family members often experience feelings of confusion, fear, numbness, anger, despair, and anxiety. Somatic symptoms are likewise familiar companions of crisis events.

The above constitute the systemic and individual bases for the family's great susceptibility to outside intervention in a state of crisis. When a family member dies, family size decreases by one, but the sociopsychological effects are multiple. In a four-member nuclear family, the father's death means the end of the marital relationship—the subsystem that plays such a vital role in establishing clear boundaries between the generations. It is in the marital relationship that parents find their primary sense of intimacy, companionship, and support. These are experiences that feed and support them in their often demanding tasks of parenthood. The surviving spouse (now a single parent) is faced with the task of experiencing significant adult relationships outside the nuclear unit, not to mention the role of handling the parental tasks alone. The children face the loss of possibly the most important male model in their culture, including the loss of his companionship, guidance, and of his physical and economic support.

This description of the bases for the personal and interpersonal dislocation involved in the loss of one member, in this case, the father, could be continued and yet simply scratch the surface. Previous discussions of the systemic nature of the person should help the reader in supplying their own elaborations and implications. The basic perspective to keep in mind, from the point of view of systems, is that the death of a member means the loss of a family position, e.g. husband-father or daughter-sister, and the role performed by, or expected of, the occupant of that position, e.g. companion, disciplinarian, sex partner, and provider. Such a loss implies a rather radical restructuring of the family system, the matrix of human identities.

This rather theoretical and clinical description of the death of a family member may seem emotionless and "out-of-emotional-context," given the usually painful and heavy emotional surroundings of the death of a loved one. However, it seems that these systemic factors are the existential fibers that weave the personal fabric of human experience. Each event has an impact at the biological, psychological, interpersonal, and social levels. The death of a family member (an intimate par excellence) is one of the most impactful events.

Grief and Mourning

Grief may be defined as that "peculiar amalgam of anxiety, anger, and despair following the experience of what seems to be an irretrievable loss" (Maddison and Raphael, 1976, P. 200).* Grief, then, is conceptualized as an individual event, with particular focus on the person's feeling or affective response to the loss of a loved one. Mourning is the process a person goes through in dealing with grief. Paul (1967, P. 188) defines *mourn-*

---

* This definition by Maddison and Raphael is a restatement of the definition given by Bowlby (1961).

ing as the "psychological process that is set in motion by the loss of a loved object and which, when completed, is associated with the relinquishing of that object." Paul's definition includes what he sees as the goal of mourning—psychologically letting go of the lost object. This point will be reemphasized because it has direct bearing upon therapy. It deserves elaboration and, in our judgment, a slight modification.

Bowlby (1961) describes mourning with a crisis theory backdrop. He conceives mourning as the complex of psychological processes with the following phases: (1) the early yearning and protest, (2) behavioral disorganization, and (3) behavioral reorganization.

YEARNING AND PROTEST: This phase, according to Bowlby, is marked by crying, anger, and appeals for help. He claims that this reaction to grief parallels the infant's instinctive cry for mother in response to separation experiences. "Of cardinal importance for those who work with bereaved people is Bowlby's assertion, amply documented from our experience, that the expression of angry strivings to recover the lost object represents a sign of health, enabling the object in due time to be relinquished" (Maddison and Raphael, 1976, P. 202). Bowlby then, like Paul, also sees relinquishing of the object as an important outcome of normal or healthy mourning. The manifestation of anger is seen as a healthy process precisely because it is seen as aiding the movement toward relinquishing the object. In our view, the awareness and acceptance of anger in the bereaved is a healthy sign because it implies the beginning of a realistic evaluation of the lost object without unduly idealizing or scapegoating the dead person.

BEHAVIORAL DISORGANIZATION: In this phase, the fact and permanence of the loss are accepted, with an accompanying tendency to dwell on feelings of despair. Painful as this phase might be, it is important for the therapist to allow the clients to experience this. It is important for the therapist to show concern and empathy but not overresponsibility. As we said, it is when a system is jarred or disorganized that new pathways for coping and relating can be more easily activated.

REORGANIZATION PHASE: According to Bowlby, the end of a

normal mourning process is marked by a person's ability to take renewed interest in the outside world and to begin to establish and maintain new intimate relationships. At the family system level, this phase is manifested by discovery and maintaining new relationship patterns for meeting the members' needs. The family achieves a modified sense of identity as a family, thus enabling the members to experience a sense of belongingness—so threatened by the loss of a member. In the beginning of this stage, it is natural for the couple or family to stress belongingness more than separateness. As the mourning progresses, there is a gradual shift toward stressing the individuation moves of each member until a relatively comfortable balance is once again achieved.

Effective and Ineffective Mourning*

Implied in the discussion so far is the assumption that mourning proceeds in a relatively effective way. This, of course, is not always the case. When seen from a family perspective, the process can become extremely complicated. Some members may attempt the manifestation of grief in the manner described above, while others may thwart such attempts. One person may be overly attentive to another member's grief and in the process not attend to their own grief. Just as one family member can be scapegoated into the role of expressing the family's aggression, so one or several family members can be recruited to express most of the family's grief. The nongrievers, however, may feel left out or pressed to be the "strong" ones. It seems to us that it is with this system context in mind that individual mourning is best understood and treated.

Direct acknowledgment and expression of grief in the family setting by all members is a characteristic of effective mourning. Ineffective mourning generally follows two major paths: (1) denial or suppression of grief, often leading to indirect grief-

---

* The literature in this area usually talks of healthy versus pathological mourning. We make an effort to diminish the impact of the medical model (disease) by referring to effective and ineffective ways of mourning. The medical model often implies a good-bad or right-wrong dichotomy that tends to concentrate on what works or does not work in a certain direction without implying that every person or family should go through such a process. The reader will probably note that we are not entirely successful in escaping the field.

work (depression, psychosomatic effects, or pseudo-hostility) and (2) overly focusing expression of grief in one or more members. The latter, of course, presupposes the presence of members who are indirectly mourning their grief.

It is important to note that couples and families differ in the degree to which they deny or overfocus on grief. A family's mourning resources are significantly shaped by previous responses to loss (including but not limited to death). Although, as W. C. Becker (1973) cogently argues, death is the foundation of all our anxieties and fears, it is important to note that the loss experience has ramifications beyond the death experience. Normal growth and development (at the family and individual levels) provide numerous confrontations with loss. Marriage, for instance, often means the loss of primary loyalty and interaction with one's family of origin. Then, of course, there are all of the usual family developmental stages with the arrival and launching of children and beyond. The manner in which family members cope with these loss experiences often determines their ability to cope with death in the family. This impact extends into one's family of origin. The manner in which a person's parents mourned their own losses while growing up influences that person's mourning style (Paul, 1967, P. 188). In general, the more open the family system, the more effective the family members are in coping with grief.

Lewis et al. (1976) examined the role of a family's potential for dealing with death in their extensive research on families. One of their primary findings was that those families that were most open to discussing death were also the families determined to be most functional in other regards as well.

Because the death of a loved one goes to the heart of the belongingness-separateness experience, the event is usually accompanied by behavior that is unusual. In that context, therefore, the following reactions are considered normal and even healthy: shock, denial, anger, tension, loneliness, sadness, disorientation, and guilt. Kübler-Ross talks about the bereaved as going through stages similar to those that the dying person goes through. Surviving family members may struggle to deny the reality of the loss and become angry at the dead for "leaving" them behind. This resentment is often accompanied by a sense of guilt. Beyond these are those painful feelings of sadness, loneliness, and despair. This is the point where a good dose of plain, old-fashioned caring, empathy, and compassion is helpful. According to Kübler-Ross, to talk about the love of God at this point is cruel and inhuman. We add that it is equally inhuman to talk about self-actualization, self-reliance, and self-love at a moment like this. With time, effective mourning generally leads to acceptance of the situation and the accompanying meanings.

It should be stressed that all of those manifestations of grief, including somatic distresses, are normal and considered components of effective mourning. It is important for the family therapist to have a deep sense of respect for these processes, because they are significant pathways toward a new homeostasis for the individual and for the family. Ineffective mourning involves fundamentally getting stuck somewhere between the experience of the loss and its acceptance. As mentioned, one or several aspects of the process are either denied or overfocused upon, resulting in abortive mourning.

Mourning: Letting In or Letting Go?

Much of the mourning literature is woven around the concept of "letting go" of the beloved object. Even the concept of *acceptance* refers to accepting the loss and accepting the reality that that person is no longer able to relate in the usual way. This attitude has a ring of validity in it, but it also hides an equally valid element of psychological reality. The hidden truth is that no experience, especially a long-term relationship, is ever really lost. The assumption made is that an emotional investment is forever. Even divorce, which is usually replete with anger and moves toward emotional separation, only dimly hides the remnants of contrived investment.

Mourning, then, is better conceived as a process of working toward acceptance and integration of the meaning of a particular relationship in one's life. The meaning that my dead father holds for me is a significant aspect of my life. Rather than think that I have to give him up, I can think instead of accepting him and my relationship with him as fully as I can. In this sense, too, mourning is a continuous process, because as I grow, I go through new levels of psychological integration. Acceptance and integration, in a paradoxical fashion, allow us to "move on"—a process of "letting go" of the previous relationship gestalt. It seems that this moving-on aspect of mourning in the literature is sometimes distorted to "giving up" or "letting go" of the person.

Because the meaning of events belongs to second-order reality (as opposed to first-order reality, the physical manifestations of events), it is subject to change at any time. This implies the past can be mentally changed. More accurately, present meanings of the past physical events are changed. The present, then, remains the point of power and leverage for change. The assumption is that nothing is unchangeable in terms of second-order reality.

Therapy With Those Who Are Grieving

Elisabeth Kübler-Ross (1969, p. 157) writes, "We cannot help the terminally ill patients in a really meaningful way if we do not include his family." The principle behind this conclusion can be extended to include the bereaved person. The bereaved is best and most fully helped if the family is included in the mourning process. Many people do this healthily and naturally. The implication here is not that everyone needs family therapy. However, if therapy is sought, then the therapist would do well to encourage and facilitate dialogue of family members on the issue of the dying or dead member.

The family systems approach indicates that it is important to get a sense of how the entire family is organized and what role and functions each member in the family plays. This sensitivity to a person's "interpersonal space" is crucial in joining the family system and in determining the mode and timing of the intervention. This is perhaps yet another time to say that each family is unique and that intervention strategies must be uniquely designed for each family. However, we can offer some general guidelines.

With Bowen (1976), we believe that it is important for therapists to have their own emotional life under reasonable control and without an undue amount of denial. As Becker

(1973) points out, some amount of denial is normal and healthy, because of the difficulty in living under the constant awareness of death. Therapists' awareness and acceptance of their own eventual deaths, however, is a critical factor in their ability to help the bereaved and dying without unbearable discomfort and with a mature tolerance for other people's momentary need to deny their pain and loss.

The ability to empathize is important in all forms of therapy, but it perhaps takes a unique focus in handling loss through death. Family therapists do well to draw from their past experiences of loss, hurt, anger, and loneliness, and the sensitivity required for adapting to these difficult emotions. The terror of loneliness can sometimes strike with a sense of sinking into some deep lonely hole from which there is no rescue. At such moments, a comforting word or touch can go a long way, especially if it comes from family members. The beginning family therapist may become scared or impatient at this apparent lack of response to therapeutic efforts. It is unhelpful at this point to back off prematurely or to take the initiative away from the family. The experienced therapist recognizes this as a process and thus accepts and facilitates its course of development.

Empathic and comforting behaviors do not imply the use of deceit or euphemistic language. Direct, straight, and complete communication is of utmost importance in the exchange involving the therapist, the physician, the dying, and the family members. This holds for children as well as adults—the sooner and the more direct, the better. Bowen (1976) emphasizes that the use of direct words (such as "death," "die," and "bury," instead of "passed on," "deceased," "expired'") signals to the client that the therapist is comfortable with the subject of death. This invites the client to talk in comfort as well. Kübler-Ross emphasizes the same concept of directness with the family members, as well as with the dying. She encourages direct communication even with those who are in a coma, cautioning never to classify anybody as a so-called vegetable, even when a person seems nonreactive. Subconscious processes are still in effect, and communication at some level is still possible.

Direct acceptance tends to facilitate the acceptance (by the survivors) of the reality of a loved one's dying, a process that facilitates the latter's dying in peace and dignity. We believe, with Kübler-Ross (1969), that every person has a right to die in peace and dignity. Directness is also the best preparation for the mourning that takes place after the death of the loved one. Secrecy, avoidance, and indirectness only help to create a paranoia that is destructive to the element of trust in relationships.

The role of mourning in therapy is not limited to the moments immediately before and after death. A great deal of grief and pain are sometimes denied or otherwise left unresolved. This unmourned grief often emerges in varied symptoms—headaches, depression, impotence, uncontrolled anger, and so forth. Part of the family therapist's task, therefore, is to explore important loss experiences (especially through someone's death) the family members have gone through in the past.

Norman Paul (1967) talks about the concept of a belated mourning reaction. The technique employed to induce such a reaction he calls *operational mourning*. Paul writes (p. 188), "Through repeated directed inquiry about recollectable responses to loss, the therapist invites the exposure and expression of intense feelings in the member involved." The therapist's empathic dialogue with the belated mourner has a critical impact upon the spouse's ability to empathize with that person. The presence of other family members during the process of operational mourning is important because of the therapist's goal to facilitate the development of an empathic response in the other members of the family.

There is a sense in which grief therapy, when extended to include belated mourning, is a part of all forms and phases of therapy, because therapy, at some level, is a process of getting unstuck from the pain of loss.

Summary

This chapter presented information on the impact of sex, alcohol, and death on the family and their therapeutic management. Sex and death inevitably affect all families for better or worse, and alcohol is increasingly becoming a disrupting factor in millions of American families.

The role of sex in marital relationships was discussed, along with a preferred philosophical set for its treatment. The most common sexual dysfunctions observed in a clinical setting, along with their treatment, were then offered.

Alcoholism was explained from a family theory perspective designed to understand alcoholism as a potential symptom of family dysfunction. Considerations for treatment of the family with alcoholism as a concern were presented. Special attention was devoted to the children of the "alcoholic family" and the types of problems they typically experience. The section on alcoholism was concluded with an exposition of the typical stages families undergo when a member is an alcoholic.

The final section was devoted to death and its impact on the family. Death was identified as a time of crisis for the family— a time when rules and roles require change. The stages of mourning normally observed were identified with considerations for the family therapist.

CHAPTER 12

THE MAKING OF THE FAMILY THERAPIST

Looking back over this experience, there were a number of significant differences from the previous therapy training encountered by most of the student therapists. First, this training took place within a group setting rather than the normal dyadic setting. Second there were two supervisors present rather than one. Third, training in therapy was done with a peer in a co-therapy model. Fourth, audio-visual feedback was used in the supervision process within the group setting. And fifth, therapeutic intervention was oriented primarily at a family system level, not at an individual or group dynamics level. [O'Hare et al., 1975, P. 162]

With the above analysis, the writers summarized their perceptions of the training they had just completed. This quotation seems to be an appropriate introduction to this chapter for two reasons: (1) It catches essential benchmarks for effective training and (2) the quotation comes from the point of view of those whose perceptions are often neglected, the consumers of a training experience.

There is a rapidly growing element of the professional literature that is devoted to the training of marriage and family therapists. As most often is the case, the direction of the professional literature seems to suggest the focus of professional concerns and interests. This body of literature not only consists of reports and observations by students but also by some of the leading practitioners in the field (Beal, 1976; Ferber and Mendelsohn, 1969; Haley, 1976; Nichols, 1968; Vincent, 1968; Winston, 1968). This movement and interest in marriage and family therapy training seems to be attached to observations such as the following: (1) Family systems therapy has gained far greater exposure and acceptance by professionals of different orientations. (2) Mental health clinics, social service agencies and other employers that used to place heavy reliance on M.S.W.'s are now beginning to advertise for individuals with either master's degrees in social work or in marriage and family therapy-counseling. (3) Six states have legislated licensing procedures for this relatively new profession and many other states are in various stages of the licensing issue. (4) National health insurance carriers, such as CHAMPUS, provide for coverage of marriage and family counseling services and major commercial insurance companies are evaluating the desire of the public to have this service covered by insurance. (5) Business and industry are acknowledging the value of providing this service to their employees as far as increased productivity and employee satisfaction is concerned. Even though the interest and demand for training is mushrooming, there is a significant shortage of adequate training programs to date. For example, at the start of 1977 the American Association of Marriage and Family Therapists Accreditation Committee had only eleven training programs in the country on their list of those programs that had received their accreditation. The program we developed (University of Wisconsin-Stout) annually has about nine to fifteen applicants for each available opening. With few exceptions, most other training programs seem to be experiencing a similar demand. While waiting for an increase in numbers of training facilities available, many people are forced to rely upon reading, attending conferences and workshops, and receiving whatever informal supervision and training they can arrange.

ELEMENTS OF THE TRAINING PROCESS

The actual training process seems to be best characterized by referring back to the quotation cited at the outset of this chapter. In that passage, former family therapy trainees identify the following as significant differences for them from past training received: (1) the setting in which training was delivered; (2) supervision; (3) co-therapy; (4) the place of audiovisual feedback; and (5) the level of intervention was the family system. We believe training programs that do not offer at least the following characteristics should be looked at carefully before one is committed to them.

The first element is that of setting and, normally, the process employed for delivering the training. Most creditable programs we are familiar with rely on the group setting for training, as opposed to reliance on the traditional didactic method. Through the group process, the training opportunity can definitely be enhanced. As the students become familiar with one another, they frequently begin helping each other apply family systems theory to their respective families of origin. This process provides them with the opportunity to apply many principles, such as Bowen's construct of triangulation ("Toward the Differentiation of a Self," 1972) and Minuchin's (1974) ideas regarding family boundaries and other similar constructs. Along with the potential for facilitating training the actual process of group development, including trainees and supervisors, is in many ways dynamically similar to what occurs with the therapist and family. As a result, the natural evolution of the group process provides a model for learning dynamics of family theory. This process was recently presented concisely by Dell et al. (1977) as they recounted their training experiences. The group also provides many different models in doing therapy for each trainee. As each student engages in clinical work with families, the others have the chance to observe the idiosyncratic style of the trainee, and vice versa. The various trainees in the group also provide each the opportunity for receiving considerably more feedback than if they were working in isolation.

The supervision process constitutes the second element that seems appropriate in consideration of family therapy training. Most marriage and family therapy training programs provide the trainee with the opportunity for exposure to at least two different supervisors. The American Association of Marriage and Family Therapists suggest that a training program has at least three supervisors in order to qualify for accreditation by their accreditation committee. By having more than one supervisor available to the students, a depth that is absent in the presence of only one supervisor is provided in their training. The students are exposed not only to different theoretical orientations but to different therapeutic styles as well. The different orientations and styles of the supervisors provide the trainees with alternative ways of perceiving families as well as themselves. An example of this is the student who receives feedback from a supervisor who is psychodynamically oriented, one who is behaviorally oriented, and one who is experientially oriented. Each provides input regarding the trainee's behavior and self that can further stimulate growth and change.

The prevalence of co-therapy as a source of training for the student in marriage and family therapy is another element that is more idiosyncratic to this training. This kind of training facilitates the student becoming involved clinically as soon into his or her training as possible. The co-therapy model serves as a source of support and encouragement in the early stages of initial contact with families. A frequent model that is utilized consists of having the neonate working with a more experienced family therapist so they are initiated to the family therapy process. The co-therapy model provides a source of strength to the trainee that seems to result in greater freedom to experiment with new insights and means of intervening. This model also provides each of the individuals with a source of continuous feedback and monitoring of their behavior. The end result of this element of training seems to definitely contribute to the enhancement of the trainees professional and personal experience that varies from the traditional individual approach.

Heavy reliance upon the use of videotape equipment and live observation of clinical work, are elements of training especially identified with the family therapy field. While thought of as relatively novel, live observation is really an old practice that has only recently been revised as a training tool for the helping professions. In the nineteenth century, the trainee in hypnosis frequently had the instructor in the room to observe the hypnotic induction and accompanying process. Quality training most often provides facilities that allow for live observation of the sessions conducted by the trainees. The live observation also facilitates the trainee getting feedback regarding the therapeutic process at the most important time—notably as it is happening. Immediate feedback is provided either by the use of a telephone hookup, a "bug-in-the-ear," or a means for the trainee to exit the room or supervisor to enter. Through these means, the trainee can monitor interventions immediately, and the clients are assured of an increased quality of service. As Haley (1976, p. 194) states, "With live supervision we finally are able to protect clients from incompetence and overintrusion and also teach how to do therapy at the moment when the therapist is doing just that."

The videotaping of the sessions is not only an excellent adjunct to training, but carries the potential for enhancing the therapeutic process. Ian Alger (1976) and Norman Paul (1976), among others, have written of the therapeutic efficacy of utilizing videotape equipment in therapy. Specific family interactions can be captured and replayed for the family to observe and apply their own interpretations and resultant applications to facilitate change. Videotape also allows the trainee to record a session that is not supervised live and receive feedback at a later date. Many trainees have also found the use of videotape before and after sessions of benefit to themselves and their clients. Through this vehicle, all involved can observe excerpts of initial and then later sessions, to perceive variables that have been changed.

The five preceding elements of training in family therapy seem to be the keys to assuring a sense of realism and aliveness to the learning process. Although this is not an exhaustive description of training in this area, it is representative of the process elements. The reader may have perceived that this form of education is expensive because of the equipment required, such as one-way mirrors and videotape hardware; the heavy investment in providing adequate supervision on a live basis; and a therapy service to the geographic area is provided in conjunction with the more traditional educational dimensions of the program.

Selection of Trainees

Considering that the trainee will be dealing with stressful situations in the real world, it seems wise to carefully select students with appropriate characteristics. In advanced education. there seems to be the traditional consideration given to the grade point average and perhaps standardized test scores, such as those obtained on the Graduate Record Examinations. Although intelligence and ability to learn are important considerations, other variables seem to be at least as important, if not more so. Haley (1976, P. 180) has stated, "Besides a modicum of intelligence, the student should have a wide range of behavior so that he or she can adapt to a wide range of therapeutic approaches. At times a therapist must be authoritarian, at times playful, at times flirtatious, at times grim and serious, at times helpless, and so on. A student lacking skills in different kinds of social behavior will be more difficult to train than one who had a range of experience."

We concur with Haley in believing that the student with a variety of life experiences and sufficient maturity is the one most likely to benefit from training. These students are better able to endure the stress and chaos that they may be exposed to in working with families and to move on to successful intervention. Along with the life experience, professional experience in a helping profession is an advantage. Past professional experience is a documentation of the person's commitment and interest to working with people. In addition, this experience has probably refined the person's basic sensitivity and ability to provide necessary conditions for effecting change.

Although much of this data can be gathered by written communiques, it seems the personal interview is also essential. The interview process should be conducted by more than one person, so that perceptions could be cross-validated. It is through the interview process that the best determination can be made regarding how the potential trainee presents him or herself in a situation that is at least somewhat stressful for most. This seems to be valuable data considering that family therapists may find themselves in many stressful situations while working with families. Through this process, variables such as the potential trainee's ability to present him- or herself with clarity, sufficient confidence, and competence, nonabrasively, can be assessed. With a group-conducted interview, these determinations can be made, especially with the assistance of at least a rough, structured interview guide for the interviewers to provide a more systematic and standardized procedure, for organizing their perceptions.

Models of Training

Just as there are various orientations and models for conducting therapy, there are also varying training orientations. The person who is considering entering training is wise to survey potential training programs regarding orientation. Through this process, potential trainees could select a program that is perceived to be most consonant with themselves and their own self-perceptions.

Beal (1976) has adapted a way of looking at the spectrum of theoretical approaches for understanding and treating families, to analyzing training centers. For his purposes, he places training centers on a continuum from A to Z, which represents various elements of philosophy and practice. He states:

> It [the continuum] demonstrates contrasting ways of understanding the expression of emotional tension or affect in a family. As one moves from A to the Z end of the scale, less theoretical and technical emphasis is placed on the direct expression of affect and more on the structure of family relationships. The theory at the A end of the scale is categorized as more experientially oriented, the theory at the Z end as more structurally oriented, and the theory in the middle (M) as a combination of these two orientations. The experiential-versus-structural approach as a method of comparison has been increasingly used in the past few years. [P. 4]

Those who espouse the theoretical framework at the A end of the continuum place significant emphasis on the expression of affect and working with emotional tension. To facilitate working in the affective domain, much emphasis is placed on the therapeutic relationship between therapist and patient. To guide the therapeutic process, attention is accorded to the subjective nature of therapy, and the subjective awareness and intuitions of the therapist are valued. Examples of techniques advocated in these training programs are: psychodrama, gestalt techniques, family sculpting, encounter group techniques, and interpretation of the unconscious conflicts.

Some have indicated that training centers at the A end of the continuum are deficient in providing an adequate diagnostic nomenclature, as well as a deficient conceptual framework. While this is most typically true of these centers, we want to emphasize that students must determine what they are most in need of from their own perspectives. If they are not concerned with nomenclature or a clear-cut conceptual framework, these programs may be ideally suited for their training.

Training programs at the Z end of the theoretical scale focus their attention on the structure of family relationships. Their interventions are directed at altering the structure of the family in a fashion that results in more functional behavior. Advocates of this approach seem to gear their interventions at two different levels, but both with the goal of changing the family structure. One point of view concentrates on changing communication pathways and feedback systems. The other point of view advocates changing the family relationship system by helping one individual alter his or her role and behavior in the system, which then results in other changes throughout the system.

Advocates of the Z theoretical orientation base their interventions on theories, as opposed to subjective intuitions. Theoretical constructs, such as family boundaries, coalitions, alliances, and communication pathways, are employed extensively to determine therapeutic goals. Often, individuals in this school of thought indicate they are problem centered and attempt to resolve what the clients state they want changed, although the preceding theoretical constructs are continually present as they map means of interviewing with the specific client presented problems. Directives, suggestions, and homework assignments are frequently employed in this approach.

Training programs at the M point of this continuum are those that combine aspects of both the A and Z orientation. Just as exposure to this orientation can be advantageous in exposure to various ways of helping families change, it also has its hazards. The student in this program may not receive in-depth training in any orientation, but rather a superficial overview. Another possibility is that the student may be caught in the midst of power struggles between supervisors as they battle for disciples and adherents of their thinking.

Just as it was indicated most programs screen their applicants carefully, it seems wise to emphasize the advisability of the applicant to screen potential programs carefully. When one considers the amount of sacrifice most educational endeavors demand, it is judicious to make every effort to ascertain the potential return from an investment in a specific training program. The information in this chapter may be used to effectively evaluate programs considered.

Competencies Developed in Training

It seems important for the training to provide a combination of both didactic theory sessions and experiential clinical contact. Either one without the other results in a deficient learning experience. When the two are offered simultaneously, they result in a synergistic experience. Ferber and Mendelsohn (1969, P. 26) seem to have captured the essence of this belief in the following as they describe their training philosophy: "These first hand contacts with families must be experienced within a framework of didactic and supervisory experiences. Contact without teaching is overwhelming, confusing, and frightening to trainees. It usually leads to avoidance of further direct family work. Teaching about families without contact with families becomes sterile, preoccupied with individual psychodynamic issues and is experienced as meaningless or trivial by the trainees."

Along with knowledge of the availability of this kind of learning environment—combining didactic with experiential—the students should be informed of what they will learn through involvement in the training program. If the program has identified competencies they hope their trainees will attain, what the students might expect to learn can be determined by simply reviewing the program's list of competencies. Competency-based education has recently become popular in higher education, so it is likely that many university-based training programs have this information readily available.

Cleghorn and Levin (1973) have identified three classes of competencies to be identified by family therapists. On the basis of our own experience of training others, we have found these categories to be appropriate. The levels they identify are perceptual, conceptual, and executive.

The *perceptual level* consists of the skills required in diagnostic assessment. In family therapy, the emphasis in diagnosis is on perceptions of interactions and the meaning and effect of them in the family system. These skills can best be assessed by supervision and live observation.

Conceptual skills include the ability to formulate one's observations of the family as a whole; how the family functions as a system. Examples of such skills are those of identifying rules that govern the family's behavior, a means of ascribing and maintaining roles within the system, and other similar operational principles. The level at which the student has mastered competencies of a conceptual nature can be evaluated by reading case notes, supervision, and in case staffings.

The last category of competencies identified by Cleghorn and Levin (1973) is in the area of *executive skills*. These skills comprise the means used to facilitate the family demonstrating the way it functions and then intervening to help them alter the way they operate. To assess attainment of these competencies, supervision and observation are imperative.

Not only do established objectives help trainees identify what they might learn in a program, they also facilitate the assessment of progress once involved. The identified competencies can be used as a checklist for evaluating progress and charting future training emphasis. The trainee's future training focus can then be developed into a contract with him- or herself or perhaps entered into and agreed upon with a supervisor. This contract can identify not only the end result, but the process to be employed to reach the end point.

Role of Personal Therapy in the Training Process

The issue of therapy for the trainees is one that has been a point of contention for a number of years among trainers. The arguments vary from those such as Haley (1976), who advises trainees to steer away from programs concerned with personal problems, as opposed to educating; to those such as Nichols (1968), who makes a strong case for training and professional functioning being enhanced through the trainee receiving required therapy. Our view is such that we believe a therapeutic experience should be available in the training process if the trainees believe there would be value in it for them. Our belief is based on the assumption that, especially in those programs that have a screening process operational for selecting applicants, trainees with any evident psychopathology are not selected. Even though stable individuals would be selected as trainees, we want to acknowledge the potential value of therapy in facilitating the development of more mature professionals and enabling them to receive greater benefit from the training process.

The American Association of Marriage and Family Therapists (AAMFT), one of the primary accrediting groups for training programs, seems to advocate a belief similar to ours. In their manual on accreditation the AAMFT Accrediting Committee (1975, P. 29) states: "Recognition of the role and value of personal psychotherapy and the encouragement of trainees to secure such assistance to their personal and professional development is recommended. Whenever possible the institution should provide opportunity for the trainee to secure such assistance." The Committee's stance of acknowledging the value of personal therapy and encouraging institutions to have this option available for trainees is one we have held as a model in our training experience.

Nichols (1968) identified a number of points as benefits to both the trainee, trainers, and programs as a result of the trainee receiving therapy during training. He indicates that intensive training can result in stress that might impede the trainee receiving the full benefit of the program. When therapy is available to the trainee, the stress can more successfully be resolved and integrated to facilitate the educational process. Another benefit of personal psychotherapy is that the trainee's own therapeutic effectiveness may be enhanced. Acknowledging that major personality restructuring is not the goal of this type of therapy, through the therapeutic process, the trainees may learn to expand their own personal limits and growth resulting in enhanced effectiveness in conducting therapy. Another concomitant advantage is that the trainee can learn something from personal experience about the process of undergoing psychotherapeutic treatment. Nichols also identifies the value of personal therapy in helping the trainee struggle in evolving a more firm professional identity.

This seems to be especially important for those trainees who are returning to a position in a clinic or agency that has been predominantly oriented to working only with individuals. Without the development of a firm sense of professional and personal selfhood, the trainee may simply accommodate to the orientation that predominates in the work environment and not utilize the training just completed. The last value of personal therapy in a training program identified by Nichols, is directed at those trainees who may not be suited for treatment of relationships. There are individuals who, for various reasons, are not prepared personally to be involved in working with relationships. They may be strong individuals and adequate in therapy with individuals, but because of their own relationship difficulties, they experience particular stress in intervening at the relationship level with others. These individuals may be assisted in leaving training for intervention at the relationship level without significant damage being incurred by both their personal and professional egos.

Various Settings in Which the Trainees May Be Located

Where might the individuals trained to do family therapy find themselves working? The first settings that one thinks of are clinics, social service agencies, and psychiatric hospitals. These are three settings that have traditionally been the domain of the social worker. Recently, more employers are looking for that person with concentrated and specific training in family therapy. Typically, the social worker's exposure to family therapy is more general in nature and focus.

As family theory and family therapy as a means of operationalizing the theory have gained more creditability, the prevalence of family therapists has increased in clinics. Many individuals trained as social workers, psychologists, and psychiatrists who have been employed in clinics are in search of family therapy training. Probably as long as clinic staffings have existed, a commonly heard statement has been: "This patient comes from a crazy family, and I am spinning my wheels in my attempts to effect change." Today, more clinic practitioners are acting on this statement by including "the patient's" family in the treatment process. These same ideas are equally appropriate for psychiatric hospitals. As explained earlier, many of the constructs of family theory evolved out of work with schizophrenics and their families. Today, more than ever, families of hospitalized schizophrenics are being seen in the hospital for reasons other than just history gathering.

Social service agencies are generally identified as the one service agency specifically designated to provides services to families. This is another group that has expressed intense interest in enhancing effectiveness in intervening by adding family therapy skills to its inventory of means available for helping clients. Even if social service agencies are not defined as the agency with primary responsibilities for providing therapy, knowledge of family therapy aids social workers in making more timely and effective referrals. While becoming involved with families for reasons such as determination of welfare assistance status, child custody studies, and foster placement, etc., they are exposed to many families and thus possess fantastic potential for developing insight into the level of functioning characteristic of those units.

Other settings that have just recently begun to indicate interest in more active family involvement are general hospitals, industry, and schools. All three of these settings are significantly involved with individuals in western society, and their involvement has a profound impact on the families from which those individuals have come. Hospitals are involved in life-and-death decisions that ripple out into the patient's family, industry affects the standard of living that has impact upon every family in the country, and schools are involved in skills, knowledge, and facilitating the enculturation process that has impact on the family of each youngster. In each of these settings, there is the potential for increasing the positive, reciprocal effect between them and families by attending to family relationships.

John Elderkin Bell (1975) has commented that three-fourths of the countries in this world encourage, and in some cases demand, the family of the patient to be heavily involved in the

The Theory and Technique of Family Therapy

hospitalization process. After visiting over 150 medical facilities in "developing countries" that emphasize family involvement he stated,

Where families are allowed freely in the hospitals, patients are more comfortable. They are insulated by their relatives when they need to be sheltered; when they are lonely their relatives help them have contact with other patients, with other members of their families, with the hospital staff, and the community at large. Psychologically they feel secure. We noticed how relaxed the children were: they seldom cried, banged their heads, or rattled the bars of their cribs. In fact, mostly they were on big beds that gave them comfort and scope. They could remain as active as was good for them under the watchful supervision of their mothers or other relatives. The noisiest children's wards were those in which mothers were not allowed. [P. 314]

Bell further states that patient care was also enhanced by the families' increased understanding of the illness being treated and posthospital care. In this sense, the hospital becomes an educational facility in working for medical advancement and public health through the homes of patients.

Hospital staff trained in family theory and family therapy could be a valuable addition to the hospital health care team, not only in facilitating the suggestions just identified by Bell, but in other dimensions as well. It is easy to think of the stressful situations about which many hospitalizations revolve. The terminally ill patient, emergency room situations, and death immediately come to mind. The staff member familiar with family therapy could provide a valuable service to these families in their time of stress and discomfort.

One of us can remember an incident that may illustrate the value of a family therapist on the hospital staff. An emergency developed with his oldest daughter, who was four years of age at the time. A growth was discovered on her body and, through a routine examination, the family physician expressed profound concern and made immediate arrangements for her to be seen the next day at the Mayo Clinic in Rochester, Minnesota. (Many readers may be familiar with this clinic because of its worldwide reputation for excellence in medical diagnosis and treatment.) The immediacy of the referral and obvious concern of the family physician resulted in considerable stress for the parents. The trip to Mayo Clinic was a goodly distance and required being removed from all semblance of support systems available in the home community. The following day at the clinic was one marked by several hours of diagnostic tests on the daughter while the parents waited in stressful suspense. While this particular day ended in knowledge that the daughter's growth was benign, the authors cannot help but speculate. Had the diagnostic procedures been prolonged over several days, or the growth been diagnosed as malignant and required surgery, how effectively would the parents have been able to adapt to the increased stress without outside intervention? There is no doubt in our minds that a staff member trained in family therapy could have been of great value in this situation.

Perhaps more general hospitals will begin to recognize the wisdom of employing at least one staff member with therapeutic training. It seems that both systems, the hospital and family, would benefit. The hospital could benefit through improved health care, both physicially and psychologically for the patients, and the families could be given acknowledgement for their curative power and would not be so prone to respond to hospitalization as a time of shock and mystery.

The authors have spoken with many personnel managers in industry who are sensitive to the reciprocal impact of industry and family life of employees. Just as problems in employees families can stimulate problems and loss of productivity on the job, industry can produce stress that ripples into families of employees and others.

Skidmore and Skidmore (1975) gathered descriptive data from the world of industry and found the following: (1) Industry is opening its doors to marriage and family counseling for humanitarian and financial reasons; (2) a variety of services are being offered; and (3) preliminary reports indicate the services are helping families and improving employee productivity. This study is the most authoritative study completed to date and definitely points in the direction of the potential for a functional and complimentary "marriage" between industry and the field of family therapy.

At least one training program in the United States has begun to address itself to the potiential relationship between marriage and family counseling and industry. Purdue University's training program seems to be directed at industry and an attempt is being made to ascertain the potential for productive interface (Figley, Sprenkle, and Denton, 1976). As more evidence is gathered as to the efficacy of this approach in an industrial setting, this will probably become a fertile setting for those trained in family therapy.

This nation's schools will probably prove to be another vital area where family therapy principles will become more prominently evidenced. Both of the authors have frequently been involved in family therapy in-service activities for school personnel. It is probable that, as long as there have been schools, school personnel have been alluding to the need for family involvement in order to facilitate change in children's behavior. In this day of increased accountability, schools appear to be looking at how they can more successfully involve families in the process.

As one reviews the literature of school counselors and psychologists, there appear many more references to ways of intervening with families. The authors believe this is a movement that is long overdue, when considering the school and family as the most important social systems in a youngster's life for facilitating the enculturation process. The school and family systems share a significant common element in the form of each child. Through increased interface between the two, all elements concerned stand to benefit. The school's responsibility for educating the youngster is facilitated by gaining family involvement. For example, the power of the family can become activated into the role of ally in changing children's behavior, whether that comes in the form of educational tutoring or alleviating stress that results in the child acting out. The family no longer perceives the school as an outside agent to be destroyed or neutralized, but rather recognizes it as a valuable resource in the maturation and development of children. The children benefit by having the two most important social forces in their lives working together to stimulate their educational process.

Considering settings such as industry, general hospitals, and schools as potential sites where those trained in family therapy may practice in the future, it is advisable to look for training programs that acknowledge this. It seems natural to expect that the more traditional settings, such as clinics, psychiatric hospitals, and social service agencies, will continue to be given the greatest place of prominence, but there is now legitimate cause to give the others recognition and acknowledgment. Those programs not acknowledging other potential sites for practicing may be functioning too strongly with their eyes on the past. It seems important to remember that the field of family therapy evolved as a result of the early pioneers, who were able to benefit from past experience, but were ever mindful of the application of that experience to new vistas.

SUMMARY

This chapter examined elements of training programs for family therapy. Elements of family therapy training that vary from training for working with individuals were presented and discussed. Among these elements were the place of co-therapy, audiovisual feedback, live supervision and observation, and the use of the group process to facilitate learning. The process of screening applicants to training programs was given attention in this chapter, along with the perceived role of psychotherapy for trainees. Various theoretical models of training were presented in addition to the identified advantage of trainees screening training programs to determine their orientation. The role of identified competencies in training programs and the training process was discussed. This chapter concluded by examining the settings in which family therapists currently function and where they may be found in the future.

REFERENCES

Ackerman, N. W. "Interlocking Pathologies in Family Relationships." In *Changing Concepts In Psychoanalytic Medicine*, edited by S. Rado and G. Daniels. New York: Grune & Stratton, 1956.

————. *The Psychodynamics of Family Life*. New York: Basic Books, 1958.

Ackerman, N. W.; Beatman, F. L., and Sherman, S. N., eds. *Exploring The Base For Family Therapy*. New York: Family Service Association of America, 1961.

————. *Treating The Troubled Family*. New York: Basic Books, 1966.

————. *Expanding Theory And Practice In Family Therapy*. New York: Family Service Association of America, 1967.

————. "Child Participation In Family Therapy." *Family Process*, Sept. 1970.

Ackerman, N. W.; Lieb, J., and Pearce, J. K., eds. *Family Therapy in Transition*. International Psychiatry Clinics Series, vol. 7, no. 4. Boston, Little, Brown & Co., 1970.

Albee, E. *Who's Afraid of Virginia Woolf?* New York: Atheneum Publishers, 1962.

The Alcoholic American. Madison, Wisconsin: Wisconsin Physician Services, 1973.

Alduous, J. and Hill, R. *International Bibliography of Research in Marriage and the Family*, Vol. 1. 1900-1964. Minneapolis: University of Minnesota Press, 1967.

Alduous, J. and Dahl, N. *International Bibliography of Research in Marriage and the Family*. Vol. II, 1965-1972. Minneapolis: University of Minnesota Press, 1972.

Alger, I. "Integrating Immediate Video Play Back in Family Therapy." In *Family Therapy: Theory and Practice*, edited by P. J. Guerin. New York: Gardner Press, 1976, pp. 530-548.

Andres, F. D. and Lorio, J. F., eds. *A Collection of Selected Papers*. Georgetown Family Symposium. Vol. 1. 1971-1972. Washington, D.C.: Georgetown Medical Center, 1974.

Andrews, E. E. *The Emotionally Disturbed Family*. New York: Jason Aronson, 1974.

Ansbacher, H. L. and Ansbacher, R. R. *The Individual Psychology of Alfred Adler: A Systematic Presentation in Selections from His Writings*. New York: Harper Torch Books, 1964.

Auerswald, E. "Families Change and the Ecological Perspective." In

The Book of Family Therapy, edited by A. Ferber; M. Mendelsohn, and A. Napier. New York: Science House, 1972, pp. 684-705.

Anderson, C. M. and Malloy, E. S. "Family Photographs: In Treatment and Training." *Family Process*, 15(2):259-264, 1976.

Anderson, R. *I Never Sang for My Father*.

Anthony, E. J. and Benedek, T., eds. *Parenthood: Its Psychology and Psychopathology*. Boston: Little, Brown & Co., 1970.

Anthony, E. J. and Koupernik, C., eds. *The Child in His Family*. New York: Wiley-Interscience, 1970. (Note: This is first of series on *The Child in His Family*.)

Aponte, H. J. "The Family-School Interview: An Eco-Structural Approach." *Family Process*, 15(3):303-311, 1976.

Ard, B. N. and Ard, C. C., eds. *Handbook of Marriage Counseling*. Palo Alto, California: Science & Behavior Books, 1969.

Bach, G. and Deutsch, R. *Pairing*. New York: Avon Books, 1970.

Bach, G. and Goldberg, H. *Creative Aggression*. New York: Doubleday & Co., 1974.

Bach, G. and Wyden, P. *The Intimate Enemy*. New York: William Morrow & Co., 1968.

Bandler, R. and Grinder, J. *The Structure of Magic: A Book About Language and Therapy I*. Palo Alto, California: Science & Behavior Books, 1975.

————. *The Structure of Magic: A Book About Language and Therapy II*. Palo Alto, California: Science & Behavior Books, 1976.

Bandura, A. *Principles of Behavior Modification*. New York: Holt, Rinehart and Winston, 1969.

Barron, F. "Family Relationships, Problem Drinking and Antisocial Behavior Among Adolescent Males." Master's thesis, Ann Arbor, Michigan State University, 1970.

Barten, H. H. and Barten, S. S. "Children and Their Parents." *Brief Therapies*. New York: Behavioral Publications, 1972.

Bateson, G. "A Theory of Play and Fantasy." *Psychiatric Research Reports*, 2:39-51, 1955.

Bateson, G. *Steps to an Ecology of Mind*. New York: Ballantine Books, 1972.

Beal, E. W. "Current Trends in the Training of Family Therapists." *American Journal of Psychiatry*, 133:137-141, 1976.

Becker, E. *The Denial of Death*. New York: Free Press, 1975.

Becker, W. C. *Parents Are Teachers: A Child Management Program*. Champaign, Illinois: Research Press Co., 1973.

Bell, J. *Family Group Therapy*. Public Health Monograph no. 64. Public Health Service Publication no. 826. Washington, D.C.: U.S. Govt. Print. Office, 1961.

————. *Family Therapy*. New York: Jason Aronson, 1975.

Bell, N. "Extended Family Relations of Disturbed and Well Families." *Family Process,* 1(2):175-195, 1962.

Bell, N. and Vogel, E. S., eds. *A Modern Introduction to the Family.* Glencoe, Illinois: Free Press, 1961.

Belliveau, F. and Richter, L. *Understanding Human Sexual Inadequacy.* Boston: Little, Brown & Co., 1970.

Belson, R. "The Importance of the Second Interview in Marriage Counseling." *Counseling Psychologist,* 5(3):27-31, 1975.

Bennis, W. et al. *Interpersonal Dynamics.* Homewood, Illinois: Dorsey Press, 1964.

Berger, M. M. *Videotape Techniques in Psychiatric Training and Treatment.* New York: Brunner/Mazel, 1970.

Bergman, I. *Scenes from a Marriage.* New York: Pantheon, 1974.

Berne, E. *Games People Play.* New York: Grove Press, 1964.

Bertalanffy, L. Von. "General System Theory and Psychiatry." In *American Handbook of Psychiatry,* edited by S. Arieti. New York: Basic Books, 1966.

─────. "The Meaning of General System Theory." *General System Theory.* New York: George Braziller, 1968.

Bettelheim, B. *The Empty Fortress.* New York: Free Press, 1967.

Birdwhistell, R. *Kinesics and Context.* Philadelphia: University of Pennsylvania Press, 1970.

Bloch, D. A. "The Clinical Home Visit." In *Techniques of Family Therapy: A Primer,* edited by D. A. Bloch. New York: Grune & Stratton, 1973.

─────, ed. *Techniques of Family Psychotherapy.* New York: Grune & Stratton, 1973.

─────. "Including the Children in Family Therapy." In *Family Therapy: Theory and Practice,* edited by P. J. Guerin. New York: Gardner Press, 1976, pp. 168-181.

Boas, C. V. E. "Intensive Group Psychotherapy With Married Couples." *International Journal of Group Psychotherapy,* 12:142-153, 1962.

Bodin, A. M. "Conjoint Family Assessment: An Evolving Field." In *Advances In Psychological Assessment.* Vol. I, edited by P. McReynolds. Palo Alto, California: Science & Behavior Books, 1968.

─────. "The Use of Video-tapes." In *The Book of Family Therapy,* edited by A. Ferber, M. Mendelsohn and A. Napier. New York: Science House, 1972.

Bohannan, P. *Divorce and After.* Garden City, New York: Doubleday & Co., 1970.

Bosma, W. *Featured Speakers at NCA Meeting Discuss TV, Drinking, Alcoholism Funds, Family Therapy.* Special Report. Rockville, Md., NIAAA Information and Feature Service, July 14, 1974, p. 4.

Bossard, J. H. S. and Boll, E. S. *The Large Family System.* Philadelphia: University of Pennsylvania Press, 1956.

320   The Theory and Technique of Family Therapy

Boszormenyi-Nagy, I. "Relational Modes and Meaning." In *Family Therapy and Disturbed Families,* edited by G. H. Zuk and I. Boszormenyi-Nagy. Palo Alto, California: Science & Behavior Books, 1967.

Boszormenyi-Nagy, I. and Framo, J. L. *Intensive Family Therapy.* New York: Medical Division of Harper & Row, 1965.

Boszormenyi-Nagy, I. and Spark, G. *Invisible Loyalties.* New York: Medical Division of Harper & Row, 1973.

Bott, E. *Family and Social Network,* 2nd ed. London: Tavistock Publishers, 1971.

Bowen, M. "The Use of Family Theory in Clinical Practice." *Comprehensive Psychiatry,* 7:345-374, 1966.

————. "Principles and Techniques of Multiple Family Therapy." In *Systems Therapy,* edited by J. Bradt and C. Moynihan. Washington, D.C.: Groome Child Guidance Center, 1972.

————. "Family Systems Approach to Alcoholism." *Addictions, 21*(2): 28-39, 1974.

————. "Principles and Techniques of Multiple Family Therapy." In *Family Therapy: Theory and Practice,* edited by P. J. Guerin. New York: Gardner Press, 1976, pp. 338-404.

Bowlby, J. *Attachment and Loss.* Vols. 1 and 2. New York: Basic Books, 1961.

Bradt, J. O. "Evolution of Research Observation of a Multiple Family Group." Paper read at Georgetown University Symposium of Family Psychotherapy, Nov. 1, 1968. Department of Psychiatry, Georgetown University School of Medicine, Washington, D.C.

Bradt, J. O. and Moynihan, C. J., eds. *Systems Therapy.* Washington, D.C.: Groome Child Guidance Center, 1972.

Brenner, C. *An Elementary Textbook of Psychoanalysis.* New York: International Universities Press, 1973.

Brodey, W. "Some Family Operations of Schizophrenia: A Study of Five Hospitalized Families Each with a Schizophrenic Member." *Archives of General Psychiatry, 1*:379-402, 1959.

Brody, W. M. *Changing the Family.* New York: Clarkson N. Potter, 1968.

Brown, E. "Divorce Counseling." In *Treating Relationships,* edited by D. Olson. Lake Mills, Iowa: Graphic Publishing Co., 1976.

Buber, M. *The Knowledge of Man: A Philosophy of the Interhuman,* edited by M. Friedman. New York: Harper & Row, 1965.

Buckley, W. *Sociology and Modern Systems Theory.* New Jersey, Prentice-Hall, 1967.

————. *Modern Systems Research for the Behavioral Scientist.* Chicago: Aldine Publishing Co., 1968.

Burns, R. C. and Kaufman, S. H. *Kinetic Family Drawings.* New York: Brunner/Mazel, 1971.

Buros, O. K. *The Seventh Mental Measurement Yearbook.* Vol. 2. Highland Park, New Jersey: Gryphon House, 1972.

Burton, A., ed. *Operational Theories of Personality.* New York: Brunner/Mazel, 1974.

Burton, G. and Kaplan, A. M. "Marriage Counseling with Alcoholics and Their Spouses. II. The Correlation of Excessive Drinking Behavior with Family Pathology and Social Deterioration." *British Journal of Addiction,* 63:161-170, 1968.

Burton, G.; Kaplan, A. M., and Mudd, E. H. "Marriage Counseling with Alcoholics and Their Spouses. I. A Critique of the Methodology of a Follow-up Study." *British Journal of Addiction,* 63:151-160, 1968.

Carson, R. C. *Interaction Concepts of Personality.* Chicago: Aldine Publishing Co., 1969.

Chafez, M. E.; Blane, H. T., and Hill, M. J. "Children of Alcoholics: Observations in a Child Guidance Clinic." *Quarterly Journal of Studies on Alcohol,* 32:687-698, 1971.

Chance, E. *Families in Treatment.* New York: Basic Books, 1959.

Charny, I. *Marital Love and Hate.* New York: Macmillan Publishing Co., 1972.

Chayefsky, P. "The Catered Affair" and "Marty." *Television Plays,* New York: Touchstone Books, 1970.

Chekhov, A. *Uncle Vanya.* New York: Oxford Univ. Press, 1965.

Chesler, P. *Women and Madness.* New York: Doubleday & Co., 1972.

Christensen, O. "Education: A Model for Counseling in the Elementary Schools." *Elementary School Guidance and Counseling,* 4:12-19, 1969.

————. Read Before Annual Family Workshop, Brigham Young University, Provo, Utah, 1971.

Clayton, R. R. *The Family, Marriage, and Social Change.* Lexington, Massachusetts: D.C. Heath & Co., 1975.

Cleghorn, J. and Levin, S. "Training Family Therapists by Setting Learning Objectives." *American Journal of Orthopsychiatry,* 43:439-446, 1973.

Cohen, I. M. *Family Structure, Dynamics and Therapy.* Psychiatric Research Report no. 20. Washington, D.C.: American Psychiatric Association, Jan., 1966.

Cohen, P. T. "A New Approach to the Treatment of Male Alcoholics and Their Families." *American Journal of Orthopsychiatry,* 36:247-248, 1966.

Comfort, A. *The Joy of Sex.* New York: Simon & Schuster, 1972.

Cooper, D. *The Death of the Family.* New York: Vantage Books, 1971.

Corder, B. G.; Corder, R. F., and Laidlaw, M. A. "Intensive Treatment Program for Alcoholics and Their Wives." *Quarterly Journal of Studies of Alcohol,* 33(4):1144-1146, 1972.

Coughlin, F. and Wimberger, H. C. "Group Family Therapy." *Family Process,* 7(1):37-50, 1968.

Cox, H. *The Feast of Fools*. Cambridge: Harvard University Press, 1969.

Cromwell, R. and Olson, D. *Power in Families*. New York: Halsted Press, 1975.

Cromwell, R.; Olson, D., and Fournier, D. "Diagnosis and Evaluation of Marital and Family Counseling." *Treating Relationships: Bridging Research Theory and Practice*. Lake Mills, Iowa: Graphic Publishing Co., 1975.

Cronbach, L. *Essentials of Psychological Testing*. Englewood Cliffs, New Jersey: Prentice-Hall, 1960.

Davis, M. S. *Intimate Relations*. New York: Free Press, 1973.

Dell, P. and Applebaum, A. S. "Trigenerational Enmeshment: Unresolved Ties of Single-Parents to Family of Origin." *American Journal of Orthopsychiatry*, 47:52-59, 1977.

Dell, P.; Sheely, M., and Pulliam, G. "Family Therapy Process in a Family Therapy Seminar." *Journal of Marriage and Family Counseling*, 00:43-48, 1977.

Despert, J. L. *Children of Divorce*. Garden City, New York: Doubleday & Co., 1962.

DeWolf, R. *The Bonds of Acrimony*. New York: J. B. Lippincott Co., 1970.

Dicks, H. V. *Marital Tensions*. New York: Basic Books, 1967.

Drechsler, R. J. and Shapiro, M. I. "Two Methods of Analysis of Family Diagnostic Data." *Family Process*, 2(2):367-379, 1973.

Duberman, L. *The Reconstituted Family: A Study of Remarried Couples and Their Children*. Chicago: Nelson-Hall Co., 1975.

Duvall, E. *Family Development*. Philadelphia: J. B. Lippincott Co., 1971.

Ehrenwald, J. *Neurosis in the Family and Patterns of Psychosocial Defense*. New York: Harper & Row, 1963.

Einstein, V., ed. *Neurotic Interaction in Marriage*. New York: Basic Books, 1956.

Elbert, S. et al. "A Method for the Clinical Study of Family Interaction." *American Journal of Orthopsychiatry*, 34(5):885-894, 1964, pp. 885. 894.

Eliot, T. S. *The Cocktail Party*. New York: Harcourt, Brace & World, 1950.

Ellis, A. and R. A. Harper. *A Guide to Rational Living*. Englewood Cliffs, New Jersey: Prentice-Hall, 1961.

Ellis, A. "Sex Problems of Couples Seen for Marriage Counseling." In, *Handbook of Marriage Counseling*, edited by B. Ard, and C. Ard. Palo Alto, Calif.: Science & Behavior Books, 1969.

Epstein, J. *Divorced in America*. New York, E. P. Dutton & Co., 1974.

Erickson, G. D. and Hogan, T. *Family Therapy: An Introduction to Theory and Techniques*. Belmont, California: Brooks/Cole Publishing Co., 1974.

Erikson, E. *Childhood and Society*, rev. ed. New York: W. W. Norton & Co., 1964.

Fairbairn, W. R. *An Object Relations Theory of the Personality*. New York: Basic Books, 1954.

Familization Therapy Treats Relatives as Co-patients. Rockville, Md., NIAAA Information and Feature Service, Sept. 19, 1975, p. 3.

Family Counseling Enhances Chance of Early Identification, Treatment. Rockville, Md., NIAAA Information and Feature Service, Apr. 26, 1975, p. 1.

Family Life Literature and Films. An annotated bibliography, 1972; and supplement, 1974. Minneapolis: Minnesota Council on Family Relations, 1975.

Family Therapy Helpful, Social Workers Say. Rockville, Md., NIAAA Information and Feature Service, Apr. 1, 1975, p. 3.

Farson, R. E. et al. *The Future of the Family*. New York: Family Service Association of America, 1969.

Feldman, L. B. Goals of Family Therapy. *Journal of Marriage & Family Counseling*, April: 103-114, 1976.

Ferber, A. and Mendelsohn, M. "Training for Family Therapy." *Family Process*, 8:25-32, 1969.

Ferber, A.; Mendelsohn, M., and Napier, A., eds. *The Book of Family Therapy*. New York: Science House, 1972.

Ferber, A. and Ranz, J. "How to Succeed in Family Therapy: Set Reachable Goals—Give Workable Tasks." In *The Book of Family Therapy*, edited by A. Ferber, M. Mendelsohn, and A. Napier. New York: Science House, 1972.

Ferreira, A. J. "Decision-Making in Normal and Pathologic Families." *Archives of General Psychiatry*, 8:68-73, 1963.

Ferreira, A. J. et al. "Some Interactional Variables in Normal and Abnormal Families." *Family Process*, 5(1):60-75, 1966.

Festinger, L. "Cognitive Dissonance." *Scientific American*, May:93-107, 1962.

Figley, C. R.; Sprenkle, D. H., and Denton, W. "Training Marriage and Family Counselors in an Industrial Setting." *Journal of Marriage and Family Counseling*, April:167-178, 1976.

Fine, T. *Children of Alcoholic Parents Need Professional Evaluation*. Rockville, Md., NIAAA Information and Feature Service, Oct. 10, 1975, p. 4.

Fischer, L. "Dimensions of Family Assessment: A Critical Review." *Journal of Marriage and Family Counseling*, 2(4):367-382, 1976.

Fisher, E. O. "A Guide to Divorce Counseling." *Family Coordinator*, Jan., 1973.

————. *Divorce: The New Freedom*. New York: Harper & Row Pubs., 1974.

Fitzgerald, R. V. *Conjoint Marital Therapy*. New York: Jason Aronson, 1973.

Fogarty, T. "Family Structure in Terms of Triangles." In *Systems Therapy*, by J. Bradt and C. Moynihan. Washington, D.C.: Groome Child Guidance Center, 1972.

Foley, V. *An Introduction to Family Therapy.* New York: Grune & Stratton, 1974.

Framo, J. "Symptoms From a Family Transactional Viewpoint." In *Family Therapy in Transition*, edited by N. Ackerman, J. Lieb, and J. Pearce. Boston: Little, Brown & Co., 1970.

————. *Family Interaction: A Dialogue Between Family Researchers and Family Therapists.* New York: Springer-Verlag New York, 1972.

————. "Symptoms from a Family Transactional Viewpoint." In *Progress in Group and Family Therapy*, edited by C. Sager and H. S. Kaplan. New York: Brunner/Mazel, 1972.

————. *Marital and Family Therapy.* Twelve one-hour audio-tapes. Behavioral Sciences Tape Library. Sigma Information, Teaneck, New Jersey.

————. "The Therapist Interviews the Family. The Therapist is Interviewed." *Perceptions.* Color videotape series. Family Institute and ETL Video Publishers, Boston.

————. "Family of Origin as a Therapeutic Resource for Adults in Marital and Family Therapy: You Can and Should Go Home Again." *Family Process, 15*(2):193-210, 1976.

————. *Advanced Family and Marital Therapy.* New York: Jason Aronson, In preparation.

Franks, V. and Vasanti, B. *Women in Therapy.* New York: Brunner/Mazel, 1974.

Freeman, D. S. "Phases of Family Treatment." *Family Coordinator, 25*(3):265-270, 1976.

Friedman, A.; Boszormenyi-Nagy, I.; Jungreis, J.; Lincoln, G.; Mitchell, H. E.; Sonne, J.; Speck, R. V., and Spivack, G. *Psychotherapy for the Whole Family.* New York: Springer-Verlag, New York, 1965.

Friedman, A. et al. *Therapy with Families of Sexually Acting-Out Girls.* New York: Springer-Verlag, New York, 1971.

Frohlich, N. *Making the Best of It.* New York: Harper & Row Pubs., 1971.

Fullmer, D. "Family Group Consultations." *Elementary School Guidance and Counseling, 7*(2):130-136, 1972.

Fulweiler, C. "No Man's Land! An interview with Charles R. Fulweiler." In *Techniques of Family Therapy*, by J. Haley and L. Hoffman. New York: Basic Books, 1967.

Gallant, D. M.; Rich, A., and Bey, E. "'Group Psychotherapy with Married Couples: A Successful Technique in New Orleans Alcoholism Clinic Patients." *Journal of the Louisiana State Medical Society, 122*(2):41-44, 1970.

Gardner, R. *The Boys and Girls Book About Divorce.* New York: Science House, 1970.

Gilroy, F. D. *The Subject Was Roses.* New York: Random House, 1965.

Glass, M. C. "Who Would Abuse a Child?" *Social Scope, 36*:4-10, 1970.

Glasser, P. H. and Glasser, L. N., eds. *Families in Crisis.* New York: Harper & Row Pubs., 1970.

Glick, I. D. and Haley, J. *Family Therapy and Research: An Annotated Bibliography of Articles and Books Published.* New York: Grune & Stratton, 1971.

Glick, I. D. and Kessler, D. *Marital and Family Therapy.* New York: Grune & Stratton, 1975.

Goldberg, M. "The Uses of Dreams in Conjoint Marital Therapy." *Journal of Sex and Marital Therapy, 1*:75-81, 1974.

Goodrich, D. W. and Boomer, D. S. "Experimental Assessment of Modes of Conflict Resolution." *Family Process, 2(1)*:15-24, 1963.

Goode, W. *After Divorce.* New York: Free Press, 1956.

Gordon, T. *Parent Effectiveness Training,* 1975. New York: Peter H. Wyden, 1970.

Gray, W.; Duhl, F. J., and Rizzo, N. D., eds. *General Systems Theory and Psychiatry.* Boston: Little, Brown & Co., 1969.

Greene, B. L. *The Psychotherapies of Marital Disharmony.* New York: Free Press, 1965.

Grinker, R. R. *Psycho-Somatic Concepts.* New York: Jason Aronson, 1973.

Grotjahn, M. *Psychoanalysis and the Family Neurosis.* New York: W. W. Norton & Co., 1960.

Group for Advancement of Psychiatry. *Treatment of Families in Conflict.* New York: Jason Aronson, 1970.

————. *The Field of Family Therapy.* New York: Jason Aronson, 1970.

Grunebaum, H. and Christ, J., eds. *Contemporary Marriage: Structure, Dynamics and Therapy.* Boston: Little, Brown & Co., 1976.

Guerin, P. *Family Therapy: Theory and Practice.* New York: Gardner Press, 1976.

Guntrip, H. *Personality Structure and Human Interaction.* New York: International Universities Press, 1961.

Gurman, A. S. "Couples' Facilitative Communication Skill as a Dimension of Marital Therapy Outcome." *Journal of Marriage and Family Counseling, 1(2)*:1975.

Gurman, A. S. and Rice, V. *Couples in Conflict.* New York: Jason Aronson, 1975.

Haley, J. "An Interactional Description of Schizophrenia." *Psychiatry, 22*:321-332, 1959.

————. "Whither Family Therapy?" *Family Process, 1*:69-100, 1962.

————. *Strategies of Psychotherapy.* New York: Grune & Stratton, 1963.

————. "Research on Family Patterns: An Instrument Measurement." Family Process, 3:41-55, 1964.

Haley, J. and Hoffman, L. Techniques of Family Therapy. New York: Basic Books, 1967.

————. Changing Families: A Family Therapy Reader. New York: Grune & Stratton, 1971.

————. Uncommon Therapy. New York: Ballantine Books, 1973.

————. Problem Solving Therapy. San Francisco: Jossey-Bass, 1976.

Harris, T. I'm OK, You're OK. New York: Harper & Row Pubs., 1967.

Hartman, W. and Fithian, M. Treatment of Sexual Dysfunctions: A Bio-Psycho-Social Approach. Long Beach, California: Center for Marital and Sexual Studies, 1974.

Howells, J. G. Principles of Family Psychiatry. New York: Brunner/ Mazel, 1975.

Jackson, D. D. "The Question of Family Homeostasis." Psychiatric Quarterly [Supplement], 31:79-90, 1957.

————. "Family Rules: Marital Quid Pro Quo." Archives of General Psychiatry, 12:589-594, 1965.

————, ed. Therapy, Communication and Change. Palo Alto, California: Science & Behavior Books, 1968.

Jackson, D. D. and Lederer, W. J. Mirages of Marriage. New York, W. W. Norton & Co., 1968.

Jackson, J. "The Adjustment of the Family to the Crisis of Alcoholism." Quarterly Journal of Studies of Alcohol, 15(4):1954.

Jellinek, E. M. The Disease Concept of Alcoholism. New Haven, Connecticut: College and University Press, 1960.

Jourard, S. The Transparent Self. New York: Van Nostrand Reinhold Co., 1971.

————. "Marriage is for Life." Journal of Marriage and Family Counseling, July:199-208, 1975.

Kalter, N. "Children of Divorce in an Outpatient Psychiatric Population." Journal of Orthopsychiatry, 47:40-51, 1977.

Kamback, M. Family Therapy is Primary Treatment for Children and Their Alcoholic Parents. Rockville, Md., NIAAA Information and Feature Service, Jan. 7, 1976, p. 5.

Kammeier, M. L. "Adolescents from Families with and without Alcohol Problems." Quarterly Journal of Studies on Alcohol, 32:364-372, 1971.

Kantor, D. and Lehr, W. Inside the Family. San Francisco: Jossey-Bass, 1975.

Kaplan, H. S. The Illustrated Manual of Sex Therapy. New York: Quadrangle/New York Times Co., 1975.

————. The New Sex Therapy. New York: Brunner/Mazel, 1974.

Kavanaugh, R. E. Facing Death. Baltimore: Nash Publishing Co., 1972.

Kelly, D. "Alcoholism and the Family." Maryland State Medical Journal, 22(1):25-30, 1973.

Kelly, J. B. and Wallerstein, J. W. "Brief Interventions with Children in Divorcing Families." *Journal of Orthopsychiatry,* 47:23-39, 1977.

Kemp, C. G. *Foundations of Group Counseling.* New York: McGraw-Hill Book Co., 1970.

Kempler, W. *Principles of Gestalt Family Therapy.* Costamesa, California: Kempler Institute, 1973.

Kilgo, R. D. "Counseling Couples in Groups: Rational and Methodology." *Family Coordinator,* 24:337-362, 1975.

Klein, M. *Contributors to Psychoanalysis, 1921-1945.* London: Hogarth Press, 1948.

Knox, D. *Marriage Happiness: A Behavioral Approach to Counseling.* Champaign, Illinois: Research Press, 1971.

————. *Dr. Knox's Marital Exercise Book.* New York: David McKay Co., 1975.

Kohut, N. C. *Therapeutic Family Law.* Chicago: Family Law Publications, 1968.

Kramer, C. et al. *Beginning Phase of Family Treatment.* Chicago: Family Institute of Chicago, 1968.

Krantzler, M. *Creative Divorce.* New York: Evans & Co., 1973.

Krumboltz, J. and Krumboltz, H. *Changing Children's Behavior,* Englewood Cliffs, New Jersey: Prentice-Hall, 1972.

Kübler-Ross, E. *On Death and Dying.* New York: Macmillan Publishing Co., 1969.

Laing, R. D. *The Self and Others.* London: Tavistock Publishers, 1961.

————. "Mystification, Confusion and Conflict," In *Intensive Family Therapy,* edited by I. Boszormenyi-Nagy and J. Framo. New York: Harper & Row Pubs., 1965.

————. *The Politics of the Family.* New York: Pantheon Books, 1967.

————. *The Self and Others,* 2nd rev. ed. New York: Pantheon Books, 1969.

————. *The Politics of the Family.* New York: Vintage Books, 1972.

————. *The Facts of Life.* New York: Pantheon Books, 1976.

Laing, R. D. and Esterson, A. *Sanity, Madness and the Family.* London: Tavistock Publishers, 1964.

Laing, R. D.; Phillipson, H., and Lee, A. *Interpersonal Perception.* London: Tavistock Publishers, 1966.

Langlsey, D. G. and Kaplan, D. M. *The Treatment of Families in Crisis.* Grune & Stratton, 1968.

Laqueur, H. P. "Mechanisms of Change in Multiple Family Therapy." In *Progress in Group and Family Therapy,* edited by C. Sager and H. S. Kaplan. New York: Brunner/Mazel, 1972a.

————. "Multiple Family Therapy." *The Book of Family Therapy,* edited by A. Ferber, M. Mendelsohn, and A. Napier. New York: Science House, 1972b.

————. "Multiple Family Therapy." In *Family Therapy, Theory Practice*, edited by P. J. Guerin. New York: Gardner Press, 1976, pp. 405-416.

Laquer, H. P.; LaGurt, H., and Morong, E. "Multiple Family Therapy: Further Developments." In *Changing Families*, edited by J. Haley. New York: Grune & Stratton, 1971.

Lebedun, M. "Measuring Movement in Group Marital Counseling." *Social Casework, 51*:35-43, 1970.

Lederer, W. *The Fear of Women*. New York: Grune & Stratton, 1968.

Lederer, W. and Jackson, D. D. *The Mirages of Marriage*. New York: W. W. Norton & Co., 1968.

Leichter, E. "Treatment of Married Couples Groups." In *Marriage and Family Therapy*, edited by W. Nichols. Minneapolis: National Council on Family Relations, 1974.

Lennard, H. and Bernstein, A. *Patterns in Human Interaction*. San Francisco: Jossey-Bass, 1969.

Levy, D. *Maternal Overprotection*. New York: Columbia University Press, 1943.

Lewis, J. W.; Beavers, W. R.; Gossett, J. T., and Phillips, V. A. *No Single Thread: Psychological Health in Family Systems*. New York: Brunner/Mazel, 1976.

Libby, R. W. and Whitehurts, R. N., eds. *Renovating Marriage: Toward New Sexual Life Styles*. Danville, California: Consensus Publications, 1973.

Lidz, T. *The Family and Human Adaptation*. New York: International Universities Press, 1963.

Lidz, T. and Fleck, S. "Family Studies and a Theory of Schizophrenia." In *Schizophrenia and the Family*, edited by T. Lidz, S. Fleck, and A. Cornelison. New York: International Universities Press, 1965.

Lidz, T.; Fleck, S., and Cornelison, A. *Schizophrenia and the Family*. New York: International Universities Press, 1965.

Lieberman, R. "Behavioral Approaches to Family and Couple Therapy." *American Journal of Orthopsychiatry, 40*:106-118, 1970.

Lief, H. *Medical Aspects of Human Sexuality*. Baltimore: Williams & Wilkins Co., 1975.

Lomas, P., ed. *The Predicament of the Family*. New York: International Universities Press, 1967.

Ludi, T. *Youth Hostels Stress Family Involvement*. Rockville, Md., NIAAA Information and Feature Service, May 20, 1974, p. 2.

Luthman, S. G. and Kirschenbaum, M. *The Dynamic Family*. Palo Alto, California: Science & Behavior Books, 1974.

Lynn, D. B. *The Father: His Role in Child Development*. Belmont, California: Brooks/Cole, 1974.

McDowell, F. K. "The Pastor's Natural Ally Against Alcoholism." *Journal of Pastoral Care, 26*(1):26-32, 1972.

MacGregor, R.; Ritchie, A. M.; Serrano, A. C.; Schuster, F. P.; McDonald, E. C., and Goolishian, H. A. *Multiple Impact Therapy with Families.* New York: McGraw-Hill Book Co., 1964.

Mace, D. *Getting Ready for Marriage.* Nashville: Abingdon Press, 1972.

Mace, D. and Mace, V. *How to Have a Happy Marriage.* Nashville: Abingdon Press, 1977.

McGilvray, T. *Children's Behavior Problems Often Alcohol Related.* NIAAA Information and Feature Service, Aug. 4, 1975, p. 3.

Maddison, R. and Raphael, T. "Conjugal Bereavement and the Social Network." In *Bereavement: Its Psychosocial Aspects,* edited by B. Schoenberg et al. New York: Columbia University Press, 1976.

Madsen, C. K. and Madsen, C. H. *Parents-Children-Discipline: A Positive Approach.* Boston: Allyn and Bacon, 1972.

Mahrer, A. R. and Pearson, L., eds. *Creative Development in Psychotherapy.* Cleveland: Press of Case Western Reserve University, 1971.

Maltz, M. *Psychocybernetics.* Englewood Cliffs, New Jersey: Prentice-Hall, 1960.

Mann, J. *Time-Limited Psychotherapy.* Cambridge: Harvard University Press, 1973.

Martin, P. A. *A Marital Therapy Manual.* New York: Brunner/Mazel, 1976.

Mash, E. J.; Hamerlynck, L. A., and Handy, L. C. *Behavior Modification and Families.* New York: Brunner/Mazel, 1975.

Masserman, J., ed. *Science and Psychoanalysis.* Vol. 2. *Individual and Family Dynamics.* New York: Grune & Stratton 1959.

Maslow, A. *Motivation and Personality.* New York: Harper & Row Pubs., 1970.

Masters, W. H. and Johnson, V. E. *Human Sexual Response.* Boston: Little, Brown & Co., 1966.

————. *Human Sexual Inadequacy.* Boston: Little, Brown & Co., 1970.

————. *The Pleasure Bond.* Boston: Little, Brown & Co., 1975.

Menninger, K. *Love Against Hate.* New York: Harcourt, Brace and Jovanovich, 1958.

Midelfort, C. F. *The Family in Psychotherapy.* New York: Blakiston, 1957.

Milgram, S. "City Families." *Psychology Today,* 00:59-63, 1977.

Miller, A. *Death of a Salesman.* New York: Viking Press, 1949.

Miller, J. B., ed. *Psychoanalysis and Woman.* New York: Brunner/Mazel, 1974.

Miller, S.; Nunnally, E., and Wackman, D. *Alive and Aware: Improving Communication in Relationships.* Minneapolis: Interpersonal Communication Programs, 1975.

————. *Couple Communication: Trainer's Manual.* Minneapolis: Interpersonal Communication Programs, 1977.

Minuchin, S. *Families and Family Therapy.* Cambridge: Harvard University Press, 1974.

Minuchin, S. et al. *Families of the Slums.* New York: Basic Books, 1967.

Minuchin, S. and Montalvo, B. "Techniques for Working with Disorganized Low Socioeconomic Families." *American Journal of Orthopsychiatry,* 37:880-887, 1967.

Mishler, E. G. and Waxler, N. E. *Interaction in Families.* New York: John Wiley & Sons, 1968.

Missildine, W. *Your Inner Child of the Past.* New York: Simon & Schuster, 1963.

Murstein, B. I. *Theories of Attraction and Love.* New York: Springer-Verlag, New York, 1971.

Napier, A. and Whitaker, C. *The Family Crucible.* New York: Harper & Row Pubs., 1978.

National Council on Alcoholism: *Alcohol and the Family.* Rockville, Md., 1974.

Nichols, W. C. "Personal Therapy for Marital Therapist." *Family Coordinator, 17*:83-88, 1968.

O'Hare, C. et al. "Group Training in Family Therapy—The Student's Perspective." *Journal of Marriage and Family Counseling,* April:157-162, 1975.

Olson, D. "Marital and Family Therapy: Integrative Review and Critique." *Journal of Marriage and the Family, 32*:501-538, 1970.

—————, ed. *Treating Relationships.* Lake Mills, Iowa: Graphic Publishing Co., 1976.

Olson, D. and Dahl, N. *Inventory of Marriage and Family Literature,* 1973 and 1974. St. Paul: Family Social Science, University of Minnesota Press, 1975.

O'Neal, P.; Robins, L., and King, L. "Parental Deviance and the Genesis of Sociopathic Personality." *American Journal of Psychiatry, 119*(2): 1114-1124, 1962.

O'Neill, E. *Long Day's Journey Into Night.* New Haven: Yale University Press, 1955.

O'Neill, G. and O'Neill, N. *Open Marriage.* New York: Evans & Co., 1972. Distributed by J. B. Lippincott Co., Philadelphia.

Palazzoli, M. S. *Self-starvation.* London: Human Context Books, 1969.

Papajohn, J. and Spiegel, J. *Transactions in Families.* San Francisco: Jossey-Bass, 1974.

Papp, P. *Family Therapy: Full Length Case Studies.* New York: Gardner Press, 1977.

Papp, P.; Silverstein, O., and Carter, E. "Family Sculpting in Preventive Work with Well Families." *Family Process, 12*:197-212, 1973.

Parsons, T. and Bales, R. F. *Family, Socialization and Interaction Process.* Glencoe, Illinois: Free Press, 1955.

Patterson, G. R. *Families: Applications of Social Learning to Family Life.* Champaign, Illinois: Research Press Co., 1971.

—————. *Families.* Champaign, Illinois: Research Press Co., 1972.

Patterson, G. R. and Gullion, E. *Living with Children.* Champaign, Illinois: Research Press Co., 1968.

Patterson, G. R.; Reig, J. B.; Jones, R. R., and Conger, R. E. *A Social Learning Approach to Family Intervention.* Eugene, Oregon: Castalia Publishing Co., 1975.

Paul, N. "The Use of Empathy in the Resolution of Grief." *Perspectives in Biology and Medicine, 11*:153-169, 1967.

Paul, N. and Grosser, G. "Operational Mourning and Its Role in Conjoint Family Therapy." *Community Mental Health Journal, 1*:339-345, 1965.

Paul, N. and Paul, B. *A Marital Puzzle.* New York: W. W. Norton & Co., 1975.

Pavenstadt, E. and Bernard, V. V. *Crisis of Family Disorganization.* New York: Behavioral Pubns., 1971.

Peck, B. *A Family Therapy Notebook.* Roslyn Heights, New York: Libra Pubs., 1975.

————. "The Extruded Third: An Interpersonal Approach to Couples Treatment." *Psychotherapy: Theory Research and Practice, 10(1)*:62-65, 1973.

Pollak, O. and Friedman, A. S., eds. *Family Dynamics and Female Sexual Delinquency.* Palo Alto, California: Science & Behavior Books, 1969.

Rabkin, L. "Patients' Family: Research Methods." *Family Process, 4(1)*: 105-132, 1965.

Rabkin, R. *Inner and Outer Space.* New York: W. W. Norton & Co., 1970.

Rainwater, L. *Behind Ghetto Walls: Black Families in a Federal Slum.* Chicago, Aldine Publishing Co., 1970.

Rappaport, A. and Harrell, J. "A Behavioral-Exchange Model for Marital Counseling." In *Couples in Conflict,* edited by A. Gurman and D. E. Rice. New York, Jason Aronson, 1975.

Reiner, B. S. and Kaufman, I. *Character Disorders in Parents of Delinquents.* New York: Family Service Association of America, 1969.

Reiss, I. L. *The Family System in America.* New York: Holt, Rinehart & Winston, 1975.

Riskin, J. "Family Interaction Scales: A Preliminary Report." *Archives of General Psychiatry, 11(5)*:448-494, 1964.

Rogers, C. *On Becoming a Person.* Boston: Houghton Mifflin Co., 1961.

Rooney, E. D. *Alcoholism and the Family.* CosCob, Connecticut: National Council on Alcoholism—Southwestern Connecticut Area, 1975.

Rosenbaum, S. and Alger, I., eds. *The Marriage Relationship.* New York: Basic Books, 1967.

Roszak, B. and Roszak, T. *Masculine/Feminine.* New York: Harper Colophon Books, 1969.

Rubinstein, D. and Weiner, O. R. "Co-Therapy Teamwork Relationships in Family Therapy." In *Family Therapy and Disturbed Families,* edited by G. Y. Zuk and I. Boszormenyi-Nagy. Palo Alto, California, Science & Behavior Books, 1967.

Ruesch, J. and Bateson, G. *Communication: The Social Matrix of Psychiatry.* New York: W. W. Norton & Co., 1951.

Sager, C. J. *Marriage Contracts and Couple Therapy.* New York: Brunner/Mazel, 1976.

Sager, C. J.; Brayboy, T. L., and Waxenbert, B. R. *Black Ghetto Family in Therapy.* New York: Grove Press, 1970.

Sager, C. J. and Kaplan, H. S., eds. *Progress in Group and Family Therapy.* New York: Brunner/Mazel, 1972.

Sampson, H.; Messinger, L., and Towne, R. *Schizophrenic Women: Studies in Marital Crises.* New York: Atherton, 1963.

Satir, V. *Conjoint Family Therapy,* 2nd ed. Palo Alto, California: Science & Behavior Books, 1967.

————. *Conjoint Family Therapy.* Didactic no. 1. Big Sur Recordings, Big Sur, California, n.d.

————. *Peoplemaking.* Palo Alto, California: Science & Behavior Books, 1973.

Satir, V.; Stachowiak, J., and Taschman, H. *Helping Families to Change.* New York: Jason Aronson, 1975.

Scheflen, A. *Stream and Structure of Communicational Behavior. Behavioral Science.* Monograph 1. Philadephia: Eastern Pennsylvania Psychiatric Institute, 1965. (Context analysis of Family Therapy session of Whitaker and Malone.)

Schoenberg, B. et al. *Bereavement: Its Psychosocial Aspects.* New York: Columbia University Press, 1975.

Schutz, W. C. *Elements of Encounter: A Body-mind Approach.* Big Sur, California: Joy Press, 1973.

Seligman, M. E. *Helplessness: On Depression, Development and Death.* San Francisco: Freeman, Cooper & Co., 1975.

Senn, J. E. and Hartfor, C., eds. *The Firstborn: Experiences of Eight American Families.* Cambridge: Harvard University Press, 1968.

Shade, R. H. and Hendrickson, W. J. "Pill-culture Parents and Their Drug-using Teenagers: A New and Frightening Therapeutic Challenge." *American Journal of Orthopsychiatry, 41*:297-298, 1971.

Shapiro, R. J. *Family Therapy.* Six one-hour audiotapes. Behavioral Sciences Tape Library. Sigma Information, Teaneck, New Jersey.

Sheresky, N. and Mannes, M. *Uncoupling—The Art of Coming Apart.* New York: Viking Press, 1972.

Sherwin, R. V. *Compatible Divorce.* New York: Crown Publishers, 1969.

Sigal, J. J.; Rakoff, V., and Epstein, N. B. "Indicators of Therapeutic Outcome in Conjoint Family Therapy." *Family Process, 4*(2):215-226, 1967.

Skidmore, R. A. and Skidmore, C. J. "Marriage and Family Counseling in Industry." *Journal of Marriage and Family Counseling,* April:135-144, 1975.

Skynner, A. C. R. *Systems of Family and Marital Psychotherapy.* New York: Brunner/Mazel, 1976.

Smith, J. R. and Smith, L. G. *Beyond Monogamy: Studies of Sexual Alternatives in Marriage.* Baltimore: Johns Hopkins Press, 1974.

Smith, R. S. and Alexander, A. M. *Counseling Couples in Groups.* Springfield, Illinois: Charles C Thomas, Publisher, 1974.

Smoyak, S. A. "Therapeutic Approaches to Alcoholism Based on Systems Theories." *Occupational Health Nursing, 21 (4)*:27-30, 1973.

————. *The Psychiatric Nurse as a Family Therapist.* New York: John Wiley & Sons, 1975.

Spark, G. "Grandparents and Intergenerational Family Process." *Family Process, 13*:225, 1974.

Speck, R. and Attneave, C. "Network Therapy." In *The Book of Family Therapy,* edited by A. Ferber, M. Mendelsohn, and A. Napier. New York: Science House, 1972.

————. *Family Networks.* New York: Pantheon, 1973.

Spiegel, J. *Transactions: The Interplay Between Individual Family and Society.* Edited by J. Papajohn. New York: Science House, 1971.

Stack, P. L. *How to Do Family Therapy.* Yankton, South Dakota: Published personally, 1976.

Steele, B. F. and Pollock, C. B. "A Psychiatric Study of Parents Who Abuse Infants and Small Children." In *The Battered Child,* edited by R. Helfer and C. H. Kempe. Chicago: University of Chicago Press, 1968, pp. 103-147.

Steinzor, B. *When Parents Divorce.* New York: Pantheon Books, 1969.

Stierlin, H. *Conflict and Reconciliation.* Garden City, New York: Doubleday & Co., Anchor Books, 1969.

————. "Group Fantasies and Family Myths—Some Theoretical and Practical Aspects." *Family Process, 12*:111-125, 1973.

————. *Separating Parents and Adolescents: A Perspective on Running Away, Schizophrenia, and Waywardness.* New York: Quadrangle/The New York Times Co., 1974.

Stream, H. *New Approaches in Child Guidance.* Metuchen, New Jersey: Scarecrow Press, 1970.

Stuart, R. "Behavioral Remedies for Marital Ills: A Guide to the Use of Operant-Interpersonal Techniques." In *Couples in Conflict,* edited by A. Gurman and D. Rice. New York: Jason Aronson, 1975.

Sugar, M. *The Adolescent in Group and Family Therapy.* New York: Brunner/Mazel, 1975.

Tharp, R. and Wetzel, R. *Behavior Modification in the Natural Environment.* New York: Academic Press, 1969.

Thorman, G. *Family Therapy: A Handbook.* Los Angeles: Western Psychological Services, 1971.

Toman, W. *Family Constellation,* 3rd ed. New York: Springer-Verlag New York, 1975.

Toomim, M. "Structured Separation for Couples in Conflict." In *Couples in Conflict,* edited by A. Gurman and D. Rice. New York: Jason Aronson, 1975.

"Toward the Differentiation of a Self in One's Own Family." In *Family Interaction: A Dialogue Between Family Researchers and Family Therapists,* edited by J. Framo. New York: Springer-Verlag New York, 1972.

Wahtroos, S. *Family Communication.* New York: Macmillan Publishing Co., 1974.

Wallace, A. and Fogelson, R. "The Identity Struggle." In *Intensive Family Therapy,* edited by I. Boszormeni-Nagy and J. Framo. New York: Harper & Row Pubs., 1965, pp. 365-406.

Waller, W. W. and Hill, R. *The Family: A Dynamic Interpretation.* New York: Dryden Press, 1951.

Wallerstein, J. S. and Kelly, J. B. "Divorce Counseling: A Community Service for Families in the Midst of Divorce." *American Journal of Orthopsychiatry,* 47:4-22, 1977.

Waskow, I. E. "Counselor Attitudes and Client Behavior." *Journal of Consulting Psychology,* 27:405-412, 1963.

Watzlawick, P.; Beavin, J. H., and Jackson, D. D. *Pragmatics of Human Communication.* New York: W. W. Norton & Co., 1967.

Weiss, R. S. *Marital Separation.* New York: Basic Books, 1975.

Weakland, J.; Fisch, R.; Watzlawick, R., and Bodin, A. "Brief Therapy: Focused Problem Resolution." *Family Process,* 00:114-168, 1974.

Whitaker, C. *Hillcrest Film Series of Family Diagnostic Interviews.* Philadelphia: Eastern Pennsylvania Psychiatric Institute, 1969.

————. *Marital and Family Therapy.* Cassette audiotapes. Chicago: Instructional Dynamics, 1970.

————. "The Territory Chart as a Platform for Family Therapy." *Voices,* 2:95-97, 1970.

————. "Psychotherapy of the Absurd: With a Special Emphasis on the Psychotherapy of Aggression." *Family Process,* 12:1-16, 1975.

————. Personal communication with the authors, 6/74.

Whitaker, C. and Malone, C. P. *The Roots of Psychotherapy.* New York: Blakiston, 1953.

Winch, R. F. and Goodman, L. W. *Selected Studies in Marriage and the Family.* New York: Holt, Rinehart & Winston, 1968.

Winer, L. "Some Efforts in Defining and Assessing Group Change." In *Systems Therapy,* edited by J. Bradt and C. Moynihan. Washington, D.C.: Groome Child Guidance Center, 1972.

Winnicott, D. W. *The Child, the Family and the Outside World.* Baltimore and New York, Penguin Books, 1975.

Winter, W. D. and Ferreira, A. J. *Research in Family Interaction*. Palo Alto, California: Science & Behavior Books, 1969.

Wolpe, J. and Lazarus, A. *Behaivor Therapy Techniques*. New York: Pergamon Press, 1966.

Wynne, L.; Ryckoff, I.; Day, J., and Hirsch, S. "Pseudo-Mutuality in the Family Relations of Schizophrenics." *Psychiatry, 21*:205-220, 1958.

Yalom, I. D. *The Theory and Practice of Group Psychotherapy*. New York: Basic Books, 1970.

Yudin, L.; Holms, J., and Heinemann, S. *Children of Alcoholic Parents Need Professional Evaluation*. Rockville, Md., NIAAA Information and Feature Service, Oct. 10, 1975, p. 4.

Zilbach, J. J.; Bergel, E., and Goss, C. "The Role of the Young Child in Family Therapy." In *Progress in Group and Family Therapy*, edited by C. J. Sager and H. S. Kaplan. New York: Brunner/Mazel, 1972, pp. 385-399.

Zuk, G. "The Go-Between-Process in Family Therapy." *Family Process, 5*:126-128, 1966.

————. "The Side-taking Function in Family Therapy." *American Journal of Orthopsychiatry, 38*:553-559, 1968.

————. "Family Therapy." In *Changing Families*, edited by J. Haley. New York: Grune & Stratton, 1971.

————. "Family Therapy: Formulation of a Technique and Its Theory. *International Journal of Group Psychotherapy, 28(1)*:1968.

————. *Family Therapy: A Triadic-Based Approach*. New York: Behavioral Publications, 1972.

————. *Process and Practice in Family Therapy*. Haverford, Pennsylvania: Psychiatry and Behavioral Science Books, 1975.

Zuk, G. and Boszormenyi-Nagy, I., eds., *Family Therapy and Disturbed Families*. Palo Alto, California: Science & Behavior Books, 1968.

INDEX

337